LEAD
WITH EMPATHY

Published by SuccessBooks®, Lake Mary, FL.
SuccessBooks® is a registered trademark.

ISBN: 979-8-9918645-9-6
LCCN: 2026904551

For more information, please write:

SuccessBooks®
3415 W. Lake Mary Blvd. #950370
Lake Mary, FL 32795
or call 1.877.261.4930

Visit us online at: www.CelebrityPressPublishing.com.

Lake Mary, FL

CONTENTS

CHAPTER 1

THE LEADERSHIP ADVANTAGE YOU CAN'T AFFORD TO IGNORE

BY CHRIS VOSS

INTRODUCTION: THE MOST POWERFUL TOOL YOU'RE NOT USING ENOUGH

"There are three sides to every story: Your side, my side and the truth."

Robert Evans

"Empathy is about the transmission of information. Sympathy and compassion are reactions to that information."

Steven Kotler

For the effective leader to inspire positive, durable, low-maintenance, self-sustaining, and problem-solving behavior, the critical information to transmit is "their side."

Like me, Steven Kotler focuses on human performance. Leadership is about human performance.

(As a side note, I always recommend Steven's books *The Rise of Superman* and *Stealing Fire* for those who believe in getting the best out of themselves and those around them.)

It's hard to grasp the full power of tactical empathy until you apply it and watch its transformative effect. Why don't you use it enough? It's a stealth tool. You never notice it unless you're using it or it's being used with you. Even when it is being used with you, you really don't know what happened.

It's leading quietly.

And leading quietly is often just what great leadership is about. It makes people feel empowered. When you empower them, they keep going in the direction you set them in. They become low-maintenance. You, as a leader, get on to other important tasks.

They also bond with you. It inspires tremendous loyalty.

Leading via authority only creates fear-induced compliance. They perform only when you are there to "crack the whip," and they are happy to let you get blindsided by problems. Loyalty that is fear-induced is an illusion.

WHAT TACTICAL EMPATHY ISN'T

Tactical empathy is not what most people think of. It's not soft affirmations. It's not "I hear you" (which, in fact, is a dismissive thing to do).

Tactical empathy is intentional demonstration/articulation of an understanding of their perspective...without agreement. It's the *description* of their point of view back to them. It's that simple and often extremely hard (the first few times).

Why is this hard? You have to limit yourself to *only* describing it. No judgement. No evaluation. No agreement. No disagreement.

Just describe it.

The first time you do this, in the moment of doing it, it will feel inadequate. Even imagining doing it will cause your amygdala (fear center) to envision things going horribly wrong, until you try it.

And then you'll be delighted by their reaction. They will step to your side.

This is the kind of empathy I used as an FBI hostage negotiator. The kind I honed to a science. The kind that makes people feel heard in the most volatile environments imaginable. And the transformative power that it has.

Carl Rogers, the American psychologist and really the father of this approach, described it as "releasing potent forces for change" within someone. When you want your people to change their behavior, if you quietly release those potent forces for change within them, that change gains momentum and sustains itself.

This chapter isn't theory. It's how I've brought tactical empathy from the field to the boardroom. It's how I've closed deals, defused conflict, built unshakeable partnerships, and led teams...all by making tactical empathy my competitive advantage.

THE MYTH OF SOFT SKILLS

For too long, empathy has been dismissed as a "soft skill." Something fluffy. Optional. But in the high-stakes world of business where everyone's distracted, loyalty can be fleeting, and relationships are often fragile...empathy isn't soft. It's strategic.

When I define tactical empathy, I say it's the ability to understand/comprehend the feelings, perspective, or mindset of another, and to say it out loud back to them. With no agreement or judgment, just comprehension.

The feeling of being heard, not agreed with, but simply being heard, is what releases those potent forces for change. This is what builds lasting influence.

And that word...**influence**...is the key. Not leverage and *not* authority.

Derek Gaunt, the Head of Coaching and Training for The Black Swan Group, wrote a must-read book entitled *Ego, Authority, Failure*[1] on this topic. I highly recommend it.

When I started applying this definition in leadership conversations, I stopped trying to fix people. I started understanding them. And that single shift changed everything.

[1] https://www.amazon.com/Ego-Authority-Failure-Intelligence-Negotiator/dp/1544526849/ref=sr_1_1?crid-1MJNC7IRZE2LS&dib=eyJ2IjoiMSJ9.ZfLrZhd21h1LUd-MReCg-D2rfkZ9Jc2b1Arf04Ra6py4rcG8oNoZ-eFrdJL4DCrBzrev17e5dxO9AiD5gVpV2CR5P8XDTMPROpqpAjCvvxOw.7jxPp76dEKtg7fi-292pwqkcNYXwzT_bFjfVpZnRVSU&dib_tag=se&keywords=ego+authority+failure+book&qid=1762103672&sprefix=ego+authority%2Caps%2C177&sr=8-1

EXAMPLES: WHEN EMPATHY CAN SAVE A DEAL

1. Mirroring
When someone says, "We're doing the best we can with the resources we have," you mirror back with a gentle downward inflection…

"The best you can…"

They will pause and likely begin to unload. "Yeah, our team was cut in half. We're drowning."

Mirroring is simple. But it lowers defenses and pulls the truth to the surface.

2. Labeling
You follow with:

"Sounds like your team's under a ton of pressure."

They will most often sigh, deep and loud. "You have no idea."

Labeling unspoken emotions makes people feel seen. And when people feel seen, they stop bracing for a fight.

3. Tactical Empathy in Action
Make sure you pause and share the silence for about 6 seconds, then:

"How can we help you look like a hero to your team while still getting what we need?"

That one calibrated question will reframe the whole dynamic.

Tactical empathy doesn't make us weaker. It makes us dynamic.

TACTICAL EMPATHY AT THE LEADERSHIP TABLE

I've seen these techniques work in life-or-death crises. But they're just as potent in performance reviews, strategy sessions, and everyday leadership.

Mirroring to Get to the Root

A high performer may say to you, "I don't think I'm growing."

You mirror: **"Not growing?"** (Use an upward inflection of gentle curiosity.)

That simple response will unlock the deeper truths. You'll hear what is really going on.

Labeling to Create Safety

Before a tough organizational change, you can open with:

"This is going to feel sudden. You'll probably think we've lost our minds."

"You're going to be worried about how this affects your job."

Naming fears deactivates the power of their impact. Human beings are incredibly resilient if given the warning to brace themselves. Once the warning is given, don't prolong delivering the message. No more than three seconds. Rip the band-aid off. They'll be ready.

THE SCIENCE OF FEELING HEARD

Why do these techniques work?

Why do these techniques work so powerfully? Why can a simple "It sounds like..." or "What's the biggest challenge you're facing?" completely change the trajectory of a conversation?

Because humans are *wired* for connection, which is almost completely satisfied by the feeling of being understood.

This is not some abstract, feel-good way. This is biology. This is neuroscience.

Neuroscience shows that when people feel genuinely understood, the brain releases **oxytocin** (the "bonding hormone") and **serotonin** (the drug of satisfaction, well-being, and emotional stability).

And oxytocin has an interesting kicker...people open up and tell the truth when they get a good hit of it.

These neurochemicals build trust and fuel candor in relationships.

JUST BECAUSE YOU DO UNDERSTAND, DOESN'T MEAN THEY *FEEL* UNDERSTOOD

I didn't rely on charm or charisma as a hostage negotiator. I relied on brain chemistry. My job was to get violent, desperate people to lower their guard...not by force, but by *feeling heard.* I knew that when the amygdala (the brain's threat-detection center) is clouding thinking, facts don't matter. People are in survival mode.

What calms the amygdala? *Tactical Empathy.*

When you use **labeling**...saying "It seems like you're frustrated," or "It sounds like you're under a lot of pressure"...you trigger a response that tells the brain: *This person gets me. I feel connected. I can relax now.*

The moment that happens, the brain stops preparing to fight or flee...and starts opening up to influence.

That's why I say:

> "Tactical empathy is understanding the feelings and mindset of another in the moment, hearing what is intertwined in those feelings, and describing it back to them. This greatly amplifies your influence."

Let that sink in: *the demonstration of understanding amplifies influence.* Not authority. Not expertise. Not even charisma. The *demonstration* of understanding.

Understanding is both essential and inadequate. Without the demonstration/description/articulation of their perspective back to them without evaluation, understanding alone will always fall short.

EMPATHY IS A PERFORMANCE MULTIPLIER

Over the years, tactical empathy has been used to:

- Cut client churn
- Raise team engagement
- Turn around underperforming business units without top-down pressure

Empathy isn't fluff. It's fuel.

EMPATHY IN A JUNGLE: KIDNAPPING IN THE PHILIPPINES

If you're still questioning whether empathy truly drives results, let me tell you about the time I used it to build trust with terrorists. Yes, actual terrorists who had kidnapped an American.

In 2000, I led the team negotiating the release of Jeffrey Schilling, taken hostage by Abu Sayyaf in the southern Philippines. Held under brutal conditions for over seven months, his life hung in the balance. We didn't threaten. We used tactical empathy.

We listened to understand the captors' worldview; their pride, motivations, and need for recognition. We mirrored, labeled, and asked calibrated questions. Not to agree, but to influence.

One moment stands out: We described their perspective completely back to their negotiator/leader, focusing on all the aspects he stated justified his position. Then our negotiator went silent. Letting the moment have its impact.

That single shift caused the ransom demand to completely disappear. The standoff could've ended in tragedy. Instead, a life was saved because we led with tactical empathy.

Why share this in a chapter on leadership?

Because if empathy can work in a jungle with armed militants, it can absolutely work in your boardroom. The stakes may differ, but the psychology is the same.

Empathy isn't weakness. It's influence. It's what turns leaders into difference-makers.

TACTICAL EMPATHY AMPLIFIES INFLUENCE

A common misconception is that leading with empathy means surrendering authority. That couldn't be further from the truth.

Tactical empathy *amplifies* influence. Authority becomes far less important because the use of "authority" is essentially a threat and therefore extremely high-maintenance. Tactical empathy makes your message more relatable, your decisions more trusted, and your influence more sustainable.

When your team knows you get them, truly get them, they'll run through walls for you. Not because they have to. Because they *want* to.

TACTICAL EMPATHY AS YOUR BRAND

In today's transparency-driven world, how you lead is how you're perceived. Leadership is no longer just about your quarterly numbers or your strategic decisions; it's about *how you make people feel while you're achieving those numbers*. Command-and-control leadership is out because it's mediocre.

It's a cliche, and it's true: People don't just remember what you said. They remember how you made them feel. They remember if you made space for their voice. They remember if you looked them in the eye during a tough conversation, or if you rushed past them on your way to something more "important."

That's why tactical empathy isn't just a skill. It's a *signature*. It becomes the watermark on every interaction you have. It's visible in how you give feedback, how you run meetings, how you celebrate wins, and how you handle setbacks.

Tactical empathy has become part of my brand. Not because I set out to make it so, but because over time, people noticed. Clients have told us, time and again, that they choose to work with us not just because of what we deliver, but because of how we make them *feel* in the process: safe, seen, and valued. It's not just about the solution, it's about the *relationship*.

I don't always get it right. I'm still learning (which is actually one of the delightful aspects of this). I still fall into problem-solving mode or let urgency override curiosity. But I come back to this center: **How can I make the people I work with feel deeply understood, especially when the stakes are high?**

That question has become my leadership compass. It's influenced our onboarding process, our performance reviews, and our leadership development tracks. We've embedded tactical empathy not as a soft layer around hard conversations, but as the very structure that supports them.

And here's the surprising thing: when tactical empathy becomes part of your brand, it has a *magnetic effect*. Partners refer you. Clients renew with you. Because in a world of noise and ego and exhaustion, being known as someone who leads with tactical empathy is not just rare, it's *irresistible*.

Tactical empathy doesn't make you "the nice boss." It makes you the *trusted* one. The one people follow when the path is unclear. The one people lean on when decisions get messy. The one whose reputation travels further than your résumé ever could.

So ask yourself:

- What do people feel when they leave a meeting with you?
- What do they say about you when you're not in the room?
- What emotional footprint are you leaving behind?

That's your brand. Whether you intended it or not.

When you lead with empathy, you guide that narrative, and you elevate every person you work with along the way.

YOUR TURN: START WITH ONE CONVERSATION

You don't need to overhaul your style overnight. Start small. In your next conversation:

- Mirror once.
- Label once.
- Ask one calibrated question.

See how it changes the tone. See how it opens the other person up. See how it makes *you* feel more connected.

Tactical empathy isn't just a tactic. It's a mindset. It's leadership at its highest level.

CONCLUSION: LEAD THE WAY FORWARD

Tactical empathy is no longer optional. It's the operating system of modern leadership. In a world where trust is scarce and attention is fleeting, the ability to connect deeply, quickly, and authentically is what sets the best apart.

I gave you the tools. Now it's your job to use them. To listen without solving. To reflect without judging. To lead without bulldozing.

In every boardroom, negotiation, team huddle, and client call, tactical empathy is your edge.

Lead with it. And watch everything change.

About Chris

Chris Voss is the best-selling author of *Never Split the Difference*, a former lead international FBI kidnapping negotiator, and the CEO and founder of The Black Swan Group.

During his twenty-four-year career with the FBI, Chris served as the FBI's hostage negotiation representative for the National Security Council's Hostage Working Group and has represented the US at two international conferences. He's been recognized for a number of awards, including the Attorney General's Award, and the FBI Agents Association Award for Distinguished and Exemplary Service. He has received negotiation training from the FBI, Scotland Yard, and Harvard Law School.

Since retiring from the FBI, Chris has earned his master's in public administration from Harvard University and taught at a number of esteemed institutions, including the University of Southern California Marshall School of Business, Georgetown University, Harvard University, Northwestern University, the IMD Business School in Lausanne, Switzerland, and the Goethe Business School in Frankfurt, Germany.

Following the success of his book *Never Split the Difference*, Chris coauthored a book with real estate guru Steve Shull, *The Full Fee Agent*, which provides practical and skillful negotiation techniques for real estate agents—both experienced and expert. Chris has been featured on podcasts and media outlets such as Time magazine, CNN, CNBC, the Lex Fridman podcast Inc., and others.

His company, The Black Swan Group, established in 2008, aims at pro- viding negotiation coaching for professionals all over the world through corporate and individual coaching, as well as live events.

When he isn't coaching or giving keynote speeches, Chris is passionate about learning, working out, reading, and spending time with his family. He currently lives in Las Vegas.

To connect with Chris and his company, you can go to blackswanltd.com. You can also follow him on LinkedIn and Instagram.

CHAPTER 2

THE PASSAGGIO MOMENT: FINDING POWER THROUGH TACTICAL EMPATHY IN HIGH-STAKES NEGOTIATIONS

BY GARETH WITTEN

Newark Airport, 4:30 a.m., dead of winter. The black cab cut through the darkness toward Manhattan, and I could feel my chest tightening with each mile. In a few hours, I'd be sitting across from some of the sharpest minds in global finance, including PhDs from MIT, MBAs from Wharton, people who'd built multibillion-dollar businesses before turning forty. My mission: represent my clients' portfolio, address significant performance challenges, and somehow negotiate a fee reduction with managers who eat people like me for breakfast.

The cab pulled up to 200 West Street, Goldman Sachs towering above me in the predawn darkness. Then another stop at one of the world's largest quant hedge funds. My hands were trembling, not from the cold, but from knowing I was about to face the very best in their field, people who'd literally written books on building successful corporate cultures and investment strategies.

What the hell was I doing here?

FROM SURVIVAL MODE TO STRATEGIC EMPATHY

Growing up non-white in apartheid South Africa, on what we called "the wrong side of the railway line," you learn one thing above all else: survival is about power, and power is about domination. In my neighborhood, there was no tactical empathy. There was no sitting down to understand the other person's perspective. You fought for everything—a decent education, food on the table, sometimes just the right to exist. The strong survived. The weak didn't. Simple as that.

This mentality carried me from the townships through a PhD in applied mathematics, through building businesses and academic institutions. I became what the corporate world rewards: an A-type personality who dominated discussions, ate first, and got promoted. When I landed in Canada less than a decade ago, I thought I had the formula figured out. Be tougher. Be louder. Never show weakness.

Then something strange happened. Canada, as I discovered, is... very nice. Suddenly, my South African directness—what Elon Musk embodies from our shared homeland—felt like bringing a machete to a tea party. I swung hard to the other extreme, becoming apologetic, subservient, trying to out-nice the Canadians.

Neither approach worked. I was either too harsh or too soft, struggling to find that sweet spot where real influence lives. (And by the way… it looks like the Canadians are figuring this out too!)

THE BILLION-DOLLAR LESSON IN LISTENING

The transformation started during a negotiation that should have been simple. We'd invested in a hedge fund, and I needed them to provide monthly valuations instead of quarterly. Our stakeholders needed timely information. The manager wanted to protect their trading strategies from competitors who might front-run their positions.

My old self would have gone in guns blazing: "We're paying you millions in fees. Give us what we need, or we walk."

Instead, sitting across from this manager who controlled billions, I heard myself saying something different: "It seems like you're concerned we might compromise your competitive advantage. Help me understand what specific risks you're seeing?"

The room changed. The manager's defensive posture softened. He leaned back, surprised, then started really talking. He spoke about the copycats monitoring their every move, about positions that took months to build and seconds to destroy if the wrong information leaked.

As I listened, really listened, not just waited for my turn to attack, something shifted. We weren't adversaries anymore. We were two people trying to solve a problem together.

Six months and several conversations later, we were the only investor getting monthly valuations. But here's the kicker: the relationship didn't just survive the negotiation; it thrived. That manager became one of our strongest partnerships, later giving us a first look at new opportunities specifically because, as he put it, "You actually wanted to understand our challenges, not just extract concessions."

THE PASSAGGIO PRINCIPLE

I'm going to share something that might sound strange coming from a finance guy: I used to sing opera. Seriously. Performed on major stages, the whole thing. In classical singing, there's this concept called the *passaggio*—Italian for *passage*. It's that terrifying transition point where a tenor must navigate from the lower register to the upper register. Navigate it wrong, and your voice cracks in front of thousands. Navigate it right, and you access extraordinary power and resonance.

Here's what Luciano Pavarotti wrote about the passaggio: Even after decades of performing, he never knew with absolute certainty whether he'd successfully navigate it. What he relied on wasn't certainty. It was preparation, technique, and trust in the process.

Every high-stakes negotiation has its passaggio moment. The conversation narrows. Tension builds. Everything feels like it's about to crack. Your survival instincts scream to either retreat or attack. But if you can stay present, stay curious, and push through with tactical empathy rather than force, you access a completely different level of power.

That morning at Goldman Sachs, discussing one of our funds' significant underperformance, we hit the passaggio forty minutes in. The lead partner's jaw clenched. His team was defensive. The room felt like a powder keg.

The old me would have lit the match or run for the door. Instead, I slowed everything down, dropped my voice to what Chris Voss calls the "late-night DJ voice," and said: "It sounds like this has been an incredibly challenging period for your team. Walk me through what it's been like on the inside?"

The lead partner's shoulders dropped. He started talking, not the rehearsed investor relations script, but the real story. A key portfolio manager who'd left at the worst possible time. A strategic pivot that looked brilliant on paper but collapsed in practice. The crushing weight of managing billions while everything went sideways.

As he spoke, I realized something profound: He wasn't just explaining to me; he was processing it himself. My tactical empathy had created space for honesty, his and mine.

THE POST-MORTEM MIRROR

Here's what nobody tells you about learning tactical empathy when you come from a survival background: The hardest negotiation isn't with the person across the table. It's with yourself.

After every major negotiation, I run the same four-step process on myself that I use with counterparties:

Step One: I sit quietly for five minutes and let my emotions flow, no judgment, no control. Just observe the ping-pong ball of thoughts bouncing around my head.

Step Two: I identify my inner critic. I call him Arthur. Arthur is brutal. "You gave away too much." "You should have pushed harder." "They played you." Instead of fighting Arthur, I negotiate with him: "It seems like you feel I was weak in that second discussion. Help me understand what you saw?"

Step Three: I ask open-ended questions of Arthur. "How could I have handled that differently?" "What would it take for you to feel we succeeded?" This transforms criticism into coaching.

Step Four: I find something to genuinely praise myself for. "I'm proud that I recognized when to pivot." "I'm glad I stayed curious when they got defensive." This isn't empty self-congratulation; it's building the emotional muscle memory that lets you stay present during the next passaggio moment.

THE ACCUSATION AUDIT THAT CHANGED EVERYTHING

Investment committees are battlegrounds. Smart people with strong opinions fighting over billions of dollars. I recall a time when I was chairing one where two teams were going at each other's throats. The kind of aggressive questioning that breaks cultures and destroys working relationships.

The old me would have either joined the fight or tried to shut it down through authority. Instead, I started with what Chris calls an accusation audit: "I know some of you probably think I'm being too soft on their investment process and potential risks their strategy is taking. Others might feel I'm not giving them enough room to execute their strategy."

Then I shifted to the thinking questions: "How do you think we could structure this to address both concerns?" "What would have to be true for everyone to feel good about this path forward?"

The room transformed. Instead of attacking each other, they started problem-solving together. We ended with genuine appreciation, not corporate pleasantries, but real recognition of the difficulty of what we were all trying to achieve.

FROM ASYMMETRIC INFORMATION TO AUTHENTIC CONNECTION

When you're negotiating with fund managers who control billions, you face a brutal reality: asymmetric information. They know infinitely more about their positions, strategies, and portfolio companies than you ever will. They've spent thousands of hours building competitive advantages you can barely comprehend.

Early in my career, I tried to overcome this through being tough—the same approach that had kept me alive in South Africa. It occasionally worked, but more often destroyed relationships, closed doors, and left value on the table.

Tactical empathy flips the script. Instead of pretending you know everything, you acknowledge the asymmetry and make it work for you. "I realize you've spent years building this strategy, and I'm seeing a snapshot. Help me understand what I'm missing?"

This isn't weakness; it's strategic vulnerability. When you genuinely try to understand their world, they stop protecting information and start sharing it. The asymmetry doesn't disappear, but it becomes bridgeable.

THE NELSON MANDELA MOMENT

There's profound irony in my journey. I grew up under apartheid, a system built on the complete absence of empathy, where understanding the *other* was not just discouraged but illegal. Every instinct I developed was about protection, dominance, and survival.

Yet my greatest successes have come from doing exactly what apartheid forbade—genuinely trying to understand another person's challenges, fears, and needs.

Nelson Mandela exemplified this transformation. After twenty-seven years in prison, he had every right to seek revenge. Instead, he chose to understand his oppressors' fears about losing power, their concerns about their future in a new South Africa. He met them where they were and created a path forward that acknowledged both sides' humanity.

That's tactical empathy at its most powerful, not capitulation, but strategic understanding that creates possibilities neither side imagined.

THE COMPOUND EFFECT OF CONNECTION

A recent phone call crystallized everything for me. A portfolio manager I'd negotiated with several years ago—a particularly difficult restructuring of a private asset—called out of the blue.

"Gareth," he said, "we have a new deal opportunity. Before we talk to anyone else, I wanted to give you a first look. Not because you're the biggest investor, but because you're the only one who really understood what we were trying to do."

This is the paradox of tactical empathy in high-stakes negotiations: When you stop trying to win at someone else's expense and start trying to understand their world, you don't get less, you get more. More information, more trust, more opportunities, more sustainable success.

That scared kid from the townships still lives in me. But now, instead of letting fear drive me to aggression or submission, I let it remind me that everyone in that negotiation room carries their own fears, their own pressures, their own passaggio moments to navigate.

The balance isn't easy. It's not about being nice. When you grow up where I did, you learn that *nice* can get you killed. It's about being strategic. Tactical empathy isn't weakness masquerading as kindness. It's strength expressed through understanding.

Every negotiation still presents that narrow passage where everything might crack. The difference is now I know it's coming. I prepare for it. Most importantly, I trust that on the other side lies not just a successful deal, but strengthened relationships and expanded possibilities.

The mathematically trained part of my brain wants to quantify this, to create an equation for empathy's ROI. But the truth is simpler and more complex: In a world of asymmetric information and high-stakes decisions, the most powerful position isn't knowing everything. It's creating conditions where others feel safe to share what they know.

That morning at Goldman Sachs that had me trembling in the cab? It led to a restructured investment benefiting both parties and opened doors to three new opportunities. More importantly, the lead partner became a friend whose guidance shaped my career trajectory.

The scared PhD from the townships still feels the pull of old instincts when negotiations get tense, when someone seems to be taking advantage. Arthur whispers that empathy is a luxury I can't afford.

But I've learned that navigating the passaggio moment isn't something you master once. Every negotiation presents a new passage. The difference is trusting that tactical empathy, that strange alchemy of strength and understanding, creates outcomes that pure power never could.

About Gareth

For more than 25 years, Gareth has advised businesses and built functional units within companies and academic institutions. He has guided global businesses through complex competitor and market environments and negotiated large private and public investment deals.

He has the unique ability to negotiate and use practical problem-solving skills (both qualitative and quantitative) to navigate a complex transaction. He has been brought into businesses to provide industry insights, to "fix" investment strategies, and risk oversight functions.

He was part of expert teams managing multi-asset investment portfolios of large public assets (e.g., nuclear funds for the province of Ontario, Canada). He helps businesses navigate challenging competitive environments and guides them to focus on the real versus perceived challenges, both technically and with Tactical Empathy®.

He has a PhD in applied mathematics and currently teaches in the Mathematical Finance Programme at the University of Toronto. He has published many journal and industry peer-reviewed articles and actively contributes to industry conferences globally. He currently serves on the Board of Weizmann Canada.

CHAPTER 3

MANAGE THE MELTDOWN: HOW TO PROJECT MANAGE VIRTUALLY ANYTHING

BY RACHEL LOSSER

"I cannot keep doing this…something needs to change."

I stared at my computer screen, eyes burning, legs aching from hours of sitting still, my stomach twisted into a knot that never went away. I had been working eighteen-hour days and barely sleeping. I woke up exhausted and went to bed wired, anxious, unable to shut my mind off. My stress level wasn't just high; it was unsustainable. My mental health was unraveling, and eventually, a doctor put a name to it: depression.

I was a project manager, managing everything except myself. Every deadline met, every crisis averted, every impossible expectation handled. And somewhere in the middle of all that competence, a clarity surfaced. I was killing myself to make someone else look good!

When that project ended, I took a vacation to think deeply about starting my own consulting business.

Then the phone rang. The company was offering voluntary separation packages. Great severance. A clean exit. It felt like the universe was calling me to something bigger. It was time!

People often ask how I got into project management, and the truth is, I never got into it. It was already in me.

From the time I was nine, I was managing businesses. My first was a neighborhood mailbox-washing empire. I recruited kids on the street. I pitched homeowners, closed deals, delegated tasks, checked quality, and paid "staff" while keeping a cut for myself.

In college, I wrote and sold study guides. The project management qualities were already taking root: identify the need, design a solution, manage the process.

Years later, when I entered the corporate world and found myself managing massive, messy, global projects, it didn't feel foreign.

The divine intervention that prompted me to start my own business gave me the runway to finally do what I was born to do: lead in my own way, build something meaningful, and move the entire profession forward.

What came next validated what I knew: project management isn't about checklists or timelines; it's about restoring order. And after helping cascades of clients recover and succeed, I know one thing for sure: I can project manage my way into and out of anything.

* * *

The room was already on fire when I got there. Not literally, but in the world of project management, figurative flames can burn just as fast. In this case, the fire was consuming the Accounts Payable department. As a project management consultant, I had been brought in to rescue a manufacturing company hurtling toward a shutdown. The leadership team didn't recognize that there was a problem. It was a ticking time bomb. They were two weeks from shutting down, money was hemorrhaging, and morale was circling the drain.

I needed to say what everyone else was afraid to say: "This is a problem. And the consultants you brought in just aren't cutting it. We either fix this now, or we watch a company fall. I need to bring in my own team member."

The directors discussed my request and came back with an answer I wasn't expecting. "You can bring your team in. In fact, we want six new people." I didn't have six. I had one. I stayed up all night, calling the smartest people I knew, onboarding them one by one. The next day, we were on site, sleeves rolled, brains firing. And we saved that company.

Yet, most people groan when they see a project manager coming. Some people think project managers nag for status updates because we enjoy irritating people. They imagine us as hall monitors with clipboards, chasing people down like exasperated parents asking if they've cleaned their rooms. But as a project manager, I'm not a nag. I'm a scientist. And this messy, high-stakes chaos is my laboratory. In my laboratory, the approach matters. At this point, these are not experiments anymore. They are highly effective methods tested and proven to work.

You see, project management isn't just a business function. It's a way of thinking. The same structure that rescues failing projects can rescue struggling people. The same principles that keep teams aligned can keep our lives aligned.

I've managed hundreds of projects across industries, personalities, crisis levels, and degrees of chaos, and managed to do it successfully. But not because I nag, micromanage, or force compliance. It's because I've developed a methodology that blends psychology, systems thinking, empathy, and courage into one coherent approach. It's a system made up of five steps that can rescue virtually anything…

STEP 1: GET THE LAY OF THE LAND

Most struggling projects aren't suffering from lack of effort; they're suffering from lack of understanding.

Before you can fix anything, you have to diagnose. Who works well with whom? Who secretly hates whom? What political wounds are still bleeding beneath the surface? Who designed the original system and is now emotionally attached? This is where the *real* work begins.

There was a warehouse team who hated our project. They ignored our emails, avoided meetings, and seemed to purposely delay deliverables. Everyone dismissed them as difficult, lazy, and resistant. Months went by like this, and I'd had enough.

I walked into their area, sat down, and just listened. Within a few hours, I learned the truth.

It turns out that this company relied heavily on temp workers. Each group requested workers weekly, but this group was consistently eating last. They would request ten workers and get zero. Every week. They weren't lazy. They were *drowning.*

So, I flipped the hierarchy. The next week, I made sure they got the support they needed, and it didn't take long for everything to change. Timelines recovered. Productivity skyrocketed. The "difficult team" became one of the highest-performing groups in the entire department.

All I did was sit near them and listen. Getting the lay is about presence, curiosity, and paying attention to what's *really* happening beneath the surface instead of reacting to what you assume.

Every one of us has "projects" we're trying to manage. A relationship. A family dynamic. A version of ourselves we're trying to grow into.

And just like that warehouse team, the obstacles in our lives aren't always what they seem. Sometimes they're caused by exhaustion, fear, or unmet needs.

Most people fail at this step not because they lack intelligence, but because they lack restraint. They think getting the lay of the land means gathering enough information to act quickly. But this step demands discipline: the discipline to resist judgment, delay conclusions, and slow the instinct to start firefighting. Those who go deeper, listen longer, observe more carefully, and lead with empathy often see what others miss. And that difference is what separates reactive problem-solvers from trusted, effective leaders.

When you slow down long enough to listen, you stop reacting blindly and start responding wisely to what's been simmering beneath the surface all along.

STEP 2: RALLY THE TROOPS

When I step into a broken project, the first thing I do is create a *single source of truth*. Not ten spreadsheets. Not twelve email threads. One home. One shared reality where information, decisions, expectations, and responsibilities live. Then I build the cadence around it: A new meeting rhythm. A communication loop people can rely on. Clear roles. Clear escalation paths so small issues don't grow teeth and turn into monsters.

Project management teaches us that teams thrive when everyone knows where they're going, how they're getting there, and what they're responsible for. Life is no different. When you rally the troops in your own world, your habits, your energy, your people, your priorities, you stop reacting to chaos and start leading from clarity.

This is where most leaders get it wrong. They demand accountability without first creating clarity. But accountability is not something you extract from people; it's something you enable. When direction is clear, accountability stops being a struggle. It becomes the default.

STEP 3: UNDERSTAND THE ANATOMY OF A COMPLAINT

The meeting exploded into a yelling match. Again. Third time that week. I had a portfolio of critical projects and was stuck with a team branded as lazy, disorganized, and impossible.

Both sides complained. Both felt they were right. If I didn't want my projects to slip, I needed to sort out this mess.

I sat with the group that was being blamed the most. Once I followed the layers of their complaints, the truth became clear: 80% of their delays were caused by *other* teams submitting late work. They weren't the bottleneck. They were the *scapegoats.*

That insight changed everything. I built a new system with total transparency that revealed where the real delays were happening. And that team began to consistently deliver on time.

That wasn't coincidence. That was understanding the anatomy of a complaint. In our personal lives, it works the same way. The surface complaint is just a flare, while what really needs tending is hidden beneath it.

People rarely voice the real problem first. They voice the nearest one, the one sitting on the surface. But behind every complaint, if you're willing to peel back the layers, there's always something valid. A truth. A pressure point. A frustration that makes sense once you see it from their point of view.

This is where great leaders stand apart: they don't dismiss complaints, they *study* them. They see complaints not as irritations but as breadcrumbs leading to the real issue. A complaint begins with words spoken out loud, but beneath those words is emotion: discontent, fear, frustration. Beneath that emotion is the way this issue is making their life harder. And if you keep asking "why," and keep pulling the thread, you eventually arrive at the story underneath: the unmet needs, the broken processes. And finally, if you stay patient long enough, you uncover the root cause, which Chris Voss calls the Black Swan. This is the real crux of the issue. The revelation that must be addressed, or nothing changes.

When you understand how complaints really work, you stop fearing conflict and start using it as vital data. Every complaint holds a key. You just have to dig deep enough to unlock it.

STEP 4: PRACTICE EMPATHY WITHOUT AGREEMENT

This is the step most leaders misunderstand. Ironically, it's the step that makes the biggest difference in project management, in relationships, and in life.

Empathy is not approval. Empathy is understanding. It says: "I see why you feel this way, even if I don't feel the same." Chris Voss calls this *tactical empathy*: the ability to understand someone's truth so clearly that they feel seen, safe, and disarmed even when you're holding a completely different position. Tactical empathy is powerful because it removes defensiveness. But here's the nuance most people miss: empathy doesn't require agreement. You can understand someone's viewpoint without adopting it and honor their feelings without abandoning your direction. In fact, that's what makes it *tactical*. You're not validating their conclusion; you're validating their humanity. You're lowering the emotional temperature, so progress becomes possible.

Once, in a room full of executives, a senior vice president silenced my bosses and asked me directly, "Rachel, do we have enough support to pull this off?" We didn't, so wording mattered. I had to speak with authority without throwing my bosses under the bus. I could have sugarcoated, but instead I got in front of the uncomfortable truth. "You're probably feeling anxious because the last time this was attempted, it went badly," I said. "You're wondering if history is going to repeat itself. Those concerns are valid." They nodded. Then I gave the real answer. "It won't be perfect. The support is slim. But we can make this work."

Afterward, the CEO pulled me aside. "That was a damn good answer," he said. Not because it was optimistic or safe, but because it was honest without being defeatist.

Empathy without agreement lets you say things like:

- "I can hear how overwhelmed you feel, and that makes sense. Here's the path forward."
- "This change feels unfair. Let me show you why we need it."
- "You're extremely frustrated with what's going on. Here's how we fix it together."

That's leadership. You move the needle in the direction you need it to go, not by overpowering someone's perspective, but by honoring it enough that they're willing to walk with you.

Empathy without agreement is both the bridge and the boundary. And when you master that balance, you stop managing people and start leading them.

AND FINALLY...DELIVER ON YOUR PROMISES, ESPECIALLY THE ONES YOU MAKE TO YOURSELF

Most people think delivering on your promise is just about doing what you said you'd do for a company, a client, or a team. But the real test of leadership, and the one that defines your legacy, is also about delivering on the promises you make to *yourself*.

When I stood at the crossroads of starting my own company, I felt the weight of that risk. I was young. If I followed the traditional path and waited for someone to grant me permission to move up, decades would pass, and I'd still be living a version of my life that was smaller than it could be.

I made a promise in that moment. Not to a boss or a department. To *myself.* I promised I'd build something that mattered, that I would lead differently, that I'd prove that empathy and structure together can transform any environment, and that I would become the kind of person teams could rely on to calm the waters when the ship was sinking.

Ultimately, delivering on your promise isn't about performance, it's about identity. It's about deciding who you are and then living in alignment with that decision every day.

That's why integrity matters. That's why the Say/Do ratio is sacred. People assume I close so many deals because I'm persuasive, but I close deals because I don't treat prospects like transactions. While others start with slide decks, I start with questions: "How can I make your life easier? What pressure are you under? What do you actually need to look good in front of your boss?"

When you show up with empathetic leadership and deliver on your promise, people learn that your word is a contract and your presence is a stabilizing force in their chaotic world.

The reality is that anyone can tick off boxes and manage tasks. But only a leader can stand in the heat, see the landscape clearly, rally the troops, hold boundaries with empathy, cut through complaints, and then deliver on what they said they would do. When you resist the impulse to jump to conclusions or act from self-interest, and instead apply the tools I've shared, you don't just earn more respect and greater success, you actually have more fun doing it.

At the end of the day, your greatest deliverable isn't the project you complete. It's the standard you set for how leaders should show up in a world that desperately needs them.

About Rachel

For over a decade, Rachel Losser has been a leader in project management and has consistently delivered some of the largest and most complex projects in the world. Rachel has worked with multitudes of clients to break down large-scale initiatives into structures that enable delivery, visibility, and speed. Her ability to translate vision into actionable plans has earned her recognition as a trusted partner for organizations seeking to implement global change.

Rachel Losser is the Founder and Managing Partner of Losser Consulting Solutions, a delivery focused firm that helps companies complete their biggest projects or fundamentally change how they operate. Known for her "Get Shit Done" philosophy, Rachel and her team are passionate about driving initiatives forward.

Beyond consulting, Rachel is a sought-after speaker and contributor on topics such as project leadership, organizational agility, business transformation, and driving accountability across global organizations. She is passionate about equipping professionals with the tools and strategies needed to thrive amid today's unique business challenges.

When she's not driving change for her clients, Rachel enjoys exploring new ideas, mentoring emerging leaders, visiting local Chicagoland breweries, and spending time with her husband, Jim, and troublemaker Standard Schnauzer, Siegfried.

Learn more at:
losserconsultingsolutions.com
www.linkedin.com/in/rachellosser

CHAPTER 4

FROM COURTROOMS TO CLOSING TABLES

BY TAI BIXBY

REAL ESTATE ADVISORS, LLC – SANTA FE, NEW MEXICO

The breakfast meeting almost didn't happen.

After ten years of litigation, mediation, and community opposition, Laura (not her real name) was the last holdout. Hundreds of neighbors had made peace with our church project. She was still holding a grudge. We'd won twice in federal court, built the church building, and proven every dire prediction wrong. The traffic apocalypse never materialized. The aquifer remained intact.

But Laura still carried her anger like armor.

When her mutual neighbor and I invited her to breakfast with the thought of burying the hatchet, she arrived defensive and triggered, ready for battle. For a decade, she'd built a threatening narrative about who we were. Those stories had become fortresses—nearly impossible to penetrate with logic or legal victories.

I remembered seeing her years earlier at the Hotel La Fonda, having breakfast with her elderly mother. I was there with my daughter, continuing our Sunday morning tradition of one-on-one daddy-daughter time. Two families, the same restaurant, the same ritual.

That memory became my bridge.

"Laura, remember when you saw me at La Fonda years ago? You were there with your mother."

Her defenses stayed up. "Yeah, I remember. What does that have to do with anything?"

I labeled what I'd observed. "It seems like you really love your mother."

"Of course, I love my mother." Her tone was sharp.

"I have seen you there a few times. Looks like it's a tradition for you."

Something flickered across her face. "We go on Sundays from time to time."

I mirrored her words. "Sundays? I take my kids there on Sundays too. We have the same tradition. Laura, you love your family. I love my family. We're not so different."

The armor fell away.

I watched the softening in her eyes, the crack in a decade-long wall of hostility. We weren't adversaries. We were two people who valued the same things, who showed up on Sundays at the same place to honor our most important relationships.

That's the moment Chris Voss calls "that's right." The other person feels genuinely understood, not agreed with, not defeated, but *understood.* It's tactical empathy in action, and it transforms everything.

THE JOURNEY TO THAT MOMENT

The path to rezoning our land and building a temple for our church in an upscale residential neighborhood in Santa Fe had been brutal. We became the first church application ever denied under the county's land use code. Opposition organized immediately—petitions, lawsuits, and years of hearings.

We sued under the Religious Land Use and Institutionalized Persons Act. We won. The county settled. Then, the neighbors sued the county, alleging an improper settlement. More litigation. More years.

I learned something crucial: winning legally doesn't mean winning relationally. The law might force compliance, but only empathy creates peace.

As a condition of settling the dispute, we agreed to let the neighbors monitor our well for five years. When that period ended, we sent a courteous letter thanking them, letting them know that we had complied with the terms of the settlement and that the monitoring period was over.

Laura's response: *We think you're violating covenants and the terms of your development permit.*

After proving every prediction wrong, Laura still needed to be right about us being wrong. At breakfast, she came with her grievances. Her message: *I don't like you. I'll never forgive you.*

The confrontational tactics I'd relied on early in my career weren't working. So, I got personal. That shared breakfast tradition became the handhold that pulled us both up from a decade of conflict. By labeling her love for family, by mirroring her language, I shifted the conversation from positions to values.

When Laura said, "That's right," I felt the weight of ten years lift.

WHEN THE DEAL ALMOST DIED AT CLOSING

In 2024, I was brokering two linked transactions: my client was buying a shopping center and a retail building. The seller of the two buildings was in financial trouble—foreclosure lawsuits, multiple loans, and complex debt securitization structures. First, we needed to close on the sale of the shopping center, then the retail building.

At the closing for the shopping center, the seller dropped a bomb: "We're out of cash. We need more money. We have to increase the sale price for the shopping center, or we can't close."

My buyer's attorney went into attack mode. "Don't do it. You can sue them for breach of contract."

Instead, I switched to the "late-night FM DJ voice," calm and soothing, and labeled what I heard: "It sounds like the timing of funds is tighter than we thought."

The seller said, "We can't close on either property unless we get more money today from this closing."

Then I mirrored: "More money from *this* closing?" And stopped talking.

Dynamic silence creates space for truth. The seller opened up. He didn't need more money overall. He needed more *at the first closing* to satisfy one debt knot. The problem wasn't the total price for the two buildings—it was the sequence of funds.

I used a no-oriented question: "Would it be a bad idea to walk through the exact cash waterfall you need?"

People protect their autonomy. Saying "no" feels safer than "yes." He said no, that wasn't a bad idea, and explained his real needs.

Before proposing solutions, I ran an accusation audit with my buyer: "You're going to think I'm spending more of your money. You're going to worry that this deal unfairly favors the seller. You probably think he's taking advantage of you."

That drained the defensiveness before it could start.

Then I summarized to each side:

To the seller: "You're not asking for a higher total price on the shopping center. You're asking for front-loaded liquidity to clear liens so the first deal can close."

To the buyer: "You're not being asked to overpay. You're being asked to shift value from Deal B to Deal A so both can close on schedule."

The fix became simple: increase the shopping center price and decrease the retail building price by the same amount. Move earnest money from the second deal to the first. Equal economics to the buyer. Day-one relief to the seller.

Both deals closed. What looked like a deal-killing crisis became a two-deal win because empathy revealed the real constraint.

THE LAND THAT BELONGED TO THE ANCESTORS

I was representing a nonprofit foundation that owned land with significant Indian ruins in northern New Mexico. The board decided to sell, and we identified the local pueblo as the ideal buyer, given their cultural, historic, and spiritual connection.

The timing proved providential. Under the Native American Graves Protection and Repatriation Act, a university was repatriating human remains to the tribe. They needed ancestral land for reburial. Rather than simply saying yes or no to the reburial request, we invited them to discuss purchasing the land.

The meeting felt charged. Here we were, white men in real estate, sitting across from Native American women leaders. Everybody knew there were centuries of broken treaties and land disputes.

We acknowledged the request for repatriation and presented our client's proposal for a sale. The tribe came prepared with a much lower offer. The gap was substantial. From their perspective, this land had been stolen from their ancestors, and now the seller wanted to sell it back at market rates.

Every word mattered. Taking a purely transactional approach would have been easy—push back on numbers, argue comparable sales. But I sensed this wasn't about price. It was about whether we saw them and respected who they are. The conversation took a turn into tense territory.

I paused. "Madam Governor, we are coming to you with maximum respect for your culture and for your people. We recognize what you've been through, and we want to find a way to restore these lands to your people."

Those words *respect* and *restore* mattered enormously.

I used labels: "It seems like this land carries enormous cultural and spiritual meaning for your tribe." Then: "It seems like you want to find a way to make this work."

They confirmed they did.

Then I employed dynamic silence. I stopped talking and gave the words room to breathe.

The tension softened, and the tribal elders were able to articulate what they needed. We listened. The tribal attorney spoke up at the end of the meeting: "I never imagined I would see the day where a white man would treat Native American women with respect in a negotiation setting, much less for a land-back deal for such an important tribal site."

What felt risky—slowing down, acknowledging history, and affirming respect—turned out to be essential. Instead of looking weak, empathy demonstrated strength.

The price gap remained wide. We identified a California nonprofit specializing in landback projects and introduced them to the tribe. Once the tribe engaged the nonprofit as intermediary and funding source, final terms were negotiated, and the process flowed smoothly.

By the time this book is published, that deal will likely be closed—one of the most significant landback stories in northern New Mexico in generations.

BUILDING A PLAYBOOK FROM PAIN

A junior broker on my team had worked incredibly hard on a listing—dozens of calls, hundreds of emails. We found a prospect who seemed perfect. The deal appeared lined up.

Then the sellers went into financial distress. Their lender foreclosed. Our prospect bought the property directly from the lender, circumventing us entirely. Since we didn't have a signed buyer-broker agreement, the $30,000 commission disappeared.

My junior broker was crushed. He genuinely needed the money.

I could have said, "That's the business," or blamed him for missing the paperwork. Instead, I labeled what I saw: "It seems like you're not just frustrated—you're hurting because you were counting on this income."

He opened up about how powerless he felt.

That vulnerability gave me the opening to coach effectively. "We can't control every buyer, but we can control our process."

We conducted a thorough postmortem. We discussed the importance of testing whether we're "the favorite or the fool" with every new client—a concept from Chris Voss's work. Are clients genuinely valuing our expertise, or just using us for free information?

We created a new policy: constantly test for favorite-or-fool status on first contact, and never move forward without a signed buyer-broker agreement.

The shift was powerful. Instead of walking away bitter, he walked away with a playbook. Since then, he's said no to weaker clients and closed multiple deals with stronger clients who respect our values.

What he needed wasn't sympathy or blame. He needed clarity, structure, and a path forward. The setback became the foundation for better business.

THE RELATIONSHIP THAT MULTIPLIED

Early in my career, I made a cold call that connected me with a young banker—a Marine captain turned Wells Fargo vice president. We stayed in touch over the years, developing our businesses alongside each other, raising families, sharing the ups and downs of building careers in Santa Fe.

We were just friends. I liked the guy.

He eventually left banking and became a prominent local investor. After the 2008 crash, he and his partners bought a shopping center out of foreclosure and dramatically increased its value.

When it came time to list the property, every major national brokerage competed—Colliers, JLL, Cushman & Wakefield, CBRE. He gave the listing to me.

Why? For over two decades, he knew I understood him. I understood his concerns, his goals, and his partners. We had a deep relationship built on genuine connection and history, not just transactions.

That sale became my largest commission up to that point. We marketed aggressively, generated multiple offers, and closed with a buyer in a 1031 exchange.

But the key wasn't just selling the asset. It was making sure the buyer and his broker also felt heard and understood. When people feel genuinely understood, even with contrary positions, you build a connection that allows you to work through challenges.

The ripple effects were enormous. That buyer returned for additional properties. My friend referred me to other investors. Those relationships led to more than $50 million in additional deal volume.

All from one cold call twenty years earlier—and from choosing to build a real relationship based on understanding.

THE FOUNDATION THAT NEVER SHIFTS

Tactical empathy isn't a trick you deploy when you need something. It's a fundamental way of engaging with human beings that creates trust, opens possibilities, and builds the social capital that matters more than any single deal.

Listening. Strategic silence. Making others feel heard and understood. These aren't soft skills—they're the hardest skills to master and the most powerful tools you possess.

Whether you're closing real estate deals or resolving decade-long neighborhood disputes, whether you're mentoring junior team members or negotiating sacred land transactions, the principle remains the same: people will work with you, trust you, and create opportunities for you when they feel genuinely understood.

Not agreed with. Not defeated. *Understood.*

That breakfast with Laura taught me something I'd intellectually known but hadn't fully embodied: legal victories are hollow without human connection. You can win every argument and still lose the relationship.

The same principle applies in every high-stakes moment. When the seller dropped his surprise demand at closing, traditional negotiation would have led to litigation. Tactical empathy led to a solution that served everyone's interests. When meeting with tribal leaders about ancestral lands, transactional thinking would have created an impasse. Respect and recognition built a bridge.

These aren't extraordinary stories. They're examples of what becomes possible when you slow down, listen beyond the words to what's really being said, and acknowledge the human needs underneath the conflict.

Every person you encounter—the difficult neighbor, the panicked seller, the defensive client, the struggling team member—has something they need to be heard about. Your job isn't to fix them, change them, or even agree with them. Your job is to understand them well enough that they feel it.

When you achieve that, when you get to "that's right," you transform what's possible between you. The armor falls away. The real constraints emerge. The creative solutions appear.

And sometimes, after years of conflict, you find yourself sitting across from someone at a restaurant, both of you there with family, both of you doing the exact same thing for the exact same reasons, finally able to see that you were never so different after all.

About Tai

Tai Bixby is a nationally recognized commercial real estate broker, investor, and advisor based in Santa Fe, New Mexico. With more than two decades of experience, he has built a reputation for bringing sophisticated financial analysis, tactical empathy, and creative problem-solving to complex transactions. As a dual designee of both the Society of Industrial and Office Realtors (SIOR) and the Certified Commercial Investment Member Institute (CCIM), Tai ranks among the top tier of commercial brokers worldwide.

At Real Estate Advisors, LLC, Tai leads investment sales, leasing, and advisory assignments across office, industrial, retail, multifamily, and land sectors. His work includes representing institutional investors, private equity funds, developers, law firms, banks, municipalities, and family offices throughout New Mexico and the broader Southwest. He has closed more than $500,000,000 in sales and leases, often in transactions that require deep knowledge of capital markets, land-use codes, and tax strategies.

Tai's expertise extends beyond brokerage. He has authored expert witness accounts, structured sophisticated investment models, and guided clients through 1031 exchanges, opportunity zone investments, and public-private partnerships. His approach to negotiation is shaped by Chris Voss's "Black Swan" methodology—anchored in calibrated questions, tactical empathy, and uncovering hidden variables that change the outcome of a deal. This approach, combined with his financial acumen, has helped clients unlock value in transactions ranging from historic downtown landmarks to master-planned development projects.

Raised in New Mexico and deeply rooted in its communities, Tai blends local insight with global perspective. He has advised clients on acquisitions, dispositions, and leasing strategies that shape Santa Fe's commercial landscape, from courthouse and government leases to downtown retail portfolios and industrial campuses. His work is distinguished by integrity, analytical rigor, and a commitment to helping clients achieve long-term success.

When he is not brokering deals, Tai is often engaged in thought leadership, professional mentoring, and developing his own investment portfolio. Out of the office, he volunteers at his religious center and spends time with his family, traveling and sailing. His combination of strategic vision, ethical focus, and tactical negotiation skills makes him a trusted advisor to investors, owners, and tenants alike.

Contact Information:
Tai Bixby, SIOR, CCIM
Real Estate Advisors, LLC
1227 Paseo de Peralta
Santa Fe, NM 87501
tai@tba.team
https://www.linkedin.com/in/taibixby/
www.reanm.com

CHAPTER 5

WHEN EMPATHY SAVED LIVES: LEADING THROUGH THE IMPOSSIBLE

THOMAS SCHACHTNER

The third wave hit Munich like a sledgehammer in winter 2021. I stood in our orthopedic hospital's conference room, watching my colleagues' faces drain of color as our medical director spoke. His voice carried something I'd rarely heard in twenty years of practice—a tremor of genuine fear mixed with desperate hope.

"The major hospitals are drowning," he said. "They're asking if we can help."

Around me, seasoned physicians and nurses shook their heads. We ran an orthopedic specialty hospital. Hip replacements. Knee surgeries. Sports injuries. Not ventilators and dying COVID-19 patients. The consensus was immediate: we weren't equipped for this. We didn't have the right facilities. The right training. The right anything.

But I heard something else in our director's voice, that special tone that only comes when someone is asking for help they desperately need but don't expect to receive. After two decades as an anesthetist and intensivist, you learn to recognize that sound. It's the same tone family members use when their loved one is coding, the same pitch in a colleague's voice when they're overwhelmed but too proud to ask directly.

"We can do this," I said.

Every head in the room turned. The silence that followed felt like standing at the edge of a cliff, knowing you're about to jump but not sure if you'll land safely.

THE WEIGHT OF "YES"

What followed was a five-month period that would redefine everything I thought I knew about leadership and medicine. Our small orthopedic hospital, built for elective surgeries and sports medicine, would take in an unpredictable number of critically ill COVID patients, mostly from Munich's overwhelmed medical centers. To prepare, we were paired with a designated partner hospital, led by senior consultant Dr. C., whose ward was already overflowing. Our COVID-instructor and I visited her unit once before starting, to see firsthand what awaited us and to discuss the basic routines. From that moment, we knew we would have to transform not only our facilities but also our entire understanding of what it means to care for people when systems fail. To meet this challenge, we involved all the consulting specialties based within our small hospital—neurology, radiology, and internal medicine. Their physicians were available, including nights and weekends, and their expertise proved invaluable. They offered the kind of clinical insight that turned uncertainty into confidence and kept our care grounded in true teamwork.

The first lesson came within days. We'd converted an entire wing into a makeshift COVID unit, but the real transformation needed to happen in our minds. My team, young orthopedic and anesthesia nurses and doctors, who'd spent careers focused on joint replacements, suddenly had to face patients dying alone, isolated behind plastic barriers, families forbidden from holding their hands.

I watched a nurse who'd worked with me for many years break down in the supply room. "I don't know how to do this," she whispered. "In orthopedics, people get better. They walk again. Here, they will just die alone."

Instead of offering false reassurance, I sat with her discomfort. "You're right," I said. "This isn't what we trained for. But maybe that's exactly why we're the right people for this moment."

She looked at me, confused.

"Think about it," I continued. "The ICU nurses at the major hospitals are burning out. They've been watching people die for months. They've had to build walls just to survive. But us? We still feel everything. Maybe that's not our weakness. Maybe it's our superpower."

WHEN PROTOCOL MEETS HUMANITY

Three weeks into our COVID unit's operation, we received an eighty-two-year-old patient with early dementia who was declining rapidly. He fought us at every turn. He pulled at his oxygen mask, cried out for his deceased wife, and became increasingly agitated with each invasive procedure.

My team gathered for rounds, uncertainty thick in the air. "We're torturing him," one nurse finally said what everyone was thinking.

In a traditional ICU setting, we'd push forward. Follow protocols. Document the resistance and continue treatment. But something about our makeshift unit, perhaps because we were already operating outside our comfort zone, gave us permission to think differently.

"Let me call his family," I said.

His granddaughter answered on the second ring. Through her tears, she painted a picture of a man who valued freedom above all else. "Opa was a mountaineer," she explained. "He climbed nearly every peak in Bavaria. Even after Oma died, he'd still hike every morning."

She told me about his other loves: good Bavarian food, especially his favorite wheat beer, and sitting in his garden watching the sunset. "Independence isn't just important to him," she said. "It's who he is."

I hung up and looked at my team. "We're fighting the wrong battle."

That afternoon, we made a decision that would have raised eyebrows in any major hospital. We stopped the invasive procedures. And when his granddaughter arrived with a small bottle of his favorite wheat beer and brought a homemade chocolate cake, we didn't cite infection control protocols. We helped him take a small sip of beer.

The transformation was immediate. He stopped fighting. He smiled, actually smiled, for the first time since admission. Finally, when he was allowed to return to his nursing home, we all felt relieved and happy for this small victory of humanity.

THE RIPPLE EFFECT OF TRUST

Not every story from those five months ended in a close call. Sometimes empathy saved lives in ways that defied medical explanation.

One patient, eighty-five, had been with us for two weeks. But isolation was killing her faster than COVID. Despite improving lung function, she was withdrawing, refusing food, and turning her face to the wall.

Every evening, we found her crying deep, body-shaking sobs that had nothing to do with physical pain.

"I'm so alone," she whispered. "Even if I survive, what's the point? No one even knows I'm here."

Instead of offering platitudes about healing, my colleague asked, "Tell me about before you were alone."

For the next hour, she talked about her partner. They'd been together twelve years but never married. A fight six months before COVID had driven them apart. Pride had kept them from reconciling.

"Would you like me to call him?" I asked.

Her eyes widened with fear and hope. "He probably doesn't want…"

"Let me try."

Her partner arrived the next morning. I'll never forget watching them before closing the door. Two people in their eighties, crying like teenagers, gloved hands pressed against each other's. He came every day, staying hours beyond the approved visiting time. The nurses and I agreed to look the other way.

Two weeks later, we discharged her. She walked out—actually walking, not in a wheelchair—holding his hand.

LEADING FROM THE GROUND UP

The most profound transformation during those five months wasn't in our patients—it was in how we learned to work together. The traditional hospital hierarchy mattered less inside our COVID unit. Titles faded quickly when everyone was wearing the same protective gear, and every task, from patient positioning to cleaning equipment, became shared responsibility. I made it clear I was not above any task, and the team responded with remarkable dedication. The nurses, physiotherapists, and cleaning staff worked under exhausting physical conditions, yet they cared for every patient with skill, patience, and genuine humanity. Many of them, I'm convinced, grew beyond what they thought they were capable of.

But the real test came with our IT department.

For weeks, we'd been struggling with communication systems. The IT department, overwhelmed with requests from every unit, kept pushing our *nonessential* needs to the bottom of the queue.

My first instinct was to escalate, to use my senior position to demand priority. Instead, I invited the head of IT to spend an hour in our unit.

He arrived skeptical, clipboard in hand, ready to explain why our requests were unreasonable. I didn't argue. I just asked him to shadow me for one morning.

He saw the daily phone-call discussions between my assistants and representatives from various public health departments. He stood beside me as we held a tablet for a quarantined woman while her son, quarantined in another country, sang her favorite lullaby.

He set down his clipboard. "What do you need?"

Within forty-eight hours, we had a working laptop. Not because of policies or hierarchical pressure, but because he had felt what we felt. He'd seen that we weren't just treating disease. We were holding onto humanity when everything else was falling apart.

THE COST OF CARING

I want to be honest about something rarely discussed in healthcare: the personal cost of leadership during a crisis. Those five months demanded everything—time, focus, and energy. I am fortunate to have a partner who understands it better than anyone. My wife, also an anesthesiologist, worked long hours herself in pediatric anesthesia at the university hospital, wearing protective gear day after day. She knew the reality behind my late calls, my missed dinners, and the nights I came home too tired to talk.

What kept us connected was a quiet kind of understanding—an empathy that didn't need words. She gave me the confidence to lead through uncertainty, knowing I could ask her for professional advice without judgment. Sometimes it was her calm that grounded me; sometimes it was her silence that gave me space to find my own words. I learned that empathy at work can only thrive when it is supported by empathy at home.

As I begin guiding other healthcare professionals, I teach what the pandemic made clear to me: empathy doesn't stop at the hospital door—it extends into how we live, listen, and care for one another. My wife and I learned to take turns carrying the weight, each of us leading and holding space for the other.

THE THANK YOU THAT CHANGED EVERYTHING

Months of effort. Dozens of patients. Hope where capacity had run out. We demonstrated that an orthopedic hospital can become a critical care unit, that sports medicine nurses can become IMC specialists, and that empathy can be as powerful as any medical intervention.

The chief physician of our designated partner hospital sent me a handwritten letter after we closed our COVID unit. Two sentences stay with me:

"You didn't just take our patients. You reminded us why we became doctors."

I keep that letter not as a trophy but as a reminder. We didn't just treat those COVID patients in an orthopedic hospital. We proved that when systems fail and protocols crumble, empathy becomes the most powerful tool in medicine.

THE PRACTICES THAT SAVE LIVES

What we learned wasn't just crisis management. It was a blueprint for leading with empathy when everything is on the line. Here's what actually works:

Listen for the Tone Beneath the Words. In twenty years of practice, I've learned that people rarely ask directly for what they desperately need. They hint. They suggest. They speak in vocal tones that betray their words. When my director asked if we could help with COVID patients, his words were uncertain, but his tone was desperate. Learning to hear that difference and respond to what's really being asked changes everything.

Make Vulnerability Operational. We succeeded not despite our lack of COVID experience, but because of it. We couldn't hide behind expertise or established protocols. Every decision required us to admit uncertainty and figure it out together. This operational vulnerability created trust that no amount of expertise could have built.

Break Rules with Purpose, Not Rebellion. We didn't break dozens of rules. Most protocols exist for good reason, especially in times of crisis. But there were moments when strict adherence would have meant losing sight of the individual behind the diagnosis. In those cases, I allowed carefully considered exceptions—extended phone calls, a brief visit under full protection, a meal that felt more human than hospital. Each decision was deliberate, guided by clinical judgment and empathy, not defiance. The key is knowing when rules protect life—and when flexibility protects dignity.

Convert Resistance Through Experience. I could have fought IT for weeks through official channels. Instead, one hour of direct experience transformed an obstacle into an ally. When facing institutional resistance, stop arguing and start showing. Let people feel what you feel, see what you see. Experience transforms in ways arguments never can.

Build Expertise Through Admission of Ignorance. The moment we acknowledged we didn't know how to run a COVID unit, we opened the door to learning. My young residents approached every new task with remarkable curiosity and humility. They asked questions far beyond their usual specialties and shared what they learned with one another. Expertise grew from the willingness to learn together. That kind of collective humility is stronger than any title or credential.

Sustain Empathy Through Balance. The real challenge is not to give endlessly, but to sustain empathy without losing yourself. During the pandemic, my wife and I learned compassion must flow both ways—sometimes you lead, sometimes you're held. Empathetic leadership lasts only when it's shared, grounded in mutual care rather than self-sacrifice.

THE LEADERSHIP MEDICINE NEEDS

Healthcare stands at a crossroads. We can continue down the path of algorithmic medicine, where protocols override judgment and metrics take precedence over meaning. Or we can remember that true healing occurs in the space between clinical excellence and genuine human connection.

As I prepare to leave clinical medicine after twenty years, it's not because I've lost my passion for healing. It's because I've discovered that the healthcare system has lost its passion for empathy. Watching brilliant clinicians burn out, seeing protocols override humanity, and witnessing the gradual erosion of genuine connection in medicine has led me to a new calling: teaching empathetic leadership to healthcare organizations that have forgotten that healing requires heart as much as science.

The transition to becoming a certified business coach isn't an escape from medicine. It's an evolution of it. Every workshop I'll lead, every healthcare executive I'll coach, every burned-out physician I'll counsel will hear the same message: when medicine is driven more by managerial profit targets, political shortsightedness, and public cynicism than by patient care, it loses its moral compass. That's what leads to burnout, to moral injury, to the quiet loss of meaning that is spreading through our hospitals. Empathetic leadership is not a luxury—it's what keeps medicine human when systems forget what they were built for.

Those four months in our makeshift COVID unit proved something vital: empathy isn't soft skills training to be squeezed in between technical modules. It's the cornerstone of effective medical practice. Sometimes it's helping a team member through exhaustion, calling a family with honest words, or staying five minutes longer to make sure a patient is comfortable. That isn't sentimental, it's essential.

About Thomas

Dr. Thomas J. M. Schachtner (b. 1976, Salzburg, Austria) is a senior anesthesiologist, intensivist, and certified business coach based in Munich, Germany. With more than two decades of clinical experience, he has combined medical expertise, leadership in crisis, and a strong commitment to education and patient safety.

He studied medicine at Ludwig-Maximilian University of Munich (1997–2003) and completed his doctoral thesis on the hemodynamic changes of ischemic preconditioning in hepatic surgery in 2006. His clinical training included anesthesiology, hemostaseology, cardiac and pediatric cardiac anesthesia, and intensive care medicine at the University Hospital of Munich. Since 2015 he has served as Consultant in Anesthesiology and Intensive Care Medicine at Schoen Klinik München Harlaching, where he also leads the immunohematology laboratory and transfusion committee.

During the COVID-19 pandemic, Dr. Schachtner volunteered to establish and lead a dedicated COVID ward in his orthopedic specialty hospital under a state emergency order. Despite limited infrastructure and a young, inexperienced team, he built a functioning unit that treated dozens of patients. His empathic leadership, focus on team cohesion, and ability to integrate diverse perspectives—medical staff, nurses, families, administrators, and even authorities—were instrumental to the ward's success. This experience remains a defining example of how empathy and structure can transform crisis into resilience.

Beyond clinical care, Dr. Schachtner has been deeply engaged in medical education and international collaboration. He is a long-standing faculty member of the ESAIC "Teach the Teachers" program, examiner for the European Diploma in Anaesthesiology and Intensive Care (EDAIC), and organizer of online assessments. His expertise includes hemostaseology, transfusion medicine, and patient safety, with a special interest in morbidity & mortality conferences and peer support.

In recent years, he has expanded his qualifications into leadership training and business coaching. Having completed internationally accredited programs (ICF & EMCC), he is preparing to support healthcare leaders, who face financial constraints and systemic change. He also explores the integration of artificial intelligence into medicine and leadership.

Outside of medicine, Dr. Schachtner is passionate about hiking, skiing, cycling, and travel. His personal and professional journey reflects a consistent theme: guiding people safely through uncertainty—whether in the operating room, on an intensive care ward, or in leadership.

Connect with Dr. Schachtner: LinkedIn or www.thomas-schachtner.de

CHAPTER 6

FROM SILENCED TO SOVEREIGN: LEADING WITH EMPATHY AFTER THE FINE PRINT TELLS THE TRUTH

BY GWEN MEDVED

I never set out to become an expert in high-stakes divorce. I was a film producer, self-help author, and the woman who believed, for thirty years, that my marriage and our businesses were built on equal partnership. Verbally, we were partners. Then the paperwork told a different story.

My forthcoming book *Million Dollar Divorce* is the exact roadmap I wish had existed the day I discovered the truth: that the position of trust I had carried for three decades had been quietly replaced by documents that erased me.

But you don't need to be going through a divorce to know what it's like to be cornered. If anyone has ever tried to pull the rug out from under you, you know the feelings. Shock. Betrayal. The intense fear that the life you've always known is about to end. Your knuckles turning white as you try to hold onto any bit of dignity you can. At least that's what happened to me when my marriage ended...

For years, the official tax records told a lie. Every Schedule K-1 listed a single individual as the owner of the company, even though the business legally belonged to our joint trust. On paper, I was erased—my ownership, my voice, my stake, quietly reassigned without my consent. That was the moment I understood the betrayal wasn't emotional alone; it had been documented, repeated, and made official. Another devastating discovery in a long list of devastating discoveries across a three-year asset-splitting journey. Since then, I have heard the stories of hundreds of women who have gone or are going through the same war. The moves are always the same. The shock is always the same. The path to sovereignty is always the same.

Maybe you're not navigating a high stakes divorce, but odds are that at some point in your life, you will be thrown into a position in which you have to advocate for yourself. This chapter is your wake-up call and your starting line. But if you are facing a divorce, with this roadmap, what you reclaim will be priceless: financially by locking in every dollar that is yours, emotionally by standing in your power instead of pleading for it, and practically by saving years of exhaustion and expense. Preparation is the ultimate act of love—for yourself and for the legacy you will leave your children.

Here is the mantra I now offer to every woman, and I offer it to you now, so you can repeat it to yourself every single day: "The love I once gave away is still alive in me. Today I turn that fierce love inward—to myself and to my children. This is not loss. This is reclamation. This is a course-correction."

You are not becoming someone new. You are becoming the person you always were, only now the love you poured outward for decades has come home. The betrayal and misalignment you discovered have removed the betrayer. Nothing else was taken.

Your love, your clarity, your purpose, your commitment to your children's future—none of it is gone. It is simply being redirected to its rightful place: inside you and inside the legacy you are building for the people who come after you.

That fierce love will keep your heart open and your mind razor-sharp. It will let you hear the fear behind every tactic, label it without contempt, and answer with calm certainty. It will let you correct misfiled K-1s, protect irrevocable trusts, and walk away whole—without ever closing your heart.

Love did not make you soft. Love made you formidable. Love and strategy are not opposites. Love is the higher ground from which strategy becomes unstoppable. And when you finally place that fierce love where it was always meant to live—inside yourself and inside the legacy you are building—the game is already won. This is not destruction. This is course-correction. And you are exactly on track.

THE EIGHT EMPATHY-LED PATTERNS THAT MOVE POWER WITHOUT LOSING YOURSELF

I didn't intend to become a master negotiator, but when the fine print erased me, learning how to hold power calmly became non-negotiable. I learned the tools of tactical empathy taught by Chris Voss. I wasn't trained to extract criminals from barricaded rooms. I was a woman sitting at a table, fighting to reclaim my dignity, my security, and the life that had quietly been rewritten without my consent. It turns out that the same tools that de-escalate hostage crises also de-escalate a war being waged on paper.

These are not just negotiation tricks. They are composure strategies. Each one restores leverage without aggression and clarity without cruelty. And here is what matters most: these tools are not limited to courtrooms, boardrooms, or high-stakes divorces. They work anywhere that power, fear, and consequence intersect—which is to say, in families, in businesses, in medical decisions, in leadership moments, and in the quiet conversations where your future is being shaped. You do not need a badge, a title, or a crisis to use them. You need clarity, steadiness, and the willingness to stay present when it would be easier to disappear. When you learn to regulate yourself and lead with disciplined empathy, you can change the trajectory of almost any conversation, including the ones that decide your life.

1. The Pause & Label

Name the fear before it hardens into resistance. When stakes are high, people speak in positions, not truths. Control. Ownership. Authority. These are usually shields, not motives. The pause is where you refuse to react and instead choose to observe. By labeling what you hear beneath the words, you interrupt escalation without conceding ground. *"It seems like losing sole control feels like losing the entire legacy."* This does three things at once:

- It slows the nervous system in the room.
- It signals that you are listening beyond the surface.

- It exposes fear without attacking character.

You are not agreeing. You are clarifying reality. And clarity dissolves power plays faster than confrontation ever could.

2. Mirror + Calibrated Question

Reflect their language. Invite correction. Retain control. Mirroring is surgical. You repeat the last few emotionally charged words—not to echo, but to focus the conversation. *"It sounds like liquidity is the real concern... have I got that right?"*

This does not corner the other party. It gives them dignity while requiring specificity.

Most importantly, it forces them to engage their reasoning brain instead of their defensive one.

You are no longer responding to accusations or tactics. You are guiding the discussion toward solvable problems. That shift alone changes outcomes.

3. The Shared-Intent Line

Anchor the negotiation to a value neither side can publicly abandon. High-conflict negotiations often collapse because each side assumes opposing goals. Shared intent reframes the conversation around what was *supposed* to be protected all along. *"I'm protecting what we both said was for the girls."* This is not sentimental. It is strategic. It narrows the field of acceptable behavior. Once shared intent is stated out loud, every move must align with it, or the other party risks being exposed as self-serving. In my case, when I shifted the focus to our girls, I was no longer negotiating as an individual fighting for fairness. I was stewarding a declared legacy.

That is a much harder position to undermine.

4. The No-Oriented Reframe

Use "no" to create safety, not shutdown. People feel safest when they can say no. This pattern gives them that safety while still advancing your objective.

"Would it be unreasonable if the K-1s were issued exactly as the trust documents require?"

Notice what's happening:

- You are not asking for permission.
- You are not demanding compliance.
- You are inviting them to object on the record.

Most cannot. Because the request is reasonable, documented, and defensible. The power of this approach is that it shifts the burden of justification. Instead of you having to argue for what is already correct, the other party must explain—out loud—why compliance with the existing documents would be unreasonable. In that moment, leverage changes hands, not through force, but through structure. "No-oriented" questions lower resistance while quietly boxing in bad faith.

5. The "That's Right" Trigger

Summarize their fear so accurately they feel understood—and exposed. This is where negotiations turn. You lay out their concern in full, without judgment, distortion, or minimization. *"So you're afraid that correcting the K-1s will open the door to endless revisions and loss of control... is that right?"* When they respond with *"That's right,"* something shifts.

They feel seen. The fear loses its grip. And the conversation moves forward. Importantly, this is not empathy as agreement. It is empathy as illumination.

Once fear is named, it can be managed.

6. The Future-Focused Empathy Close

Redirect energy from the past to the next safe step. When negotiations stall, it's often because everyone is still arguing yesterday. This pattern pulls the room forward—without bypassing concern. *"What would need to be in writing—today—for all of us to feel 100% safe moving forward?"*

This question:

- Assumes resolution is possible.

- Centers documentation, not promises.
- Forces practical solutions instead of emotional looping.

You are no longer debating intent. You are designing safeguards. That's how settlements accelerate.

This is the moment where emotion gives way to architecture. Instead of managing fear, you begin building certainty. Agreements stop living in people's heads and start living on paper, where they belong—and once safety is structured, progress becomes inevitable.

7. The Legacy Mirror

Hold up the long view when short-term tactics dominate. Legacy questions bypass ego and activate conscience. *"How do you want this chapter to read when your daughters look back on how their inheritance was handled?"* This is not manipulation. It is consequence awareness.

Legacy reframes behavior in a way numbers alone never can. It reminds everyone that records outlive emotions—and children eventually read everything. Legacy questions collapse the time horizon. They force today's decisions to stand beside tomorrow's judgment. When someone is asked to imagine how their actions will be remembered—not explained, not defended, but *read*—the room shifts from strategy to responsibility. When legacy enters the room, recklessness tends to leave.

8. Self-Directed Empathy

Regulate yourself first—or you will negotiate from injury. This is the pattern that makes all the others possible. You will feel grief. You will feel fury. You will feel betrayal in your body before you can articulate it in words. Do not bypass that.

Self-directed empathy means allowing those emotions to exist without allowing them to take the wheel. You acknowledge what is true inside you without acting from it in the room. You do not weaponize your pain against yourself, and you do not bleed it into the negotiation where it can be misread, exploited, or dismissed.

When held with discipline, emotion stops being a liability and becomes a resource. The same intensity that could have driven impulsive reactions instead sharpens your attention, steadies your nervous system, and anchors you in your purpose. Held properly, that energy becomes fuel:

- Focus instead of reactivity.
- Precision instead of panic.
- Resolve instead of collapse.

This is not emotional suppression. It is emotional mastery. And this is how love—directed inward, regulated, and intact—becomes formidable.

The New Era

This is not about winning at someone else's expense. This is about refusing to disappear quietly. The new era is documented, empathically enforced, and rooted in love—paired with the unapologetic belief that transparency is the ultimate form of wealth protection for the generations of women to come. Open the folder. Send the letters. Hire your own experts. Read every line yourself. Then lead with love—not the love that sacrifices itself to keep peace, but the love that protects truth, legacy, and the woman you have always been. The fine print has been silent about you for far too long. Let it speak now. You've got this. I've got you.

The women of this lineage are rising, and we rise together—transparent, fierce, and free.

About Gwen

Gwen Medved is a best-selling author, an entrepreneur, and an advocate for women and children, known for her deep commitment to family and impactful storytelling. Gwen works with individuals and companies dedicated to making a positive difference and is on a mission to inspire others to see the opportunities hidden inside every obstacle.

Gwen has been featured in *Forbes, USA Today, Women's Health*, and *Entrepreneur* magazine, and has appeared on ABC, NBC, CBS, and FOX affiliates nationwide, as well as Yahoo! News, CNBC, and MSNBC.

A member of The National Academy of Best-Selling Authors, Gwen is a recipient of both the EXPY and Quilly awards. She is the executive producer of the Telly Award-winning film *It's Happening Right Here*, which raises awareness about child sex trafficking in the US.

Gwen holds a BA from Purdue University and an MEd in counseling and human services from DePaul University. She is a certified Canfield Transformational Trainer, Values-Based Leadership Coach, Health Coach, and a dedicated advocate for women, children, and families.

In her personal life, Gwen enjoys traveling and spending time with family and friends in the Midwest and Santa Monica, California. Her goals include lake house living with backyard chickens.

CHAPTER 7

THE QUIET REVOLUTION: HOW EMPATHY TRANSFORMS EVERYTHING IT TOUCHES

BY KIMBERLEE LANGFORD

The man's voice boomed through the living room, sharp and commanding: "You're not doing it right. That's all wrong!"

I stood in that lakeside home, watching a daughter crumble under her father's words, her face flushing with tears as she tried to demonstrate the sterile tracheostomy care I'd just taught the family. Her mother, elegant even in terminal illness, watched from her chair with quiet sadness. The other adult children froze, not daring to move or speak.

In that moment, I saw past the volume and the power. I saw the love behind his eyes. The raw, unprocessed fear. The helplessness of a man who had always been able to fix things but couldn't fix this. He was drowning in his wife's cancer diagnosis, grasping for control where none existed.

I touched his arm gently and said, with soft but absolute authority: "You will sit down and shut up, or I will have to leave. And you don't want me to leave."

The room went silent. This prominent businessman, who commanded boardrooms, looked down at me, shocked. Then something shifted. He became quiet, malleable. And in that space, something beautiful happened. The family began to share their love, fear, and tender feelings that only those who have sat with grief truly know.

That day taught me what I've spent decades refining: empathy isn't just about feeling with someone. It's about stepping into the space between emotion and action, steadying the room, and making it safe for people to move forward together.

THE INHERITANCE OF UNDERSTANDING

I come from a long line of nurses; my grandmother, mother, aunts, and cousins all wore the same calling. Growing up, stories filled our holiday tables of healing, loss, and the quiet grace that emerges when we walk through darkness with others.

My mother had both the science and the art, the heart of nursing. While working with her at a rural Idaho hospital, I saw how she noticed everything: the way a patient's hands fidgeted under a blanket, the unspoken fear between spouses, the lost look in a child's eyes. She could walk into a room tense with worry and, within minutes, have people talking, sharing, and believing they could face what lay ahead.

One rainy night, she came home early and sat on the porch with a glass of wine. She'd helped deliver a stillborn baby that day. *Fetal demise*, the medical term that sanitizes unbearable loss. She told me how she'd cleaned and wrapped the baby, put on a tiny cap, and encouraged the parents to hold their child and take a picture. In my youth, this seemed strange. But she explained the profound comfort parents find in counting tiny toes, in having a memento of a life that touched theirs so briefly.

Years later, when I worked in labor and delivery, her wisdom echoed through me as I held space for parents saying goodbye to babies who would never come home.

THE MOMENT EVERYTHING STOPS

Before I was a nurse, before I understood the true weight of empathy, I was working at Kmart—yes, Kmart—trying to escape my own grief after my brother's death. A woman came through my checkout line during the Christmas rush. Making small talk about holiday preparations, she mentioned her daughter had died.

"Oh, that's nice," I responded automatically, then froze. Everything ceased. The whole world in my head stopped.

I came around the counter, and we embraced. That was over forty years ago, and we remain friends to this day. That moment taught me something I've never forgotten. Never ask how someone is unless you're ready to hear the answer. Really ready.

This lesson became the foundation of my nursing practice. In healthcare, there's always pressure to get things done—complete the assessment, check the boxes, move to the next patient. But I learned to shut the laptop completely when someone opens a door to something deeper. Because how can we not have time for what matters most? The emotional and spiritual aspects of well-being aren't separate from healing. They're essential to it.

WHEN EMPATHY REQUIRES COURAGE

Not everyone makes empathy easy. As a home health nurse in rural North Idaho, I had a patient who tested every ounce of compassion I possessed. Picture this: driving up to a house and finding a very large woman sitting on her front lawn, buck naked, with a rifle tucked under her pendulous breasts for safekeeping.

She was rough. Deliberately offensive. She'd tell the physical therapist she wanted to hire her for her brothel. She made everyone profoundly uncomfortable, and most healthcare workers refused to see her after one visit.

But I saw beyond the shocking behavior. I recognized the self-loathing. When you're that vulnerable, that full of self-hate, you level the playing field by making others uncomfortable, too. It's protection, not aggression.

One day, she made a particularly vicious comment about herself. Something in me shifted. I laid it out straight: No woman is ugly. No one is unlovable. I told her about the nobility I saw in her, despite everything.

Eventually, she agreed to see a social worker. When that social worker was "horribly offended" and refused to return, I was disappointed but not surprised.

Months later, when my patient admitted she'd sold her pain medication to pay her heating bill, I had to report it to her doctor. She was furious and demanded a different nurse.

Three weeks later, she called the office: "I really want Kimberlee to come back."

That's when I learned that empathy doesn't mean avoiding hard truths or accountability. Sometimes the most empathetic thing you can do is hold someone to a standard that honors their potential, even when they can't see it themselves.

THE TRANSFORMATION OF COMPETITION INTO COLLABORATION

Nursing is known for *eating our young*. It's cutthroat, competitive, especially among women who feel they must fight for limited positions of power. As I advanced in my career, I discovered that I had what others referred to as a *powerful personality*. This intimidated some managers who felt threatened rather than supported.

One manager became openly hostile toward me for no apparent reason. She knew less about our field than I did, and instead of seeing me as a resource, she saw me as a threat. My first instinct was anger. I'd done nothing but try to help.

Then I made a choice that changed everything: I decided to serve her. How could I make her successful? How could I use my knowledge to elevate her rather than compete with her?

We became the best of friends. Together, we developed a fantastic clinical team. Years later, we're still close. That experience taught me that, regardless of rank or title, everyone bears responsibility for creating a leadership culture. One person can really shift the entire dynamic, much like moving one piece of a mobile causes all the other pieces to move.

READING BETWEEN THE LINES IN THE BOARDROOM

Empathy isn't limited to bedside care. I once sat across from a healthcare executive whose plan was experiencing catastrophic claims. He came at me with accusations about our program, questioning our billing, our outcomes, everything. I had documentation to prove we were delivering exactly what we promised.

But I recognized something deeper. This wasn't really about our program. It was about fear. His budget was hemorrhaging from unrelated shock claims, and he needed to cut somewhere.

Instead of getting defensive, I asked: "It seems like you're really unhappy with what we're doing. What's the one thing you wish we did that we aren't?"

That question changed everything. We spent the next twenty minutes discussing how to strategically scale our program to work within his budget constraints while still serving his sickest members. We saved the relationship, and when his budget recovered, he scaled the program back up.

Anger and fear are often two sides of the same coin. When someone comes at you with anger, look for the fear it's protecting. Get behind the objection to find the real need.

THE PRICE AND POWER OF GRACE

My brother was sixteen when a UPS truck hit him head-on on his way home from school. My parents had just gotten him a motorcycle. We grew up riding motorcycles. My first was a little Honda three-wheeler in nursery school, but that was for dirt biking. This was his first street bike, meant for getting to and from school.

I still remember the awful feeling in the pit of my stomach when my parents told me they'd bought it for him. Something felt wrong about it, even then.

He was doing everything right that day—helmet on, lights on, following traffic laws. The UPS driver made an illegal turn without looking. Hit my brother head-on. The impact was devastating.

When it went to court in small-town Idaho, the judge was friends with the driver's lawyer. My mother went through all the accident reports. I don't think I could have done that. The sentence came down: a fifty-dollar savings bond payment once a month for a year. That was it. That was the price the court put on my brother's life.

I hated that driver with every fiber of my being. I'd never met him, but the rage and injustice of it consumed me. An illegal turn, a moment of inattention, and my sixteen-year-old brother was gone. Now, a year of fifty-dollar payments.

The anger was poisoning me from the inside. Eventually, I realized I was the only one it was destroying. I learned to let it go, to forgive. Easier said than done. Later, I discovered the driver had lost his own son in a drive-by shooting. His wife left him. His life fell apart.

Did he set out that morning planning to kill a teenager on a motorcycle? Of course not. He was probably thinking about deliveries, deadlines, and ordinary things. One moment of not looking, and it instantly destroyed two families.

Holding onto that anger would have given me ulcers, maybe worse. The person who ultimately benefits from grace isn't just the one receiving it. It's the one extending it. That forgiveness didn't bring my brother back, but it gave me my life back.

THE CENTER OF EVERYTHING

There's a scene in the movie *Little Big Man* where the chief asks young Dustin Hoffman, "Do you know where the center of the universe is?" When the boy says no, the chief draws a circle in the sand around himself: "This is the center of the universe."

We're all walking around in our own universes. When you recognize this, when you can mesh your center with someone else's center, transformation happens not just for them, but for you as well. Every patient, every difficult colleague, every challenging executive has taught me something I needed to know.

In business, healthcare, leadership, and life, I've learned one absolute truth: put the person at the center of everything you're building, and all the other stuff, such as profitability, outcomes, and savings, falls into place naturally. But you have to mean it. You have to see past the presentation to the nobility underneath, even when it's hidden under fear, anger, or a rifle tucked under naked breasts.

THE QUIET REVOLUTION

Empathy isn't soft. It's not always gentle. Sometimes it requires telling someone to sit down and shut up so healing can begin. Sometimes it means reporting a patient you love for selling their medication. Sometimes it means serving someone who's actively trying to undermine you.

But here's what I know after decades of wielding empathy as a leadership tool: it works. Team members feel safe enough to speak up, preventing errors. Turnover drops because people feel valued beyond their productivity. Innovation flourishes because people stop competing and start collaborating. Loyalty emerges that goes beyond any contract or job description.

For leaders, empathy becomes both a compass and a lifeline, keeping you connected to your *why* when budgets are tight, criticism is loud, and the work feels impossible.

None of us looks good naked, regardless of what we might think. We're all broken, flawed people. But in that brokenness lies the magnificence, the magic we can create for each other to make life a little more noble, a little more bearable, a little more beautiful.

The question isn't whether you have time for empathy. It's whether you have time for anything else. Because when you truly see people, when you hold space for them to be both broken and magnificent, everything changes. The angry father finds peace with his wife's cancer. The self-loathing patient finds dignity. The threatened manager becomes a friend. The executive saves his program while saving face.

This is the quiet revolution of empathy: it transforms everything it touches, including and especially the person brave enough to wield it.

About Kimberlee

Kimberlee Langford is a nationally recognized nurse executive, leadership and nurse coach, and wellness strategist with over two decades of experience transforming healthcare teams and organizations. Known for blending clinical excellence with human-centered leadership, Kimberlee has led high-performing teams in complex, high-stakes environments—helping organizations improve outcomes while honoring the humanity of those they serve.

Her nursing career spans hospital-based care, home health, and hospice. She currently serves as Vice President of Medical Management with Boon-Chapman, an independent third-party administrator. She is widely respected for her work with her teams, delivering robust cost savings, a frictionless, high-touch member experience, and improved member outcomes for self-funded, employer-sponsored health plans.

She is known for building transformational clinical teams in national medical, case management, and disease management programs and for consulting with brokers, advisors, third-party administrators, stop-loss carriers, providers, and employers to reduce the incidence and cost of catastrophic health claims such as dialysis, kidney and heart disease, and cancer.

Beyond the boardroom, she is a Reiki Master Teacher, Qigong and Sound Healing Practitioner, and advocate for whole-person wellness, integrating compassion, mindfulness, and energy-based practices into leadership development. She lives with her husband in Idaho and is a mother of three and a grandmother of three.

Through speaking at industry events, coaching, and writing, Kimberlee inspires professionals to lead with empathy, courage, and authenticity—believing that when leaders prioritize people and scalable processes over profits, both success and purpose flourish.

Her contributing chapter is a call to action for a new kind of leadership—one where compassion and empathy are not an afterthought but the driving force of sustainable success—in business and life.

CHAPTER 8

PRIORITIZE PEOPLE OR RISK THE MISSION

BY PRESTON HOREJSI

The evaluating provider couldn't diagnose anything that would keep him out of the field. From a medical standpoint, there was nothing concrete enough to disqualify the young soldier from the upcoming training exercise. We knew it was not the right answer to send him to the field. Reviewing the facts outside our barracks in a snowy German winter so we couldn't be overheard, we knew.

My platoon sergeant and I had watched this young soldier closely since he'd joined us fresh out of basic training. We saw it happen over the course of months of training and seven months deployed to Europe—the mental health struggles that eventually manifested as self-harm ideations, then actions. Time was short until the exercise, so we ensured he received medical care and evaluation. We argued our case to the company and battalion commanders.

The response: We need him in the field. We need the numbers.

A few days into the exercise, he harmed himself again. It was more serious this time. We evacuated him. After receiving treatment, he was placed in a position that reduced the risk to himself and others. Soon after returning home, he was discharged from the Army.

About a year later, I learned that he'd taken his own life.

I'm not going to attempt explaining why he did it. Everyone reacts to and processes stimuli differently. However, I know this: my platoon sergeant and I didn't need a medical diagnosis to understand the severity of his situation. We knew because that's the job. We'd eaten together, trained together, laughed and struggled together. He never confided in us the depth of his struggles, but we sensed it.

Our subconscious absorbs more data than we can possibly imagine, including empathetic data. When you step outside yourself and your immediate problems, with genuine curiosity, you sense people as they truly are.

Unfortunately, our intuition was right about that soldier. Decision-makers, removed from the situation, made choices that placed him and the entire platoon at risk. At least the battalion commander met his quota.

EMPATHY BEGETS EMPATHY

My platoon sergeant was phenomenal—a great leader, experienced tanker, and an invaluable mentor. I learned an immeasurable amount from him during our almost two years working together, which is rare for a platoon leader and platoon sergeant to be together that long.

He also carried the weight of over a decade of service that resulted in PTSD and myriad physical injuries. However, he grew up in an Army where strong leaders didn't need mental health treatment. It wasn't an option.

Although the Army culture around mental health has significantly improved since then, there's still a stigma against seeking help, particularly in combat arms. The stigma mostly stems from fear of seeming weak, being vulnerable when your job is to fight and win wars. There's also legitimate fear of career damage. Some positions of special trust, like drill sergeant, have restrictions if your record has any history of "emotional instability."

Towards the end of our time together, I started suggesting he talk to our Embedded Behavioral Health (EBH) team. It took time, but he eventually went. The difference was immediate. He came in the next day, saying he felt better being able to unload some of the weight, and later, after continued treatment and medication, the daily grind stopped causing him as much stress.

Eventually, he was recommended for medical retirement. He worked as a forklift driver for a while to keep busy, then went back to school.

He's a social worker now. Having known the original version of him, the guy who refused to seek help, I never would have predicted his new career choice. Except, it makes perfect sense. The best leaders in the Army, from private to general, often find themselves in the role of counselor. As a phenomenal platoon sergeant, he was also a great counselor. I see now that he modeled leading with empathy, and he did so well that I turned the lessons back on him. I've been taking credit for convincing him to go to EBH for years, but in a roundabout way, he did it himself.

YOUR LEADERS NEED EMPATHY TOO

As a company executive officer, I frequently interacted with our mechanics. One afternoon, I was in the motor pool when one of the junior enlisted mechanics approached me.

"Hey, sir, are you doing okay? You seem stressed."

My response was automatic: "I'm fine, just busy."

His question gave me pause. I had a decent working relationship with all the mechanics, but we weren't particularly close. Rank disparities in the Army tend to discourage candid conversations. I assumed it took courage to leave his comfort zone and question me with clear sincerity.

His empathy caused me to reflect on whether I truly was "fine." The answer was uncomfortable: I wasn't fine. I was able to step back and observe myself from another perspective because he spared a few seconds to show his concern.

I decided to take the advice I once gave my platoon sergeant and seek help from EBH. It was effective, and this experience impacted me profoundly.

I didn't recognize it at the time, but the previous experiences, among others, shaped how I would eventually command a One-Station Unit Training (OSUT) company. Although never explicitly stated, empathy became our core policy. Empathy as policy developed from the beginning. I referenced my experiences with mental health early and often, telling the drill sergeants and tank instructors, paraphrasing: "It is okay to not be okay. If you need help, ask. We will all support you, and if anyone in the company criticizes or mocks you for it, they won't be here very long."

EMPATHY AS POLICY

Company command is an extremely fulfilling job, but it is equally frustrating. My biggest frustration early on was my battalion commander.

He was type A, detail-oriented, and micromanaging. I was type B, laid back, and overly trusting. To him, my leadership style lacked caring. To me, he looked like a control freak, only worried about the numbers.

We fundamentally disagreed on some trainee policies. He was focused on graduation numbers and attrition rates because people above him cared about the numbers. I focused on what was best for the individual trainees, my company, and the Army. It didn't help that, despite my profession, I have rebellious tendencies.

Around this time, I'd started learning about tactical empathy. I began incorporating those lessons into interactions with the battalion commander. When we discussed trainees or cadre, I used calibrated questions, mirrors, and labels to bridge the gap between our competing perspectives. I also used anchors at the beginning of conversations to help us reach a mutually agreeable solution.

It wasn't one conversation that changed things. We interacted multiple times a week in meetings, briefings, and more serious discussions. Over time, the dynamic shifted. He seemed to understand how deeply I cared about the mission. I started to understand his position, pressures, and how much he cared about people.

Sometimes I "won" our negotiations, sometimes I "lost." Eventually, it stopped being a competition and became collaborative. When he relinquished command, he rated me highly in my evaluation. In my final counseling session, he acknowledged our rough start and the progress we had made. He even commended the culture and performance of my company.

That relationship was a small example of the many interpersonal relationships that contribute to success. Nearly every relationship improved during that time: drill sergeants and tank instructors, cadre and trainees, our company and other companies, and the list goes on. Our culture of empathy was the key to our high performance. We became a better team, better leaders, and better teachers because we followed through and built mutual trust. For empathy to work as policy, words and deeds must align, empathy must be genuine, and actions cannot tell a different story.

EMPATHY AS A FORCE MULTIPLIER

Later in my command, I came across research on the consistency principle: people tend to make choices that reinforce past actions. It's a way humans prevent cognitive dissonance. Writing a statement, even if you don't believe it, implants it in your mind and increases the chances you'll eventually believe it.

From this concept, I developed a voluntary short-essay contest for the trainees. I designed the prompts to elicit reflection on who they were, why they joined the Army, and who they wanted to become. I incentivized participation through competition.

The volume and content of the essays surprised me. The trainees shared personal experiences, feelings, and desires. They demonstrated something that's often hard to see in a 100-mph nonstop training environment: their heartfelt commitment to becoming good soldiers, or at least better people.

After selecting winners, I gathered everyone together and shared excerpts, maintaining anonymity, of parts that moved me, and shared common themes. Sharing those excerpts did two things. First, it proved I cared enough to actually read the essays. Second, it showed them they weren't alone, and their peers weren't that much different.

OSUT is intensely stressful. When you're in that environment as a trainee, you get hyper-focused on the immediate: How do I get through today? How do I make it to lunch?

Through the essays, I gave them a few minutes to step out of survival mode and reconnect with the bigger picture. They reflected on their purpose, on why they'd chosen this path, on their goals.

I only managed two iterations before I left to attend the Information Operations Qualification Course, but when I returned, that class was noticeably different. Fewer discipline issues. Better motivation. Stronger performance. Better teamwork.

My little experiment was an example of applying strategic empathy, which is actively trying to understand the motivations, beliefs, and perspectives of an "other" group so that you can make more informed decisions to achieve your strategic aims.

PRACTICE PERFECTS POLICY

One of my tank instructors was dealing with significant family stressors. His mother-in-law had moved in, adding tension to his already struggling marriage. The demands of the job were taking their toll, and the demands of home life left him feeling like he was not performing well at work. Eventually, he asked me to help him find another job, a different position somewhere else on base, so that he could focus on his family.

I didn't want to lose him. We would be diminished without him, but I had to do what was best for him and his family. Our first sergeant found some options. However, applying some tactical empathy, it became clear he didn't want to leave the company. He just saw it as the only solution. I was concerned that another unit would not support him the way we would.

We offered him an alternative. The training room needed someone. The position would give him mostly regular hours with no field time. Predictable schedule, more time at home, and guaranteed support from the team. He accepted.

Over the following months, his eyes regained their shine. He was reestablishing work-life balance, improving his marriage, and still contributing invaluable service to the company.

This success story was made possible by focusing on long-term goals: the best outcome for him, his career, his family, and the company. These events suggested that our policy of empathy was transforming into a guiding principle or a grand strategy. Grand strategy dictates how a nation (or organization) applies all available resources toward achieving long-term and overarching objectives. In this situation, we did everything we could to achieve our overarching objective of leading with empathy.

HUBRIS KILLS EMPATHY

Life prepared me for that experience because I'd been, and was, dealing with my own relationship issues.

We're indoctrinated from the very beginning as officers that company command is the most important time in our careers. We should give it everything.

Our first daughter was born two weeks after I took command.

I gave that job too much, and my family not enough. I believed I had the balance worked out, that I knew how to prioritize my time and attention for everyone's benefit.

After a shameful amount of indicators and time, my wife got through to me, and I was able to acknowledge that I didn't have anything figured out.

There's a quote from Italo Calvino: "It is not the voice that commands the story; it is the ear." What I thought I was giving to my family didn't match what they received. I withheld empathy from my family while giving it freely to others. I was using empathy as a tool. Tools can be misused. Principles are applied equitably.

This painful realization enabled me to course-correct and begin repairing the damage. We are a work in progress, and I'm still trying to make empathy my grand strategy for facing life. Mistakes and failures happen, but with empathy, we can overcome difficulties. Or as Ms. Rachel says, "You can do hard things."

GRAND EMPATHY: PUTTING IT ALL TOGETHER

The stories I've shared are meant to serve three purposes: First, to remind you, especially the military readers, of similar times when empathy played a major role in your life, even without realizing it. Second, to give you a sense of how my understanding of empathy and leadership changed over time. And third, to help you think beyond person-to-person interactions, and hopefully see how empathy can be more than tactical. Empathy can be operational, strategic, and even a nation's grand strategy.

Grand empathy is pursuing national or organizational objectives by aligning deeds with words, actions with principles, while applying instruments of power to uncover and understand counterparts' needs, wants, and desires. Thereby, decreasing uncertainty and ensuring relationships are either mutually beneficial or ended when irreconcilable differences prevent cooperation.

This concept is centered on the idea that empathy doesn't mean you have to surrender your objectives or capitulate. That you "Never Split the Difference." From this idea, I've integrated the other concepts mentioned previously: strategic empathy, word-deed alignment, empathy as policy, and grand strategy. None of which are new, but combining each concept's strengths as an overarching matter of policy, strategy, principle, etc., offers boundless potential at every level of human interaction.

Imagine running a corporation whose reputation is for always putting customers first, even at financial loss. Imagine the depth of brand loyalty that could be gained without using clever advertising or other influence methods. Imagine a corporate culture where the idea of intentionally sabotaging an older product to sell more of the new product is absolutely unconscionable.

Imagine living in a country whose reputation is one of humanitarianism and collective benefit without ulterior motives. A country where domestic and foreign policy is crafted to achieve the greatest benefit for the most people, and actions prove sincerity. Imagine healing old rivalries without conflict or resorting to conflict only when irreconcilable differences can't be resolved otherwise.

That is the potential of grand empathy, empathy as grand strategy, empathy as policy, empathy as principle. It is power through empathy.

About Preston

Preston Horejsi is a Captain in the U.S. Army with almost 10 years of active service. He graduated from the United States Military Academy at West Point in 2016 with a Bachelor of Science in Defense and Strategic Studies and was commissioned as an armor officer.

Preston served a combined seven years as an armor officer in the 1st Cavalry Division at Fort Hood, TX, and in the 194th Armored Brigade at Fort Benning, GA. His leadership positions included platoon leader, company executive officer, and company commander. Every position blessed him with the privilege of leading, training, and commanding 19K Armor Crewmen (tankers).

In 2023, Preston transitioned from the armor branch to the information operations functional area. He has since served as a planner in the 1st Multi-Domain Task Force at Joint Base Lewis-McChord, WA.

His military education includes the Armor Basic Officer Leader Course, Army Reconnaissance Course, Air Assault, Maneuver Captain's Career Course, Information Operations Qualification Course, and Army Space Cadre Basic Course.

Preston enjoys a diverse range of hobbies and pastimes, but his primary focuses are family time, reading, and martial arts.

Contact:
phorejsi6@duck.com

CHAPTER 9

UNDERSTANDING THE PEOPLE BEHIND THE NUMBERS

BY JOSEPH REYES

The look stopped me cold.

It was 9 p.m. on a Tuesday in 1993, and I was sitting at my desk in our Manhattan accounting department, surrounded by the usual chaos of ledgers and tax forms. My boss, the controller who'd hired me years earlier, walked past my office. He said good night; nothing unusual about that. We'd worked together for nearly a decade, often until late in the evening.

But something in his eyes that night was wrong.

I can't explain exactly what I saw. It wasn't anger or frustration or even exhaustion, but emptiness. A hollowness that didn't belong to the man I knew. He just stared at me for a beat too long before walking out, and every instinct I had started screaming.

I waited a few minutes after he left. Then I did something I'd never done before—I walked into his office uninvited.

On his desk, I found small drops of blood. Next to them sat a razor blade. My stomach dropped. I moved to his trash can and started searching. Crumpled at the bottom was a slip of paper with a few words written in his handwriting: "To all who I have hurt, offended..."

I grabbed the phone and called one of our VPs. "I think we have a problem," I told her, explaining what I'd found. She went up the chain of command. They contacted his family. Within hours, he was committed to psychiatric care.

He didn't come to work the next day. Or the week after. Eventually, I learned he'd been struggling with demons I'd only glimpsed the surface of—a childhood without his father, a marriage falling apart, his wife having an affair with a close friend. The pressure had built until something inside him snapped.

I became the controller in his absence. When he recovered and the company brought him back a year later, they made him VP of Finance. I knew immediately what would happen next. There was no way this man could look me in the eye every day knowing I was the one who'd found that note, who'd started the intervention. The embarrassment was too much, regardless of the outcome.

He let me go within months of his return.

But here's the thing—I'd make the same choice again tomorrow. The man didn't die. He got help. He got better. That's more important than any job, including mine. I lost my position, sure, but I landed somewhere much better eventually. And somewhere out there, that man is alive because I paid attention to what his eyes were telling me that night.

WHEN HATE TURNS TO LOVE IN FORTY-FIVE MINUTES

The husband walked into my office like he was ready for war.

I'd been working with his wife for years on their partnership business—him the majority owner, her with a smaller stake. They'd fallen behind on bookkeeping, and tensions were high. She'd warned me he was coming in hot, blaming her for the administrative mess, and by extension, blaming me. He'd never even met me, but he'd already decided I was part of the problem.

I watched him settle into the chair across from my desk, his jaw tight, arms crossed. Every line of his body language screamed hostility. This was a man ready to fire his accountant and probably torch the bridge on his way out.

So, I smiled, leaned back, and softened my voice.

I've learned something critical over my decades in this business—you never meet aggression with aggression. Fire fuels fire. To put out a blaze, you need water, calm, gentleness, and patience.

"Tell me what's bothering you," I said.

He started unloading—the books were a disaster, tax returns weren't where they needed to be, and he felt in the dark about his own company's finances. I listened, didn't defend, and didn't make excuses. When he finished, I acknowledged every single concern.

"You're absolutely right," I told him. "Here's where we are, what's happened, and how we fix it."

I laid out the whole situation with complete transparency. I explained the path forward, the timeline, what I needed from him and his wife to get their returns filed properly. Then I said something that seemed to catch him off guard.

"If you want to go to another accountant, I'm happy to help your new person get up to speed. I'll give them everything they need. The only thing that matters is that you get taken care of."

His shoulders dropped. The tension in his face eased. By the time we finished talking, we were discussing his business like colleagues, maybe even friends.

The next day, his wife called me. "Joe, he loves you. I don't know what you said, but he went from hating you to thinking you're the greatest guy in the world."

We kept the client, got their bookkeeping current, and filed their returns on time. The marriage didn't survive. They're seeing divorce lawyers now, but they're still working with me. They both trust me. I'm not taking sides, just helping them land as softly as possible through this disaster, keeping their legal fees manageable, and making sure they file their taxes in the most financially beneficial way.

Because at the end of the day, their crisis isn't about me. It's about them. My job is to calm the temperature, provide solid guidance, and help two people who are hurting navigate the financial wreckage without making it worse.

THE IRS AGENT WHO CHANGED HER MIND

People think the IRS is the enemy. I get it. Nobody likes getting that letter in the mail. You open your mailbox, and there it is—that envelope. Your stomach drops. You either rip it open immediately or you shove it in a drawer and pretend it doesn't exist.

But here's what I've learned after decades of dealing with the IRS: those agents are human beings doing a job. They want respect, not hostility. They want transparency, not games. And when you treat them like adversaries, you make everything exponentially worse.

I had a client who owed massive money—we're talking enough to liquidate his house, wipe out his holdings, destroy everything he and his wife had built. The previous accountant had gone in aggressively, treated the IRS agent like the enemy, and turned a bad situation into a catastrophe. By the time this client came to me, the damage was severe.

I called the agent. I apologized for the previous representative's approach, acknowledging mistakes. I was transparent about the client's financial situation and asked for help.

"What do you need from us? We're not hiding anything. We want to work with you to make this right."

The agent's aggression melted within minutes. We had a civil conversation. I negotiated a payment plan that didn't require liquidating assets. My client kept his house. The IRS got paid over time. Everyone walked away satisfied.

A few weeks later, the client's wife called me. "Joe, I need to tell you something. My husband was planning to kill himself over this. The stress was destroying him. Then we got your letter saying we'd worked out a solution, and everything changed. You saved his life."

I sat there holding the phone, stunned. I'd just been doing my job—staying calm, showing respect, finding a workable solution. But to them, it was the difference between life and death.

This happens more than people realize. Financial crises trigger real psychological emergencies. The weight of owing money you can't pay, the fear of losing everything you've worked for, the shame of facing your family—it breaks people. I've seen it repeatedly throughout my career.

The key is never letting aggression escalate. When someone comes at you hot, you respond with calm. It's verbal jiu-jitsu. You absorb the energy and redirect it. You don't push back. You acknowledge, apologize where appropriate, own mistakes, and work toward solutions.

THE EMPLOYEE WHO MATTERED MORE THAN ANY CLIENT

An employee had been with me for twelve years. He's what I'd call a brilliant accountant—fantastic with numbers, sees patterns others miss, makes our biggest clients happy. He's the kind of person other CPA firms would kill to have on their team.

This past summer, his family hit a crisis—mental health issues exacerbated by drug abuse. It was weighing heavily on the family. The employee needed to be present more than ever with the family, but we were in the middle of our busy season. Major clients needed work. Returns were piling up.

He came to me worried, conflicted about dropping his time during crunch time.

I looked at him and said, "Your family is more important than this business. Go take care of your family. Don't worry about the work. If we lose clients, we lose clients. We've been doing this together for many years. You helped me build this firm. Do what you need to do."

His relief was visible. We talked about what was happening, really talked. I listened to his fears about his family, about the situation potentially spiraling into legal trouble, about feeling torn between family and work obligations.

"You have nothing to worry about here," I told him. "I'd rather lose a client than lose you. You know I have your back."

He spent most of that summer with the family. We managed. The clients got serviced. Nobody died. And this employee came back knowing he's valued as a human being, not just as an employee who processes work for important accounts.

That's the thing about prioritizing people over profits—it pays off in ways you can't measure on a balance sheet. This employee works harder for me now because he trusts me completely. He knows I'll support him when things get difficult. That loyalty, trust, and mutual respect, you can't buy those things. You earn them by making hard choices that put people first.

THE HOMEWORK THAT BUILT AN EMPIRE

I was the oldest person in my master's program in finance, older than most of the professors. Late bloomer doesn't begin to cover it. But I was determined to get that degree, so there I was in my fifties, grinding through advanced coursework with students young enough to be my kids.

One of those students was about thirty years younger than me. We'd end up in the same classes, working through the same problems. He'd often ask, "Hey Joe, can I see what you did on this one?" I'd share my work freely. We were all hustling just to survive each semester.

I didn't think much of it at the time. Just being collegial, helping a fellow student get through a tough program. We graduated and went our separate ways—him to try various entrepreneurial ventures, me to continue building my accounting practice.

Then he started calling. "Hey, can you help with the books for this small business I'm starting? Can you do a tax return for me?" We'd work for low fees or sometimes for free, just helping him get his ventures off the ground. Most of those early businesses struggled or failed.

Until one didn't.

He cofounded a company that took off. He called me up: "Would you like to be our CPA firm?" We handled all the startup paperwork, created the LLC, and did the technical work to get them launched properly. For five years, we watched that company grow into a multimillion-dollar enterprise.

During the lean years when money was tight, we gave him breaks on fees and generous payment terms. We invested in the relationship, not just the transaction. As the business grew, so did our billings. Then he started referring us to other successful entrepreneurs in his network. Those clients brought more referrals. The accounting fees became substantial—the kind that make other CPA firms envious.

All because I shared my homework with a struggling student decades ago. Because I treated him like a peer rather than someone beneath me. Because I helped him when he had nothing, expecting nothing in return.

That's the long game of empathy. You don't help people as a business strategy. You help them because it's the right thing to do. But over time, over years and decades, those relationships compound. The young man you mentored becomes the successful entrepreneur who builds your practice. The struggling client you gave a break becomes your biggest advocate.

THE TEMPERATURE IN THE ROOM

I'm not always successful. My new neighbors and their dogs created conflict with my family, which I'm still trying to mediate. There are difficult relationships that don't transform into valuable alliances, arguments that don't resolve with calm conversation.

But I've learned that you can always try to lower the temperature. You can always choose to meet anger with gentleness, hostility with understanding. You can always ask yourself: What does this person really need right now? What am I not seeing?

Sometimes, like that night in 1993, what you're not seeing is written in someone's eyes. Sometimes it's hidden in trash cans and razor blades. Sometimes it's buried under aggression and blame. Your job, my job, is to look deeper, to pause before reacting, to choose empathy even when it feels risky.

Because here's what I know after decades in this profession: the stakes are almost always higher than they appear. That angry client isn't just upset about bookkeeping—he's dealing with a failing marriage. That IRS debt isn't just a financial problem—it's threatening someone's will to live. That employee struggling at work isn't just having a bad week—his family is falling apart.

We're accountants, yes. We work with numbers, tax codes, and financial statements. But we're really in the business of helping people navigate some of the most stressful moments of their lives. Money is never just money. It's security, dignity, hope, fear, shame, and pride all wrapped together.

When you understand that, when you really see the human being sitting across from you, everything changes. You stop rushing toward the fastest solution and start looking for the right one. You stop prioritizing profit and start prioritizing people. And paradoxically, that's when your practice grows, when your reputation strengthens, when clients become advocates and employees become partners.

The man whose life I saved by finding that note in his trash—he let me go, but I ended up in a better place. The hostile husband who came to my office ready for battle—we became friends, and I kept valuable clients. The IRS situations that could have destroyed people—they resolved because I chose respect over aggression. The employee I told to prioritize his family—he's more loyal and productive than ever. The student I helped with homework—he built an empire and brought me along for the ride.

None of that was strategy. It was just paying attention. It was just about seeing people clearly and responding to what they actually needed, not what was convenient for me.

That's the real work. That's what matters. The rest is just math.

About Joseph

Joseph Reyes, CPA, is the founder of Reyes Accounting, a Pennsylvania-based firm he launched in 2008. With decades of experience in finance, tax strategy, and advising business owners, Joe has developed a reputation for steady judgment, practical insight, and clear communication. He works with clients across the country and is known for helping people navigate financial complexity by breaking down issues to what truly matters—people, decisions, and long-term consequences. Joe holds a Bachelor's degree from Pace University, a Master of Science in Finance from Drexel University, and a Master of Arts in Theology and Biblical Studies. He is also a Main Street Certified Tax Advisor and maintains both a Series 65 license and a life insurance license, giving him a comprehensive perspective on financial planning and stewardship. In addition to his practice, Joe appears frequently on the Now Media On Demand TV network as a tax professional, sharing practical insights with a national audience and contributing to conversations that make financial topics more accessible.

Born in New York City and shaped by his Spanish heritage, Joe carries forward traditional values that influence both his work and his relationships: discipline, duty, faith, and personal responsibility. In January 2024, he committed to the carnivore diet and lost 40 pounds, leading to one of the most surprising changes of his life. After a 51-year battle with asthma that required daily medication, he is now 68 and completely medication-free. That transformation deepened his belief in resilience, attentive listening, and the power of intentional change—principles that have shaped his personal journey and his approach to understanding others.

Outside the office, Joe stays active through Brazilian jiu-jitsu (he holds a blue belt), kettlebell training, basketball, and Kenpo Karate. He's an outdoorsman who enjoys the mountains and has completed multiple survival courses, which have strengthened his appreciation for awareness, staying calm under pressure, and understanding others—skills directly connected to empathy and effective communication. In 2024, he also stepped into the arts, beginning piano lessons in May and singing lessons in September, embracing the humility and openness required to learn creatively. Joe is active in his church, a community filled with wonderful people who enrich his faith, support his growth, and remind him daily of the importance of compassion.

Joe lives in Pennsylvania with his wife, Carolyn, and their son, Nathaniel. To learn more, visit ReyesAccounting.com.

CHAPTER 10

THE MOMENT EVERYTHING CHANGED

BY TRICIA C. RICHARDSON

The boardroom was quiet, too quiet. Seven Senior Leadership team members sat around the polished conference table, each offering polite, technically correct insights about our turnover problem. Everyone was being professional, measured, and careful. And we were getting absolutely nowhere.

I watched as one person made a pointed comment that subtly challenged our approach. A few heads nodded quickly in agreement, but something else caught my attention: two people immediately shut down. Their shoulders tensed, their eyes dropped to their notebooks, and they withdrew from the conversation entirely. While others interpreted their silence as agreement or disengagement, I recognized something deeper happening. It was something that needed addressing if we were ever going to solve our real problem.

"Let's take a fifteen-minute break," I suggested.

During that pause, I pulled those two individuals aside. "I noticed you had more to say in there," I said gently. "Would you be willing to share what you're seeing that the rest of us might be missing?"

With visible hesitation, they opened up. Their perspective was radically different from what others had discussed in the room. They pointed to systemic issues and team dynamics that people had chosen to avoid. The conversation we'd been having was dancing around the real problems because addressing them felt too risky, too uncomfortable.

"Would you be willing to share this with the full team?" I asked.

They exchanged nervous glances. "What if it derails everything?" one asked.

"What if not sharing it means we never solve the real problem?" I responded.

When we reconvened, the conversation that followed was honest, difficult, and long overdue. It surfaced blind spots we'd all been protecting, both individually and collectively. We didn't solve everything that day, but we did something more important: we established a new standard for openness and trust. That leadership team transformed from seven people protecting their territories into a unified group committed to genuine solutions.

That moment taught me that being nice or avoiding conflict doesn't define empathy in leadership. We need to see what others miss, creating space for difficult truths, and having the courage to address what everyone else is too uncomfortable to name.

WHEN CONNECTION TRUMPS STRATEGY

Years later, at my first board retreat as a newly promoted executive, I found myself in a room full of influential leaders. Among them was the head of one of the state's largest foundations, a woman everyone wanted to meet. During breaks, I watched as board members and staff clustered around her, each taking their turn to pitch programs and angle for funding. She never got a moment's peace.

That evening, as we left the venue, I found myself walking beside her back to our hotel. We fell into an easy conversation, not about work, funding, or programs, but about life. We talked about our families, our favorite books, and the challenges of constant travel. For twenty minutes, we were just two people sharing a walk.

As we reached the hotel entrance, she stopped and looked at me with genuine surprise. "You're the first person in a very long time who hasn't mentioned their program or asked me for money. Why?"

I smiled. "I figured after everyone else vying for your attention, you could use a break. Besides, I'm new to this role. I'm more interested in learning from people like you than asking for something."

She studied me for a moment, then nodded. "Thank you for that."

I thought that was the end of it, a pleasant conversation with an interesting person. But six months later, when our organization was preparing to launch as an independent nonprofit, she called me directly. "I've been thinking about your program," she said. "I want to help."

She didn't just help. She became our biggest champion, securing the operational funding that gave us stability from day one. Without that initial investment, we might have struggled for years to find our footing. Instead, we launched strong and never looked back.

The lesson was profound: sometimes the most strategic thing you can do is forget about strategy entirely. When you see the human being beyond their position, when you offer genuine connection instead of calculated networking, you create trust that no amount of strategic planning can manufacture.

THE RISK OF HONESTY

Working with state agencies taught me that government meetings have their own special brand of tension. Everything is formal, structured, and controlled. You present facts, follow protocols, and stay within carefully defined boundaries. Emotion, intuition, and honest concern have no official place at the table.

We had a substantial contract with one state agency and were partnering with a smaller agency on a related initiative. After some leadership changes at the larger agency, the atmosphere in our meetings shifted dramatically. Suddenly, they were asking detailed and pointed questions about our methods, outcomes, and partnerships. The tone was polite but cold, professional but suspicious. It felt like we were under investigation for something, but no one would say what.

Meeting after meeting, the tension grew thicker. My team was becoming anxious, worried we might lose the contract, a loss that would affect dozens of employees and thousands of people we served. The safe play would have been to continue answering their questions, provide whatever documentation they requested, and hope the storm would pass.

Instead, I took a different approach.

"I need to be direct," I said during one particularly tense meeting. "I'm under the impression there's an issue here, but I'm not sure if it's with our work, with our partner organization, or something internal for you. Rather than continuing to dance around it, can we have an honest conversation about what's really going on?"

The room went silent. In government contracting, that kind of directness could be career suicide.

Then the lead administrator leaned back in her chair and actually smiled. That smile was the first genuine expression I'd seen from her in months. "Thank you for saying that. Yes, we need to talk."

What followed was a series of conversations that required NDAs and closed-door meetings but ultimately led to a complete transformation of our relationship. By choosing transparency over self-protection, by risking the discomfort of honest dialogue, we moved from being just another vendor to becoming a trusted partner. That decision led to multi-year contracts, pilot programs, and opportunities we never could have accessed by playing it safe.

SEEING BEYOND THE RESUME

Sometimes empathy means seeing potential where others see problems. When Sall (not her real name) applied for a position with our organization, she admitted, by her own account, to being a poor interviewee. My team had doubts. On paper and in person, she didn't present as our strongest candidate.

However, I had worked with her before in a volunteer capacity, and I had seen something that others missed: resilience, dedication, and a quiet strength that didn't always show up in traditional interviews. Before her official interview, I ran into her at Sam's Club. We chatted briefly, and I mentioned the position. Later, she called me with something she needed to share.

"I've struggled with addiction," she said, her voice barely above a whisper. "Only my immediate family knows. Not even my mom. I just needed you to know before you made any decision about hiring me."

The vulnerability in that moment told me everything I needed to know. This was someone who had fought battles most people couldn't imagine, someone who had the courage to be honest even when it might cost her an opportunity.

"Everyone deserves a second chance," I told her. "Come interview. Let's see if this is right for both of us."

We hired her, and initially, everything went well. The team loved her work ethic and dedication. But over time, I noticed troubling patterns—frequent lateness, moments of disengagement, signs of being overwhelmed. Many managers would have moved straight to disciplinary action. Instead, I chose curiosity over judgment.

"What's really going on?" I asked during a private conversation.

The floodgates opened. Her daughter was battling severe depression. Her husband was struggling with mental health issues. The weight of her past shame still haunted her. She wasn't using again, but she was drowning in the responsibilities and pain of those she loved.

What she needed wasn't discipline. It was structure paired with grace, accountability balanced with compassion. I called her in the mornings when she was running late, not to scold but to remind her that we needed her and that she mattered. We worked together to create systems that supported her success while maintaining professional standards.

Over the next eleven years, I watched her transform. She earned her degree, developed confidence she never thought possible, and became one of our strongest team members. Recently, she sent me a letter that captured the impact of empathetic leadership: "You didn't let my struggles define me. When I was the worst interviewee your team had ever seen, you saw value I couldn't see in myself. You walked with me through my darkest valleys: my struggling marriage, my daughter's depression, my own cancer diagnosis. You showed me that leadership isn't about fixing every problem. It's about walking alongside someone while they carry their load."

THE POWER OF PATIENT UNDERSTANDING

A gentleman called our center after multiple failed attempts to resolve his benefits issue through various channels. By the time he reached me, he had made numerous calls, and his frustration had transformed into rage. He was rude, accusatory, and abusive to my staff.

The easy response would have been to match his energy or simply end the conversation. Instead, I listened. Beneath the anger, I heard desperation. This wasn't just about benefits. It was about dignity, about feeling heard in a system that seemed designed to ignore him.

"I understand you're frustrated," I said calmly. "Let me look into this personally and see what's really happening with your case."

It took weeks of investigation and coordination with multiple agencies. In the meantime, I arranged for immediate support through a partner organization. This was not a complete solution, but it was enough to show him that someone cared. I called him regularly with updates, small steps of progress that proved he would not slip through the cracks.

In the end, we couldn't deliver everything he had hoped for. Some programs had eligibility requirements he didn't meet. But when we concluded our work together, his response surprised me.

"I'm still frustrated about the outcome," he said, "but you treated me like a human being. You listened. You tried. That matters more than you know."

That experience reinforced a crucial lesson: empathy doesn't always mean solving someone's problem. Sometimes it means bearing witness to their struggle, validating their frustration, and demonstrating through action that they matter.

THE DECISION THAT DIDN'T MAKE SENSE

We had just received a large grant to improve technological access for veterans. This thrilled the foundation and excited the board, as the funding would position us as innovators in our field.

But as we convened focus groups with veterans and dove deep into their actual needs, a different picture emerged. The barrier wasn't technological, but rather mental health. Veterans and their families were struggling with PTSD, depression, and suicide risk at alarming rates. Improving our application process might help us look good, but it wouldn't address what they actually needed.

I made a decision that shocked everyone: we would return the grant.

No one returned money to this foundation. My unprecedented actions were potentially relationship-ending and definitely risky. However, keeping funds meant for one purpose, knowing they wouldn't address the real need, felt like a betrayal of the people we claimed to serve.

Six months later, the foundation called. "We've been discussing your decision," the program officer said. "We want to offer you the same amount, but this time for mental health initiatives."

That pivot led to implementing Mental Health First Aid training statewide, ultimately impacting thousands of veterans and their families in ways our original technology plan never could have. By choosing people over profit, mission over money, we gained something far more valuable than funding. We earned trust.

BRINGING YOUR WHOLE SELF TO WORK

Throughout my career, people have often told me that I need to change certain things if I want others to take me seriously as a CEO. Drive a different car. Dress more formally. Keep clear boundaries between work and personal life. Maintain professional distance. The advice always came from well-meaning people who wanted me to succeed in traditional terms.

But authenticity is not a manageable weakness. Authenticity is the foundation of empathetic leadership. When you bring your whole self to work, when you create space for others to do the same, you build organizations where people don't just show up—they engage, they care, they thrive.

This doesn't mean there are no boundaries or standards. It means recognizing that the person comes before the position, that understanding comes before judgment, and that sometimes the most professional thing you can do is be genuinely human.

I've shared my struggles when appropriate. I've admitted when I didn't have answers. I've cried with employees facing tragedy and celebrated their personal victories as enthusiastically as our organizational wins. And yes, people who mistook empathy for weakness have occasionally taken advantage of me.

But for every person who exploited that openness, there were dozens like Sall who flourished because someone saw their potential beyond their problems. For every moment of vulnerability that felt risky, there were breakthrough connections that transformed our organization's trajectory.

Empathetic leadership isn't about being soft or avoiding hard decisions. It's about seeing clearly—seeing what others miss, seeing potential where others see problems, seeing the human being before the human resource. It's about having the courage to pause when everyone else is pushing forward, to speak truth when silence feels safer, and to choose connection over strategy when the moment calls for it.

The path of empathetic leadership isn't always comfortable. It requires you to feel deeply, risk genuinely, and sometimes stand alone in your conviction that people matter more than processes. But when you commit to truly seeing and serving others, when you create spaces where vulnerability and strength can coexist, you don't just build successful organizations, you transform lives, including your own.

Because empathetic leadership is not a management technique you deploy or a strategy you execute. It's who you choose to be in every interaction, every decision, every moment when you could take the easier path but choose the human one instead. In making that choice consistently, you create ripples of change that extend far beyond any metric, any contract, or any conventional measure of success.

That's the power of leading with empathy. Not just changing outcomes but changing lives. Not just building organizations but building trust. Not just achieving success but defining it in terms that actually matter.

About Tricia

Tricia C. Richardson is a leadership strategist, executive advisor, and founder of Uz and Buz Partners, LLC, where she helps leaders align purpose with measurable progress and build organizations that flourish from the inside out.

As Founder and former CEO of SC Thrive, she built and scaled a statewide nonprofit serving all 46 South Carolina counties, transforming it into a multimillion-dollar system known for strong partnerships, disciplined growth, and mission-centered execution.

Today, Tricia advises executives, boards, nonprofits, and emerging leaders navigating complexity and transition. Known for her steady presence and direct insight, she helps leaders strengthen communication, make sound decisions, and build cultures rooted in trust and accountability.

Through her writing and thought leadership, Tricia explores the deeper work of leadership, clarity, courage, stewardship, and empathy. Equipping leaders to create lasting impact in the environments they are entrusted to serve.

CHAPTER 11

EARNING THE RIGHT TO TRY

BY CHRIS DANEK

The Friday afternoon war room sessions had become excruciating rituals. Every week, my startup client and I would spend forty-five minutes hammering out adjustments to the project plan—responding to failed component inspections, manufacturing process failures, and packaging validation issues. Then we'd spend another hour on the phone with John, the project manager at our contract manufacturing partner two and a half hours away, trying to convince him that our changes were necessary to keep the program on track.

His answer was always the same: "I'll try to walk it around to the functional heads and get the new plan approved."

By the following Friday, that approval still hadn't come through. We'd lost an entire week of days we couldn't afford to lose. The pattern repeated itself week after week, and the project was dying in gridlock.

The stakes couldn't have been higher. My client, a medical device startup, was transferring their FDA-approved device into manufacturing. They needed to produce a second-generation version that was manufacturable at scale, cost-effective, and clinically reliable. Like many medical device companies, they'd discovered that a device good enough for clinical approvals isn't good enough for commercial launch.

An acquisition payment worth over $100 million hung in the balance, contingent on meeting specific manufacturing transfer milestones. These weren't arbitrary deadlines. They were formal studies, rigorous process qualifications that either passed or failed. Miss those milestones, and the deal would collapse. The company would fold. A medical procedure that produced better patient outcomes with fewer side effects would never reach the market.

I was trapped in an endless cycle of Gantt chart updates—nearly a thousand line items linked together with dependencies that became obsolete the moment reality intervened. Every time we ran a validation protocol or tested a new component, something unexpected would emerge. That's the nature of developing regulated medical devices. You must be agile and responsive while maintaining rigorous documentation and safety standards.

But our top-down project management approach made agility impossible.

THE MOMENT EVERYTHING CHANGED

I was only thinking from one perspective: my startup client's urgent need to move fast and help patients. Drive forward. Get it done. We had a breakthrough medical device, and people were suffering every day without it.

As a former founder and startup CEO, I knew the pressure firsthand. The constant questions from the board. The CEO asks a version of, "When will you be done?" daily. The weight of knowing that every delay means more patients living with inadequate treatment options.

That empathy for my client came naturally. Too naturally. It blinded me to everyone else's reality.

But then I stopped. I actually stopped and thought about John's life.

He wasn't just being difficult. John was a project manager at a contract manufacturing organization that served multiple clients across multiple continents. They had existing contracts, agreed-upon timelines, committed resources, and established processes. When we asked him to walk through changes around his organization—seemingly simple and obvious changes—it put him in an impossible situation.

From his perspective, our *simple* decisions weren't simple at all. They required him to marshal resources across multiple functions, secure buy-in from different department heads, and somehow fit our urgent needs into a system designed to serve many clients simultaneously. Every change we requested created ripple effects throughout his organization. Resources had to be reallocated. Other clients' schedules might be impacted. Functional heads needed to sign off on commitments that affected their departments' capacity.

I had been thinking about what we needed. I hadn't been thinking about what John needed.

That realization changed everything.

CREATING PULL INSTEAD OF PUSH

I met with Jason, the engineering manager, who owned the entire project at the contract manufacturer. I explained what we were trying to do and why the timing mattered so critically. But I didn't just demand faster turnarounds. Instead, I proposed a way to achieve our goals that would actually work within their organizational structure. I listened to his concerns about managing resources across multiple clients. I acknowledged that they had constraints we needed to respect.

I earned the right to try.

Next, I met with Dell, my client's COO. I needed his trust and his team's trust before making any changes to how we worked. Dell was protective of his team—he needed to know they could stay productive and positive while executing under intense pressure. I explained my plan: daily contact with the program, immediate visibility into what was accomplished each day, and a comprehensive grasp of all required activities so nothing would slip through the cracks.

He gave me the flexibility to proceed. The first step? Get buy-in from my client's CEO. The CEO supported the concept because it gave him clarity on a daily basis and gave a green light as long as I could still provide visibility to the overall timeline. This okay from senior leadership contained a hidden deadline trap. I let the CEO know that, to change the timelines he got from the team from fiction to reality, we first needed to focus on the work to be done, in the right order. As we begin delivering, we can provide more accurate estimates of the timeline. Dell and I could do that behind the scenes while letting the team focus entirely on the work.

Then I went back to John with a completely different approach.

The issue wasn't that we needed to abandon the contract manufacturer's processes. The issue was that we needed better, faster communication without creating additional work for him. Instead of forcing a wholesale methodology shift, I offered something incredibly simple—something he could control entirely on his own.

"John," I said, "I'll come to your plant. I'll set up boards with Post-it Notes—just a visual system showing what's to do, what's in progress, and what's done. All you need to do is move the notes as things progress and take a picture each day. Text it to me. That's it."

He looked skeptical. "So now I have to maintain a Gantt chart and do daily updates in a new format? That extra time is going to delay us. Moving the project forward is hard enough as it is."

"No," I said. "You won't have to write email updates anymore. You won't have to spend time crafting detailed status reports. Moving a Post-it Note and taking a picture is faster and easier than drafting an email. This actually makes your job simpler."

I watched his expression shift. He could do that. It was within his control, required no organizational commitment to new timelines or workflows, and genuinely reduced his daily workload.

That simple shift became the blueprint for transforming how both organizations worked together.

WALKING IN THEIR SHOES

Understanding wasn't enough. I needed to demonstrate commitment, and I needed to help. I knew that even though this simple workflow change would free up John and the team to deliver, the team was stuck in a classic case of "work getting in the way of work," and it would take a catalyst to make this change.

I started working on-site at the contract manufacturer during critical periods. Not to supervise or micromanage, but to be present. To help answer questions in real time. To show that I wasn't asking them to do anything I wouldn't do myself.

The contract manufacturer was a couple of hours from my client's location. I could have easily stayed close to the startup's office, where I worked daily with my client's development team. But convenience wasn't the point. Building trust was the point.

By being there in the contract manufacturer's fishbowl conference room, I turned decisions that had been taking multiple days through inbox staging into real-time action. When questions arose about design specifications or testing protocols, I could answer them immediately. When small issues emerged, we could address them before they compounded into major problems.

The results were immediate. Information that used to take a week to communicate was now visible within hours. Problems that used to compound while waiting for approval could be addressed the same day. Decisions moved to real-time. The project unlocked.

We successfully met the manufacturing transfer milestones. The acquisition payment, more than $100 million, came through. The company survived and thrived.

But perhaps the most powerful evidence came afterward: both organizations continued using the agile project delivery method we'd introduced. The contract manufacturer began implementing it with all their clients globally. They'd traded physical Post-it Notes for electronic versions to accommodate their worldwide operations, but the core principle remained.

I didn't just help my client. I helped their partner become permanently better at serving all their clients.

THE WE, NOT YOU, HYPOTHESIS

Years of leading teams and coaching competitive soccer taught me something fundamental about empathy and performance: how you frame challenges determines whether people feel blamed or empowered.

Early in my career, I used 360-degree feedback where team members ranked each other. The result? Finger-pointing. "You did this." "He did that." "She's always late." Third-person blame created defensiveness instead of growth.

I shifted to what I call the "We, Not You" hypothesis. Instead of saying, "You should be on time to meetings," feedback across the team shifts to the first-person: "We should all be on time to meetings. Here's what I'm willing to commit to making that happen."

As you go around the table with the team, something remarkable occurs. Discoveries emerge that change everything. The person who's *always late* turns out to be the backup for customer support and must remain available by phone. The person who *doesn't do their share* is actually juggling three other project teams with conflicting schedules. The person who *never speaks up* has profound insights but needs different communication formats to share them effectively.

When you take the effort to understand what's really happening for people, the team can reconstruct how it works together. You develop grace for the fact that things change constantly. You never know what someone's going through on any given day—a health crisis, a family emergency, a personal struggle that's consuming their emotional energy.

THREE CULTURES, ONE FOUNDATION

I've led and taught dozens of teams across universities and industry. The teams that achieve breakthrough impact share three interconnected cultures, with empathy at the foundation of the first.

Culture of Caring and Respect: Everyone has a voice. We practice the "We, Not You" hypothesis. We connect with each other on things inside and outside the work. When people know they're valued as whole human beings, not just as production units, they give their best work even during difficult times.

Culture of Discipline: We deliver what we say we'll deliver and drive toward daily progress. We pursue excellence in documentation, process, and continuous learning. Our disciplined documentation isn't bureaucratic paperwork; it's how we ensure patient safety and enable other teams to build on our work. It's the equivalent of making your bed in the morning: a small discipline that creates order and capability.

Culture of Achievement: We have a high drive to make an impact, and we don't accept going halfway. But achievement becomes natural when it's built on the foundation of the first two cultures. Start with the vision for breakthrough impact that serves as a call to excellence. Build the team's mutual care and respect. Add the discipline of process and continuous learning to hone expertise. Achievement takes care of itself.

360-DEGREE EMPATHY

The most powerful application of empathy extends beyond your immediate team to every stakeholder in your ecosystem.

Consider the FDA, the regulatory body every medical device company must work with. Many companies approach the FDA as adversaries, viewing reviewers as obstacles who don't understand their innovations.

But FDA reviewers are highly qualified professionals who have chosen public service to protect patient safety while approving healthcare innovations. They ask reasonable questions for reasons that are, well, reasonable. They need to ensure that devices work not just in ideal circumstances, but at scale across diverse patient populations, all without causing unintended harm.

When you approach the FDA with empathy, asking, "What will they need answered? How can I present information so they can help me move this forward? How can I help them do their job?" you create pull instead of push. You design studies that unequivocally answer their questions before they have to ask. You provide documentation that makes their review process straightforward. You make it easier for them to say yes. And in the process, you will often uncover your blind spots and develop safer, more effective procedures and devices.

The same applies to insurance companies evaluating coverage decisions. Instead of fighting and petitioning after the fact, design clinical studies during development that address the questions payers will need answered. Show a clear patient benefit. Demonstrate cost-effectiveness and economic value. Remove obstacles to adoption before they become barriers. Create pull.

This 360-degree empathy—extending to regulators, partners, suppliers, customers, and everyone affected by your work, as well as your own company—is what enables collective impact. Any breakthrough innovation requires many different people from different domains working together. If you can't work together effectively and stack wins for all of the stakeholders, you can't create a breakthrough that scales.

THE MOST POWERFUL MINDSET

I've spent years teaching design thinking and human-centered design, where empathy is a core mindset. After all that teaching and practice, I've come to believe something fundamental:

Empathy is the most powerful mindset you can develop and apply.

Is listening more important than empathy? You can't have empathy without listening and understanding, so they're deeply connected. Is communication more important? You can't speak to your audience from their point of view unless you understand them first.

Empathy is the foundation that makes everything else possible. It's the first thing you need to pursue—understanding others, what they need, what they're going through, what constraints they're operating under—so you can frame challenges from their perspective and activate your stakeholders to work on your behalf.

When I look back at how easily the contract manufacturer shifted to our new approach once I understood John's constraints, I'm still amazed. The solution seemed so obvious in hindsight, but I couldn't see it until I stopped thinking only about what we needed and started also thinking about what he needed.

That's the power of earning the right to try: you don't demand trust, you demonstrate that you understand. You offer solutions that make other people's lives better, not harder. You prove the value through small wins before asking for big commitments.

When you lead with genuine empathy for all your stakeholders, you create something remarkable. Not just successful projects or profitable outcomes, but lasting change that makes everyone involved permanently more capable.

The contract manufacturer didn't just help us succeed. They became better at helping all their clients succeed. That's collective impact. That's what happens when you stop pushing and start creating pull through 360-degree empathy.

That's what happens when you earn the right to try.

About Chris

Chris Danek is a builder, strategist, and mentor in the world of medtech innovation. Trained in engineering and business, with a career spanning decades across engineering, executive leadership, and founder roles, Chris has helped shape some of the most impactful medical technologies of the past two decades. He led the development of the first FDA-approved interventional treatment for asthma, co-founded AtheroMed (developer of the Phoenix Atherectomy System, now Philips AtheroMed), and has guided many medtech development teams through critical phases of product development, fundraising, and go-to-market readiness.

Chris believes empowering teams is a key to accelerating breakthrough impact. As the CEO of Bessel and creator of proprietary Bessel frameworks for startups and development teams, Chris teaches how to innovate with speed, integrity, and clarity. He specializes in aligning cross-functional teams, building high-impact product strategies, and helping early-stage companies avoid costly missteps by focusing on what matters most.

Chris developed the Bessel Origin program that combines real-world project-based learning with expert team mentorship. This program has achieved success for dozens of teams in industry, the classroom, and advanced research settings. Bessel's train-the-mentor program helps companies identify, develop, and retain emerging leaders.

With a Ph.D. in mechanical engineering from Stanford and an M.B.A. from The Wharton School, University of Pennsylvania, Chris is an inventor with more than 90 U.S. patents.

A frequent speaker, educator, and advisor for medtech companies, startup founders, and accelerators across the country, Chris brings a rare combination of technical rigor, strategic insight, and human-centered leadership. A simple belief drives his work: care deeply, stay disciplined, aim high.

Learn more at:
ChrisDanek.com

CHAPTER 12

EMPATHY UNBOUND

BY JOHANNA SOTO RIGSBEE

It was June in Texas, the kind of heat that makes every surface hot to the touch. I woke up early, slid into my little car, and began driving the seventy-nine miles from Austin to the San Antonio immigration office.

I was eighteen years old, and it was the first time I had ever driven outside the city limits. My palms stuck to the steering wheel, and my heart thudded so loud I could hear it over the engine. I had exactly ninety-five dollars to my name, just enough to pay the fee. I'd worked long shifts making $4.25 an hour and saved every penny. This appointment meant everything to me. This was the doorway to scholarships, to a college degree, and to the life I dreamed of but didn't yet have the language for.

But the cost wasn't just financial. My mother didn't want me to go. In her mind, becoming a U.S. citizen meant turning my back on our Honduran roots. She believed I was choosing a new identity, a new culture, a new life that didn't include the one she'd fought so hard to give me. She worried she was losing me to a world she didn't understand. I remember standing in our kitchen the night before my appointment. She was quiet, her mouth pressed into a hard line. I kept waiting for her to soften, to say she understood, but she didn't. She couldn't.

When I left the house at dawn, she did not come to the door. And when I walked into that immigration office, terrified, trembling, and about to hand over every penny I had, I walked in alone. Sitting there felt like being called into the principal's office, only I hadn't done anything wrong. The officer's badge glinted under the fluorescent lights, and even though he was kind, his presence intimidated me. I had never been in trouble a day in my life. I passed the test and, a few weeks later, returned for the swearing in ceremony. I was the youngest person in the room by five decades, but when that certificate of citizenship was pressed into my hand, something shifted inside me.

I realized that sometimes the people who love us the most will misunderstand our choices. Sometimes, pursuing your dreams requires walking alone. Sometimes choosing your future requires you to release your past.

For a long time, my mother resented my decision, but when I walked across the stage as the first in our family to graduate college years later, she was there. And she was proud. But she wasn't the only woman who shaped me. My aunt became the voice I leaned on whenever life tested me. She was the one who taught me that faith wasn't just hope, it was believing that God walks with you through every uphill climb. She prayed with me, steadied me, and reminded me that the same God who opened doors for generations before us would open them for me, too. My mother and my aunt were hardworking, wise women, and their voices became part of my journey and part of the reason I kept moving forward even when the path was steep.

In becoming an American citizen, I hadn't abandoned my heritage. I had expanded my legacy. And my decision was not made in any way to disrespect my family. It was made so that I could avoid disrespecting myself.

* * *

After citizenship came the next uphill climb: college. It took me nine years to earn my degree because I had to work full-time the entire way. I felt behind constantly, watching students younger than me graduate, get internships, and move forward while I was still juggling work schedules and tuition bills. When I finally landed my first real role in the engineering world, it felt like stepping into a foreign country. My field was overwhelmingly male, and the unspoken message was clear: You are an outsider here.

I'll never forget one interview in particular. I had applied internally for a security engineering role, which was a role I was absolutely qualified for. One of the interviewers leaned back in his chair and said, "So… why do you really want to be an engineer?" Not, "What excites you about this position?" or "Tell us about your experience." I knew instantly he wasn't asking from a place of curiosity. He was asking because he didn't think I belonged. I closed my notebook, looked him in the eye, and said, "I don't think I'm the right person for your team. If I were a man, you wouldn't have asked me that." Then I stood up and walked out. It hurt, but it taught me my first leadership truth: Empathy starts within. If I wanted others to respect my time, my effort, my talent, I had to respect it first. I had to show empathy to *myself.*

My next field job was intense. I pulled cable, crawled through ceilings, hung access points, and worked grueling hours. I studied manuals on airplanes because I didn't want to say no to any opportunity. I built my competence the hard way, by being willing to learn every inch of whatever the job required.

Over time, I realized empathy wasn't softness. It was stamina. It was self-trust. It was having your own back when other people doubted your place in the room. How often do we question our worth simply because someone else questioned it first? Looking back, I see that when I walked out of that interview, I wasn't being rebellious. I was cultivating a leadership value. I was learning that building the strength to support others begins with finding the courage to support yourself.

EMPATHY IS RESPONDING, NOT DISMISSING

Working in a male-dominated environment taught me something no textbook ever could:

Power isn't gained by raising your voice. It's gained by choosing your response.

There were moments when comments stung. Moments when I was mistaken for the secretary. Moments when I was perched precariously on a high ladder, only to hear the men snickering that I should have worn a skirt.

I could have fired back. I could have matched their tone. I could have hardened. Instead, I realized something important: Responding is far more powerful than reacting. Reacting is an emotional reflex. Responding is emotional *intelligence.* When someone questioned my qualifications, I responded with clarity. When someone underestimated me, I responded with results. And slowly, the dynamic shifted.

People learn who you are based on how you handle the moments when they *aren't* treating you fairly. Choosing dignity isn't about letting people walk over you. It's about refusing to shrink yourself into something smaller than your values.

Think of a situation where you usually react out of frustration or hurt. What would it look like to pause, breathe, and *respond* instead? What power might you regain? Sometimes the greatest act of empathy happens in the space between stimulus and response; that quiet moment where you choose who you will be next. That pause is where your power lives. It's where you decide whether you'll hand your emotions over to someone else's behavior or keep ownership of your own story. Every time you choose to respond rather than react, you aren't just defusing a moment, you're strengthening the muscle of emotional authority. And that authority becomes the backbone of your confidence, your presence, and ultimately, your leadership.

EMPATHY IS ADVOCACY

A couple of years ago, I got a message from an engineer I'd once worked with. He was older, talented, and terrified. His role was being eliminated, and he had thirty days to find a position inside the company, or he would be out of work. He said, "Jo, I don't know who else to turn to. Is there any chance there's something open on your team?"

I could hear the fear beneath the words. It wasn't the fear of change. It was the fear of being deemed irrelevant and discarded. I put myself in his shoes. I thought about every time I had been overlooked or dismissed based on assumptions. And then I did what empathy demands: I acted.

I rewrote his story for the hiring committee, translating his technical experience into a narrative that showed his value. I advocated through every obstacle and promised to train him myself if they took a chance on him. He got the role, and not only did he thrive, but he became a pivotal part of a large multimillion-dollar deal. He retired this year with honor and confidence.

Who in your life needs your advocacy right now? Where can you use your influence to help someone be seen, heard, or valued?

Empathy isn't passive. It isn't just nodding along, understanding someone's pain, or feeling compassion from a distance. Empathy can be a *verb.* It's the courage to step into someone's story long enough to help them rewrite it. It's rolling up your sleeves when it would be easier to look away. It's using your voice, your access, your credibility, or your insight to bridge the gap for someone who's standing on unsteady ground. Empathy is not softness; it's service.

And service, when rooted in truth and action, has the power to change the entire trajectory of another person's life.

EMPATHY ASKS FOR COURAGE AND CURIOSITY

When I was tasked with building a systems engineering team from scratch, I had no roadmap, no template, no precedent, and very few supporters. If it failed, *I* would be blamed.

People assume leadership means having all the answers. It doesn't. Leadership means being brave enough to admit you don't. So, I made up my mind to interview people who had already done what I was tasked to do. I knocked on the doors of C-level executives and said, "What does success look like for you? What skills matter most for this team?"

Curiosity became my most effective strategy not just for building the team, but for managing it. I matched roles to abilities, not titles. I had people on my team who were incredibly imaginative but weak in execution. I had others who were rockstar producers but lacked communication skills. No one was perfect on their own, and yet together, it was a home run.

That experience taught me something life-changing: curiosity is the purest form of empathy, because curiosity says, "I care enough to understand you. I believe your perspective matters."

Courageous empathy means being willing to get curious and ask the questions that expose your gaps rather than pretending you don't have any. That creates trust. It creates buy-in. And when leaders choose curiosity over certainty, they don't just build better teams, they build better relationships, better solutions, and better outcomes.

WHAT'S YOUR BRAND?

People often think a "brand" is something that's only for companies and influencers. I disagree. You have a brand, and so do I. Your brand is essentially how the people who encounter you experience you. Your brand is your values in motion.

It isn't your job title or your credentials. Your brand is how people *feel* after they interact with you. It's the emotional footprint you leave behind through your behavior, your choices, and the way you treat people when no one is watching.

In my world, empathy is a cornerstone of my brand. It's how I lead, communicate, and manage teams.

When I created my first team, I didn't hire just for experience but for heart, integrity, and potential. I celebrated when team members grew out of their roles. I cheered for their promotions like a proud big sister. Part of leadership, to me, is about stewarding the gifts of others. But here's the truth that matters for *you*: You're building a brand, too, whether you realize it or not. Your brand is shaped every time you choose empathy over ego, patience over pressure, curiosity over assumption. People remember how you listen. They remember whether you elevate them or diminish them. They remember whether they felt dismissed or inspired in your presence.

Ask yourself: What emotional experience do people walk away with after being in my orbit? Does the way I show up match the values I claim? When empathy becomes your brand, people trust you. They follow you. They grow with you. And perhaps most importantly, they *value* you.

EMPATHY IS CONSISTENCY

When I was seeking American citizenship, my mother looked at me and said, "I'm afraid you'll lose who you are." But the truth is, empathy *preserved* who I was. It rooted me, guided me, and kept me grounded through changes, relocations, new industries, and higher levels of leadership.

Years later, when I became a stepmother, my stepson told me something that pierced my heart in the best way. He said, "You never changed. I thought you might change after a while, but you stayed nice." Consistency is the soul of empathy. It's not how you treat people when things are easy. It's how you treat people when things are hard. And consistency creates *connection.* If I've learned anything, it's this: No matter where you go — no matter the title, income, badge, or boardroom — you're a human being first. And so is everyone else.

Looking back, everything I ever accomplished can be traced back to two things: I chased my dreams and held onto my empathy.

When I think about everything I've walked through, I realize that empathy was the fluid source behind all of it. It kept me grounded in self-respect when I needed to take care of myself. It prevented me from being bitter when I was confronted with the worst of humanity.

Empathy is what allowed me to advocate for others, guided my leadership, and helped me to foster a legacy for the generation coming after me. And if there's one message I want you to take from my journey, it's this:

Empathy didn't make me smaller. It made me *braver*. You were born with the right to become whoever you want to become. You're standing in a place rich with freedom and opportunity, one I had to fight to earn. So, pick up the baton and run your race. Legacy is built by those willing to push forward, even when they're crawling across the finish line—knees scraped, lungs burning, sweat stinging their eyes—because they know the victory on the other side is worth every bruise.

If a girl born in a rural developing country with no access to technology and no guarantees can come here and build a life simply because she said *yes* to her dreams, imagine what you can do with the advantages already in your hands. Don't wait for permission. Don't wait for certainty. Move in the direction your intuition is leading you.

Because in the end, empathy isn't just a feeling or a principle. It's a practice, and perhaps more importantly, it's a compass; one that points you towards the life you're meant to live, the person you're created to be, and the legacy you're meant to leave behind.

About Johanna

Johanna Soto Rigsbee is an experienced cybersecurity leader with more than two decades of designing secure, scalable, and business-aligned technology strategies across Fortune 100 organizations. She guides teams and enterprises through complex security challenges with clarity, strategic direction, and a leadership style grounded in empathy.

Beyond her technical achievements, Johanna supports educational and mentorship initiatives that open pathways for future professionals in computer science. She is also known for developing training and enablement programs that help individuals and organizations adapt confidently to an ever-evolving digital landscape.

Driven by curiosity and guided by empathy, Johanna approaches cybersecurity not only as a discipline of defense but as a practice of trust. She believes true resilience is built through awareness, collaboration, and the courage to lead with integrity.

CHAPTER 13

THE JACKET THAT CHANGED EVERYTHING

BY JIM ROBINSON

I was fifteen and a half years old, sleeping in a park in Oklahoma, when a restaurant manager's wife named Bert threw a Walmart bag across the kitchen table at me. "Here, you need that," she said, her voice deliberately harsh, like she was trying to maintain some kind of front. Inside was a winter jacket; nothing fancy, just basic warmth. It was January, and I was freezing my ass off. She knew I'd been sleeping in the park.

For years afterward, I couldn't tell that story without crying.

That jacket wasn't just about warmth. It was about being seen when you're trying to be invisible. It was about someone caring enough to act, even when they didn't particularly like you. Bert's awkward compassion in that moment planted a seed that would take decades to bloom fully. This one act would eventually lead me to serve over 480 homeless individuals monthly and transform a 48 percent success rate into human beings reclaiming their lives.

But I'm getting ahead of myself.

WHEN INTUITION SPEAKS LOUDER THAN WORDS

Twenty-four years ago, I had a client named Bill from Starbucks. We'd been working together for a while, and business was good, really good. But something was off. I couldn't put my finger on it, couldn't point to any specific complaint or issue, but my gut was screaming that Bill was struggling with something.

Now, when you've been in business for forty years like I have, you learn that intuition isn't some mystical power. It's a massive data bank of millions of tiny observations accumulated over a lifetime, processed faster than conscious thought. Your brain picks up on microexpressions, slight changes in communication patterns, subtle shifts in energy that your conscious mind hasn't registered yet.

I could have waited for Bill to come to me. I could have ignored that nagging feeling and focused on the numbers, which still looked fine. But instead, I picked up the phone.

"Let's get together," I said when Bill answered.

"Sure, I'll just stop by the office," he replied, and I could hear the relief in his voice, like I'd thrown him a lifeline he didn't know he needed.

When Bill sat down in my office, I didn't wait for him to explain what was wrong. Instead, I started outlining changes we were making internally. These were specific adjustments to our service delivery that I sensed were creating pain points for him. I watched his face shift from professional courtesy to genuine surprise.

"How did you know that?" he asked. "I didn't call you. I didn't say anything."

"Bill, I just felt it. Something told me we needed to make some shifts, and here's what we're doing."

That conversation didn't just save a contract. It transformed a business relationship into a twenty-four-year partnership. Bill became our best internal advocate at Starbucks, opening doors throughout the Western United States. Just last month, he retired, and we celebrated at a dinner in San Diego with his wife, my wife, and our current manager, who'd been working with him.

"Dude, I remember that moment," Bill told me over dinner. "It was like you knew me before you even knew me."

THE HIGH COST OF BEING RIGHT

Here's what nobody tells you about empathetic leadership: sometimes it means defending people who've hurt others. Sometimes it means seeing past inexcusable behavior to find the terrified human being underneath.

We had an employee, let's call him Paul, with an IQ somewhere north of 160. Brilliant guy, but socially, he might as well have been from another planet. Wouldn't shake hands, couldn't read social cues, communicated like he was programming a computer rather than talking to human beings.

One day, Paul sent a video clip to one of our female employees. She was offended and rightfully so. When she came to me, I initially made the mistake that too many leaders make.

"Well, that's just Paul," I said.

She looked me straight in the eye with a mixture of disappointment and anger. "I'm so tired of hearing 'That's just Paul.' That doesn't excuse his behavior. I feel threatened."

The moment those words left her mouth, something fundamental shifted in my understanding. She was absolutely right. Paul could have an IQ of 165 or be as dumb as a box of rocks. It didn't matter. Her emotions, sense of safety, and experience were genuine and valid. This wasn't her problem to solve by being more understanding. This was a leadership failure on my part, as I did not adequately protect my team.

We terminated Paul immediately. Sexual harassment is sexual harassment, regardless of intent or social capability.

Then Paul sued us for wrongful termination.

During the settlement negotiations, I watched the attorneys and the judge turn this into a three-ring circus, posturing and positioning while missing the actual human being at the center of it all. Finally, I'd had enough.

"Bring him in here," I said. "You guys are embarrassing yourselves. Paul and I can solve this problem."

When Paul finally entered the room, and it took some convincing to get him there, I asked him one simple question: “Paul, what are you really trying to get here?”

His answer floored everyone except me: “I don’t want this to be public.”

This brilliant man genuinely believed that a termination for sexual harassment meant it would be broadcast on the news. He thought I was threatening to destroy his entire future. He had no idea that employment records are confidential unless subpoenaed by a court.

“Paul, we’ll never make this public. I’ll sign a letter today guaranteeing that.”

“That’s all I needed,” he said.

We settled for $5,000, which was money that we should never have spent if his own attorney had simply explained the confidentiality laws to him. But here’s the kicker: the female employee he’d offended? She’s still with us twenty-four years later. She’s like an adopted daughter to me now. When we have the occasion to see each other, we always hug before we depart.

Both of these people needed to be seen, heard, and understood, just in very different ways.

BUILDING IN BLUE JEANS

Years ago, I showed up to give a speech wearing what I always wear: blue jeans. A broker named John Drummond pulled me aside with that particular brand of concerned disappointment that only someone trying to help can manage.

“Jim, could you, you know, wear some khakis and throw a blazer on?”

I looked at him, this well-meaning man in his expensive suit, and felt my irritation rise. “I wouldn’t have been comfortable giving that talk in your costume,” I told him. “This is my standard. I wear blue jeans everywhere I go.”

The conversation could have ended there, with both of us writing the other off as stubborn or clueless. Instead, it led to meeting his wife, Mary Ellen Drummond, who became my first business coach. She saw something in that irritated exchange—a man confident enough to stand his ground, clear enough about his identity to refuse to compromise it for comfort.

I'm literally writing a book about it now: *Building in Blue Jeans: It's Not About the Costume, but How You Wear the Costume.*

John, who once criticized my wardrobe, has since given speeches about me that made my wife cry, not from embarrassment, but from the power of how he described the impact of authenticity. You can show up in pajamas and make an impact, or wear a $5,000 suit and be forgotten. It's not the costume; it's the confidence in who you are underneath it.

THE FORTY-EIGHT PERCENT

Remember that homeless facility I mentioned? The East County Transitional Living Center became my life's unexpected mission. It started with Bill, the same Bill from Starbucks, inviting me to a charity event. Being the supportive business partner I was, I went along. Twenty minutes in, Bill bailed. "Peace out, dude. I'm out of here."

There I was, feet feeling like they had bricks attached to them, unable to leave despite every fiber of my being wanting to follow Bill out the door. Harold, the CEO, was talking about vacant rooms they couldn't use because they needed a plumber.

"I own a plumbing company," I heard myself say. "I can fix that today."

One phone call later, my team was there. Those rooms were ready for people to get off the streets that same day. What started as a simple repair job turned into a $150,000 renovation. Then Harold invited me to what I thought was a thank-you lunch. Half the board was there.

"The board wants you to join us," Harold said. "We think you can change things."

Five months later, they elected me chairman. I served for eight years.

During my tenure, we achieved something remarkable: a 48 percent success rate in getting people off the streets and into productive lives. That's higher than Alcoholics Anonymous. Higher than most rehabilitation programs. We served 480 people monthly, including 180 children.

But here's what made the difference: we didn't just house people. We transformed them. We taught life skills and soft skills. We partnered with restaurants to create job pipelines. Twice a year, we held black-tie galas where our program participants served as chefs and wait staff, telling their stories of transformation to potential employers.

I learned something crucial during those years: you can't help someone by enabling them to stay comfortable in their pain. That dollar bill you hand out the car window? It keeps them on the street for another day. Sometimes, the most empathetic thing you can do is let someone hit rock bottom so they're ready to climb back up.

THE FULL CIRCLE

Here's what forty years in business and eight years serving the homeless taught me: every interaction is preparing you for something. That jacket Bert gave me when I was sleeping in a park? It wasn't just about surviving winter. It was about understanding that compassion often comes wrapped in awkwardness, that help doesn't always look helpful, and that sometimes the smallest gesture creates the biggest impact.

When I stood in that facility, watching people come in looking like stray dogs and leave four months later looking like they could walk into any job interview, I understood why my path led there. Every moment of my own homelessness, every night in that park, and every struggle to build my business from nothing, prepared me to see these people not as statistics or problems to solve, but as human beings, one moment of genuine understanding away from transformation.

My father was a minister. He taught me two things: fix stuff efficiently and serve other people. I built a forty-year business on that foundation. But it took sleeping in a park to teach me the third thing: empathy isn't about feeling sorry for someone. It's about seeing yourself in their struggle and having the courage to act anyway.

Today, when I draw my business model for employees—a triangle with owner, team, and client—I flip it upside down. The team sits at the top, carrying the most weight. The client comes second. I'm at the bottom, the smallest point, holding it all up. That's not false humility. That's understanding that leadership isn't about being seen; it's about seeing others.

One of my employees lost his grandmother years ago. His family couldn't afford a funeral. I wrote a check for $15,000, money I didn't really have to spare, and paid for everything. Today, I still have the card his entire family signed, thanking me for making it possible to say goodbye with dignity. That employee? He's now running his own successful business. Some might call him a competitor. I call him a success story.

THE ROUND TABLE REVOLUTION

We need each other. That's not a feel-good statement. It's a survival imperative. Right now, we're so divided we're not even sitting at the same table, much less a round one. And that's why I insist on round tables. No one sits at the head because no one is more important than anyone else.

The table needs to be diverse, or we won't change anything. It needs people who wear suits and people who wear blue jeans. It needs those with 160 IQs who can't read social cues and those who can feel a shift in energy from across the room. It needs people who've slept in parks and people who've never missed a meal.

Because here's what I know after forty years of building businesses, eight years of serving the homeless, and a lifetime of learning to see people as they really are: empathy isn't a soft skill. It's the hardest thing you'll ever do. It requires you to set aside your ego, your assumptions, and your comfort to truly see another human being.

But when you do, when you really see them, everything changes. A twenty-four-year business relationship blooms from a single intuitive phone call. A lawsuit dissolves with one honest conversation. A homeless person becomes a productive citizen. A competitor becomes an ally.

That jacket Bert threw at me wasn't just about keeping warm. It was about being seen when you're invisible, valued when you feel worthless, and helped when you're too proud to ask. Every time I tell that story and cry, which is every damn time, I'm reminded that empathy isn't just about understanding someone else's pain.

It's about remembering your own and using it to change the world, one person at a time.

About Jim

Jim Robinson is the President and CEO of CGP Maintenance & Construction Services. With more than forty years of industry experience, Jim has grown CGP from a regional operation into a trusted national provider for some of the most well-known brands in retail, hospitality, restaurant, and commercial real estate.

Jim's journey in the construction and maintenance world began at the ground level, giving him a deep, firsthand understanding of the industry's demands. His leadership style is rooted in transparency, integrity, and a relentless focus on customer satisfaction. Under his guidance, CGP has developed a reputation for high standards, fast response times, and the ability to deliver quality outcomes in complex, time-sensitive environments.

Throughout his career, Jim has prioritized building a culture that values people just as much as performance. He believes that long-term success comes from empowering employees, fostering accountability, and continuously investing in training and leadership development. His emphasis on mentorship and professional growth has helped CGP attract and retain top-tier talent across multiple trades and disciplines.

Jim is also an active member of several professional and industry organizations, where his insights have made him a sought-after speaker at trade conferences, leadership summits, and corporate events, where he shares practical strategies for building scalable operations and delivering consistent client value in an ever-evolving market.

Outside of his professional work, Jim is a dedicated supporter of community development initiatives and nonprofit programs that provide skilled trades training and career pathways for underserved populations. He believes deeply in giving back and creating opportunities for others to grow and succeed.

Suggested Topics:

- Leadership
- Company Culture
- Facility Maintenance
- Business Growth
- Industry Trends
- Mentorship
- Management
- Innovation
- Customer Service

CHAPTER 14

THE SIZE OF THE SHOES MATTERS

BY NICK NANTON

The email landed with a thud. "I know you won't like this," it began. It was a classic accusation audit, whether the sender knew the term or not.

Before asking for more time, more edits, more patience, he named the emotion he knew I was likely to feel. Resistance. Frustration. Fatigue. By putting it on the table first, he defused it. He acknowledged the impact before making the request. That single sentence changed the temperature of the entire exchange. Instead of triggering a defensive response, it invited perspective. It slowed me down just enough to remember what Chris Voss teaches so well: when you label fear, frustration, or objection first, you take away its power. And in that pause—between irritation and insight—I chose empathy over reaction.

We were years into a project, and just weeks from completion. We were an inch away from a final draft we all believed was done. And now, he was requesting more edits. More time. More cost. More delay. My first instinct was the same one I'd had for most of my career: frustration and the urge to push back and protect what I thought was fair. And then I stopped. It wasn't just his empathy that disarmed me. It was the fact that I have learned (sometimes the hard way) that leadership often begins in the space between reaction and response.

In every unexpected curveball, there is a crossroads moment. How we react in that moment can spell the difference between a bridge irreparably burned or a relationship powerfully forged.

RUNNING AN EMPATHY AUDIT

Early in my career, when someone retracted on a commitment, I took it personally. I'd feel the surge of anger rise, and I was ready to confront or cut ties. Now, I can't say my lizard brain always handles it perfectly, but I'm constantly trying to get better at looking at things differently. When something goes south, my first step is to run an empathy audit. An empathy audit is a moment of deliberate pause, where reaction gives way to curiosity. It's the discipline of checking your own role in a situation before assigning intent to someone else. In high-stakes relationships, that pause is often the difference between resolution and rupture.

Before I react, I ask myself three questions:

- Did I offend them?
- Did I miss something?
- Is there anything I could have done better?

Most of the time, the honest answer is no. And when it's not me, I remind myself of a simple truth that took years to learn: I have absolutely no clue what else is happening in their life.

The sharp email. The delayed response. The impatience that feels personal. Any of those could be about me. But it could just as easily be about a crisis I can't see—a sick parent, a collapsing deal, a boardroom fire, a marriage under strain, or a decision they're carrying that affects hundreds of people and millions of dollars. People rarely announce the weight they're under.

That awareness changes how I show up. Instead of assuming disrespect, I assume pressure. I give the benefit of the doubt. Reacting to the surface behavior without understanding the underlying load is how relationships get damaged beyond repair. That realization creates space. Space for grace. Space to ask instead of accuse. Space to slow the moment down just enough to keep it from exploding. Now, I am by no means perfect. What I've written here in this chapter is as much advice for you as it is a reminder for me to pause before responding and to remember that behind every deal is a human being.

Empathy, in business, isn't weakness. It's restraint powered by awareness. When I finally matured enough to understand that, it allowed me to form solid relationships with some of the most iconic people in the world. When writing this out, it could appear a bit simplistic or obvious, but to state it plainly: when dealing with people who are constantly getting hit from all angles, you have to have an incredible amount of grace and understand that at any given time they may have to change course and deal with something that is, at least temporarily, more important than what they are doing with you. It sure can feel like a broken promise, or worse, when it happens to you, but if you can remember that it's not personal, you can keep your head cool and your relationships intact.

EMPATHY REQUIRES EXAMINATION

Empathy becomes more complicated the higher the stakes rise. When decisions involve reputation, legacy, and a lifetime of public scrutiny, what looks like indecision or perfectionism is often something else entirely: protection. The pressure people carry scales with the visibility of their lives. The more you work with individuals whose names, stories, and identities are known to the world, the more you realize that empathy requires imagination, not just intention. You can't evaluate someone's reaction without understanding the weight they're carrying. And you can't lead well if you forget that some people are walking in shoes far larger than your own.

The multi-year project I mentioned—the one with the "I-know-you-won't-like-this" email—was a book with a major celebrity. Someone whose life had unfolded in public for decades. From my side, I'd told dozens of life stories. I knew how to shape them, polish them, move them forward. But then it hit me. This person only had one.

This wasn't just another manuscript to him. It wasn't a deadline or a deliverable. It was his entire life condensed, preserved, and released into the world forever. Of course he was particular. Of course the details mattered. In that moment, empathy reframed the entire project.

My frustration dissolved when I realized something critical: the privilege of telling someone's story comes with a responsibility to honor it. When people trust you with their life narrative—especially public figures who have been misunderstood or reduced by the media—you don't rush them. You listen. You slow down. You lead with care. Empathy isn't about agreeing. It's about honoring what's at stake.

Walking a mile in someone else's shoes doesn't mean you surrender your standards. It means you recognize the terrain they're crossing before you judge the pace they're moving at.

In that moment, I understood that this was about legacy; about how a single life would be understood long after the ink dried. My role wasn't to rush the process. It was to steward it.

Empathy didn't slow the work down. It refined it. It clarified my responsibility. It reminded me that leadership isn't proven by how quickly you push things forward, but by how well you hold what matters most to the people who trust you. The larger the life, the bigger the shoes. And the higher you rise in business, the more often you'll be asked to walk alongside people carrying weight you cannot see. When you do, you'll have a choice: protect your ego or protect the relationship. Enforce the moment or invest in the long game.

The leaders who endure are the ones who understand that empathy, applied with discipline, isn't a detour from results. It's how the best ones are achieved.

SEPARATING THE MISSION FROM THE EGO

Not every test of empathy announces itself with drama. Some arrive quietly, disguised as inconvenience. A schedule shift. A delayed call. These are the moments where leaders reveal whether they're committed to outcomes or attached to control. I learned that lesson again on a documentary project where access, timing, and relationships were everything.

It was a film about the entertainment industry, so of course, the major players needed to be involved. I flew to Los Angeles to meet one of the biggest figures in the movie industry.

Ten minutes after I landed with my entire camera crew, my phone buzzed. He'd had an incident that was deemed an emergency that he had to deal with. Even though we were both in LA, and I had my crew with me, it would not be happening that day.

My co-producer was furious. But I'd learned something by then. There are always two things happening on a project:

1. The work
2. The ego

And confusing the two can cost you everything.

This icon didn't wake up that morning thinking, "How can I screw Nick Nanton over today?" His world bends differently. Everyone wants something from him. His decisions ripple across dozens of lives and projects. Our responsibility—to our investors, our team, and the project itself—was to keep the relationship intact. So, we rolled with it.

Leadership sometimes means absorbing inconvenience so the mission survives. The key is to keep the ego in check. The danger isn't having ego. The danger is letting it drive the decision-making. Left unchecked, it turns minor disruptions into personal affronts and replaces strategy with reaction. Leadership requires separating ego from execution. When I say there are always two things happening—the work and the ego—I'm talking about the discipline of knowing which one deserves your attention in the moment. The work asks for patience, problem-solving, and perspective. Ego asks to be seen, defended, and satisfied. Only one of those moves the mission forward.

HOW BIG ARE THEIR SHOES?

It's hard to walk a mile in someone's shoes if you've never stopped to consider how big those shoes really are. Some would say mine are big. I carry responsibility. Pressure. Visibility. But they're not Magic Johnson's shoes. Or Dolly Parton's. Or Keith Richards'.

Part of leading with empathy is understanding where you fit in business and in life. That doesn't mean diminishing yourself. It means orienting yourself accurately. I learned this lesson at the Heisman Trophy event.

I wanted to interview my favorite football player for a project I was working on. We were both scheduled to be at an event, so I flew in my camera crew to film some other stuff and try to get thirty seconds of this guy's time. As expected, there was a protocol. The player I wanted to interview was not easily accessible. There was a handler, a process, and twenty other people trying to get him on camera. We waited, but hours passed, and we were no closer to getting that interview. We decided to just enjoy the night, and at the end, as people filed out, I made my way to him, introduced myself, and simply said, "We'd love to set something up."

He smiled and said. "Absolutely, set it up." And we did. Now, I could have been annoyed that I had spent money to fly my camera guy there and walked out with no interview, but luckily, I know better now. That night validated one of the most important rules of leadership: Walk past the short game to win the long one.

The short game is tempting because it offers immediate validation. But the long game asks for patience without guarantees, restraint without applause, and decisions that won't pay off until long after the moment has passed. Empathy lives almost entirely in the long game.

When you're playing for the moment, every delay feels personal. Every unanswered request feels like a loss. But when you're playing the long game, you begin to evaluate situations differently. You ask not just, "What do I want right now?" You ask, " What relationship am I building? What access am I earning? What trust am I preserving?" That shift from immediate gratification to long-term leverage changes how you interpret power, timing, and your place in the room.

THE FINE LINE

There's a fine line between empathy and exploitation. The way I tell the difference is simple. I watch communication. Are they apologetic? Do they acknowledge the inconvenience? Does it happen repeatedly? Empathy gives the benefit of the doubt—once. Patterns tell the rest of the story.

What people often misunderstand is that empathy without honesty isn't empathy at all. It's avoidance. And honesty without empathy is just aggression dressed up as transparency. The two only work when they travel together. Real empathy doesn't require you to soften the truth. It requires you to deliver the truth in a way that respects the other person's position. That's how trust is built, not through perfection, but through clarity.

I once had to move a meeting with a PR firm twice. The second time, it was because a celebrity I'd been pursuing for months finally became available. I didn't lie. I called and said, "This is going to sound shady, and I'm sorry, but I have to move this again. I'm working with a high-profile client, and I don't control the calendar on this one." That honesty mattered. People can feel when you're managing perception instead of telling the truth. Leading with empathy doesn't mean pretending. It means telling the truth with care. They appreciated the honesty, we booked a third date, and the meeting happened.

THE REAL WHY

I've made plenty of decisions that were penny-wise and pound-foolish. Most of us have. Choices that felt efficient in the moment but were expensive over time. Moves that protected my pride but taxed the relationships I needed most.

What keeps me grounded now is a question I return to again and again, especially when pressure is high and patience is thin: Why am I really doing this?

That question has a way of stripping the noise away. When your why is clear, inconvenience stops feeling like an insult and starts looking like part of the process. Ego loosens its grip. Delays don't trigger panic. Difficult conversations don't feel like threats. Empathy becomes easier when you remember the mission is bigger than the moment.

If your goal is only to win the exchange, empathy will always feel optional. But if your goal is to build something that lasts—a relationship, a reputation, a body of work—empathy becomes essential. It's no longer about being agreeable. It's about being aligned. Just like leadership isn't about being right. It's about being effective. And effectiveness, over time, belongs to those who can pause when others rush, listen when others react, and choose understanding over impulse. It belongs to those who can separate ego from outcome and emotion from intent.

The strongest leaders don't just stand tall in their own shoes; they recognize when someone else is carrying more weight than they can see, and they lead accordingly. Leadership that lasts is built by those who know when to advance and when to walk alongside. In the long game, empathy isn't just a courtesy; it's *leverage*. You don't earn trust by demanding someone keep up with your pace. You earn it by recognizing the size and fit of their shoes and leading in a way that honors the ground they're walking on.

About Nick

From the slums of Port-au-Prince, Haiti, with special forces raiding a sex trafficking ring and freeing children, to the Virgin Galactic Space Port in Mojave with Sir Richard Branson, twenty-two-time Emmy Award–winning Director-Producer Nick Nanton has become known for telling stories that connect. Why? Because he focuses on the most fascinating subject in the world: *people.* As an award-winning songwriter, storyteller, and best-selling author, Nick has shared his message with millions of people through his documentaries, speeches, blogs, lectures, songs, and best-selling books. Nick's book *StorySelling* hit The Wall Street Journal Best-Seller List and is available on Audible as an audiobook. Nick has directed more than sixty documentaries and a sold-out Broadway Show (garnering forty-three Emmy nominations in multiple regions and twenty-two wins), including:

- *DICKIE V* (ESPN/Disney+)
- *Rudy Ruettiger: The Walk On* (Amazon Prime)
- *The Rebound* (Netflix)
- *Operation Toussaint* (Amazon Prime)

Nick has shared the stage with, coauthored books with, and made films featuring:

- Larry King
- Kathie Lee Gifford
- Hoda Kotb
- Dick Vitale
- Kenny Chesney
- Magic Johnson
- Coach Mike Krzyzewski
- Jack Nicklaus
- Tony Robbins
- Lisa Nichols
- Peter Diamandis
- And many more

Nick specializes in bringing the element of human connection to every viewer, no matter the subject. He is currently directing and hosting the series *In Case You Didn't Know* (season 1 executive produced by Larry King), featuring legends in the worlds of business, entrepreneurship, personal development, technology, and sports.

Nick's first love has always been music. He has been writing songs for more than two decades, and his songs have been aired on radio across the United States and in Canada. He is currently ranked in the top 10 percent of songwriters in the world. His songs have been recorded by Lee Brice, Darius Rucker, RaeLynn, Joe Bryson, and many more, and have amassed more than three million streams on Spotify, Apple Music, Pandora, and SoundCloud. He received three Gold records in 2018 for his work with the global touring band A Day to Remember.

Nick has written and/or produced songs that have appeared on the following shows or in promotional commercials for:

- the Fox prime-time series *Glee, New Girl, House*, and *Hell's Kitchen*
- the MLB All-Star Game
- ABC Family's hit series *Falcon Beach*
- the CBS prime-time series *Ghost Whisperer* starring Jennifer Love Hewitt

CHAPTER 15

THE POWER OF STREET-CORNER EMPATHY

BY NIRANJAN SESHADRI

I kept my head down, weaving between sweaty bodies and nameless faces as I hurried along the roadside. It was another sweltering summer day in South India. I was anxious to get home, but stopped when I noticed bare feet on the scorching pavement. I looked up to see a young man about my age. He clutched a begging bowl in one hand and a thin white cane with the other. His face was marked with pain as he shifted from one blistered foot to the other, yet he was determined to solicit donations.

I watched him for a minute. People hurried past him as if he were invisible. I couldn't get over how young he was. How much like me he seemed. It was the first time in my life I remember truly paining for the predicament of a stranger.

I approached him. He shifted his clouded eyes upward against the sun and shook his bowl, a few rupees rattling inside. I slipped off my shoes and knelt on the street corner, my knees digging into the rough heat.

"I want to give you my shoes," I said. He remained silent but lifted one foot. I helped him steady himself, slipped on one shoe, and then the other.

His face transformed. He smiled with pure, unguarded joy, then offered me his bowl of coins. I refused his offer, of course. Then I walked home barefoot. Block after block, the pavement radiated heat like a furnace. I experienced the burning he'd endured for who knows how long.

That day, I learned two fundamental truths:

1. Empathy can only manifest if we are paying attention, and by paying attention, we can discover unspoken needs that other people often miss.
2. Leadership is having the courage to act on those unspoken needs—even when it requires personal sacrifice.

GOING THE EXTRA MILE

As a cardiologist who often works in rural Kansas, I've seen firsthand how difficult it is for small-town folks to access quality medical care. Patients routinely drive hundreds of miles to see me. One young man arrived in my office with venous ulcerations on his leg—painful, non-healing wounds that his previous doctors suggested might require amputation.

I knew a procedure that could be done to save his leg. I told him and his wife that it would require multiple visits and an overnight stay. As I explained the treatment plan, his wife asked to step out to make some phone calls. That's nothing unusual, as families often need to rearrange their schedules around surgeries and such. However, when I passed her in the hallway, I overheard her on the phone asking her bank if she could delay this month's mortgage payment, as they couldn't afford a hotel room along with the house payment.

I felt sick. This man was facing the loss of his leg, and the barrier to saving it wasn't medical complexity or lack of insurance—it was the cost of travel. When I met with my patient and his wife again later that day, I chose my words carefully. "Are there challenges beyond medical costs that I could help you address?"

His wife's eyes filled with tears, and she confessed everything. I immediately arranged to cover their hotel room and the gas for their return trip home once the procedure was done.

"It's not just about the money," she said, wiping her eyes. "It's that someone finally sees what we're really struggling with. No one ever asks about that part."

That experience reinforced a critical lesson: the obvious problem often masks additional barriers. To be successful in our leadership, we must use empathy to look beyond the presenting issue to understand every issue that might prevent progress.

FROM CRITIC TO CHAMPION

Early in my career, I was working hard to establish myself as a cardiovascular specialist in an already saturated market. I met with a primary care doctor with a goal of convincing him to refer his cardiac patients to me. However, he barely looked up when I introduced myself.

"I don't have time for this," he said bluntly. "Specialists come and go all the time. They join practices and then leave as soon as there is a better offer. Why would I refer my patients to you? I don't even know you."

The dismissal stung, but I heard exhaustion beneath his irritation. Instead of pitching my credentials, I changed direction entirely. "You've been practicing here a while," I said. "What has it been like watching medicine change over your career?"

He looked up, surprised. For the next forty-five minutes, he talked about corporatization, lost autonomy, eroded patient relationships, and productivity metrics replacing actual care. I forgot about my pitch entirely, genuinely curious about his journey.

As we wrapped up, I handed him my card: "If you ever want to try sending me a patient or two, just to see, I'm here."

Six months later, he'd become my biggest referral source and strongest supporter. Years later, he told me why: "Every other specialist came talking about themselves. You were the first to ask about me."

Empathy isn't a technique to master. Instead, it comes from a genuine curiosity and concern about another person's experience. When you approach with authentic interest, trust follows naturally.

NEGOTIATING A WIN-WIN

I leaned back in my chair and stared across the desk at the software vendor. I'd been running my medical practice for a few years at this point, but negotiating business deals had never been my strong suit. In fact, I was worried about being taken advantage of.

My computer system desperately needed a software upgrade. I'd done my research, and I knew multiple vendors wanted our business. I was pressing this particular salesman hard on price, determined not to get ripped off, determined to come out on the better end of the deal.

Then something unexpected happened. The salesman's professional composure cracked. His voice broke. "Doctor, please. I've got loans piling up. I can't afford to lose this deal."

Here was an opportunity to push even harder, but all I saw was a vulnerable guy struggling under immense pressure. I backed off.

I set my notes aside and said, "Okay, let's figure out how to make this work for both of us."

The negotiation transformed from adversarial to collaborative. We structured a creative deal: a lower upfront fee within our budget, extended implementation support we genuinely needed, and a modest success bonus tied to smooth rollout. He got the sale he needed. We got better terms than we hoped.

That deal taught me something crucial: empathy in business doesn't mean giving up value. It means recognizing that sustainable success comes from creating wins for everyone involved.

WHEN ANGER IS A MASK

I could tell this patient was terrified. He'd already had his right leg amputated due to severe vascular disease. He didn't want to lose his left leg, too. Three years earlier, in the throes of the pandemic, he'd been told by his care team at the time that his left leg had an eighty percent blockage and would possibly need to be amputated. Because hospitals were overwhelmed by COVID, they released him, which postponed his treatment repeatedly. He lived with physical pain in his leg and an increasing fear that he would lose it.

The tests I ran on his leg revealed surprising results: only thirty percent blockage, nowhere near requiring intervention. The pain likely stemmed from arthritis or nerve issues. I returned to the exam room to deliver the good news.

His wife erupted with fury. "How dare you say there's no significant blockage! Another doctor said eighty percent!" She yelled at the nurses. She yelled at me. She accused all of us of incompetence. My team wanted me to discharge them immediately for the disrespect, but I declined.

I recognized something my team didn't. This wasn't anger. It was three years of fear and frustration with no outlet. This husband and wife had reorganized their entire life around an eighty percent blockage.

I let them vent and didn't interrupt. When they had exhausted their fury, I offered to show them the test results. In the reading room, I pulled up both angiograms side by side, three years ago and today. "See this?" I said. "Three years ago, this narrowing was thirty percent. Today, it's still thirty percent. It hasn't progressed at all."

The wife studied the images intently. Her expression softened. "They're exactly the same," she mused.

"Sometimes in crisis, things get miscommunicated," I offered. "What matters now is that your husband's leg is safe."

The next day, she returned to the office and apologized profusely. Leading with empathy sometimes means having to absorb fear-driven anger without taking it personally. This allows us to create a space where truth can replace terror.

IT'S NEVER TOO LATE TO CHANGE DIRECTION

Since the age of sixteen, medicine has been my focus. Always at the core of my professional life, it has been rewarding in so many ways. However, at the age of forty-eight, I began to develop an interest in law, especially how it pertains to the use of artificial intelligence within the field of medicine. This interest led me to Georgetown University Law Center, where I received my JD. From there, I attended UC Berkeley Law, where I completed my Masters in both Technology and AI Law.

At one point during law school, I played the role of a mediator between two groups of students. They were debating how to approach a legal case regarding housing discrimination. I ended up watching two brilliant groups completely miss each other's actual concerns. One faction insisted we build the case on legal doctrine. The other pushed for a data-driven approach.

The debate raged for two hours, each side talking past the other. Once I concluded nothing was getting accomplished, I silenced both sides and brought that silence front and center. After some time, I said, "It feels like you're each afraid that if your approach doesn't dominate, the case will fail because your expertise was ignored. Is that a fair assumption?"

Both sides nodded.

"So," I continued. "Perhaps the real issue isn't law versus data. Maybe it's trust. Trust that your perspective won't be lost."

More nodding.

"What would need to be true for each of you to feel your expertise is honored?" I asked.

The legal group didn't hesitate. "One section must deal directly with case law. Otherwise, it's just policy."

The data group responded immediately. "And one section needs technical metrics—false positives, disparate impact ratios. Otherwise, it's hand-waving."

I walked to the whiteboard and sketched three connected boxes: Part I: Legal Doctrine. Part II: Data and Evidence. Part III: Hybrid Approach. "Would this structure work?"

The argument transformed into collaboration. We won that case and created a framework that the team used for future cases. Empathy in professional settings isn't about being soft. Instead, it's about hearing unspoken fears, naming them without judgment, and creating space for co-creation.

PATIENTS OVER PROFITS

My law degrees have given me the opportunity to work in the field of medicine on a much larger scale. Before, I could only help one patient at a time. Now, I can potentially help millions of people by combining the power of AI technology with advances in medical science.

While building my healthcare AI startup, my co-founders and I faced a defining choice. The early AI revolution in healthcare was exploding. We could rush to market for immediate revenue or delay six months to build proper safeguards and transparency.

"You'll miss the window," investors warned. "Competitors will eat your lunch."

We decided to wait. We weren't willing to sacrifice safety. Those six months cost us immediate revenue and early market position, but something unexpected happened. Early adopters who were skeptical of AI in healthcare heard about our approach. They were willing to wait for a product that prioritized patient safety over speed. When we launched, we had a coalition of supporters who trusted us precisely because we had chosen the harder, safer path.

That experience crystallized what I'd been learning: empathy-driven decisions may initially look like poor business choices, but they build foundations for sustainable success. Trust compounds faster than quick profits.

A COMPANY BORN FROM ONE QUESTION

As a doctor, I'm grateful for the medical professionals who support me day in and day out. Many of these people are highly visible, such as nurses and technicians, but some of them work behind the scenes. One such example is a medical device representative. Medical technology is always improving, and the tools I use to perform procedures often get upgraded. For this reason, medical equipment manufacturers often send out reps who make sure that the rollout of their newest product goes smoothly.

Recently, during a complex vascular procedure, my medical device rep rushed out of the room. He didn't say a word about where he was going or what he was doing. After completing the case, I found him in the break room. He sat in a chair, hunched over, head in his hands.

"Whoa. Is everything okay?" I asked.

He was silent for a while. I could tell he was debating whether he should share his troubles. Eventually, it all came out. His son had a debilitating neurological illness. They had been to every specialist in every major hospital they could access, yet had no answers. In desperation, he'd spent three years researching genetics. Finally, he discovered that his son had a genetic variant that responded to a common supplement. His son improved within weeks.

“How many families go through exactly what you experienced?” I asked.

“Thousands. Maybe tens of thousands,” he said.

“What if we could help them avoid all of the searching you had to do?”

“It would be a godsend,” he said.

That conversation birthed HelixaHealth.ai, a company that helps people with chronic illnesses navigate medical information faster. It exists because I took a minute to ask, “Is everything okay?”

OUR UNIVERSAL THREAD

Throughout my journey, from that Indian street corner to operating rooms in rural Kansas hospitals to meetings with investors, I’ve learned empathy isn’t a soft skill or a quality that is simply nice to have. It’s one of the most powerful tools for creating genuine value in any field.

With every patient encounter, I make an unwavering commitment: when I walk through that door, nothing else exists except that patient’s needs. Not the next appointment, not paperwork piling up, not business pressures. Just two human beings—one seeking help, one equipped to provide it.

As I write this, I think about the young man and his bare feet burning on the pavement. Every significant achievement I’ve made, every successful breakthrough, negotiation, or development, came from applying that same principle: See what others miss. Feel what others ignore. Act when others hesitate.

Ultimately, we’re all pursuing the same thing—happiness, fulfillment, meaning. I’ve learned our own happiness is inextricably tied to creating happiness for others.

About Niranjan

For more than two decades, Dr. Niranjan Seshadri, MD, JD has worked at the intersection of medicine, innovation, and law to help shape the future of healthcare. Trained at the Cleveland Clinic and Beth Israel Deaconess Medical Center, Harvard Medical School, he is an interventional cardiologist and a healthcare entrepreneur committed to building advanced AI platforms that translate clinical insight into meaningful patient impact.

Dr. Seshadri is the Co-Founder and CEO of HelixaHealth.ai, an AI-driven precision wellness company that integrates genetics, lifestyle patterns, and medical records to deliver deeply personalized health guidance. He is also the Co-Founder and CEO of Nectara.ai, which develops neuro-imaging AI tools that support surgeons and neurologists in the management of drug-resistant epilepsy.

In addition to his entrepreneurial leadership, Dr. Seshadri advises international healthcare innovation efforts and translational research programs. His dual background in medicine and law enables him to bridge clinical practice with regulatory and ethical considerations, reflecting his belief that empathy, evidence, and equity must guide all meaningful advances in healthcare.

Dr. Seshadri earned his JD cum laude from the Georgetown University Law Center and went on to complete his LL.M. at UC Berkeley, where he earned Certificates of Specialization in AI Law and Technology Law. He writes and speaks on issues at the intersection of AI governance, healthcare regulation, and digital ethics.

He is the co-author of *Himalayan Tsunami*, a true account of a catastrophic natural disaster and the resilience that followed. The book examines the human, social, and environmental forces that shape survival, loss, and long-term recovery.

Learn more at:
linkedin.com/in/drseshadri

CHAPTER 16

WHEN REASON MEETS UNDERSTANDING: THE COGNITIVE PATH TO EMPATHETIC LEADERSHIP

BY BABER AMIN

The security architect sat across from me with his arms crossed, radiating hostility. I could feel the tension from the sales team beside me. We were two months into a critical deal, and this one person had the power to kill everything with three simple words: "I'm not comfortable."

My name is Baber Amin, and I work in the complex world of enterprise security products where multiple stakeholders can make or break million-dollar deals. But this moment taught me something fundamental about leadership that no business school had covered: sometimes the most powerful form of empathy isn't feeling what others feel. It's understanding what they need.

"Help me understand your worst-case scenario," I said, pushing aside the carefully prepared roadmap presentation. "What are your concerns about deploying our solution?"

The room went quiet. The sales team shifted uncomfortably. We were supposed to be showcasing shiny new features, not inviting objections. But as I watched that architect's posture relax and arms uncrossing—I knew we'd found the right conversation.

THE ZERO-EMPATHY EXECUTIVE

Here's something most leadership books won't tell you: early in my career, I scored near zero on the empathy portion of my 360-degree review. Not low. Near zero. While other executives were reading emotional intelligence books and practicing active listening, I was staring at assessment results that essentially said I had the emotional range of a rock.

That score haunted me for months. Was I really that disconnected from my teams, customers, and even fellow human beings? The answer came through an unexpected source, not from leadership seminars or coaching sessions, but from two books that a mentor recommended: *Adam Smith's Theory of Moral Sentiments* and *Marcus Aurelius' Meditations*. In those pages, I discovered something transformative: I wasn't lacking empathy. I was experiencing it differently. Over the years, this has been further refined by Ryan Holiday's writings and Paul Bloom's arguments about empathy versus compassion.

What I possess is cognitive empathy—understanding what others need.

Think of it this way: empathy is my sensor, but reason is my steering mechanism. I don't need to feel your frustration to understand that missing a product deadline affects your quarterly targets. I don't need to experience your anxiety to recognize that regulatory compliance keeps you awake at night. This cognitive approach, I learned, could be just as powerful, sometimes more so, than emotional connection.

THE CUSTOMER WHO WOULDN'T DEPLOY

Several years ago, I was pulled into a crisis. We had a customer who'd purchased our product six months earlier but hadn't deployed it, a pattern that typically signals churn risk. The sales team was pushing for an upsell opportunity, trying to expand our footprint, but they kept hitting a wall. The customer wasn't interested, and the renewal they already had was looking increasingly uncertain.

"We need heavy discounting," the sales team told me. "Maybe 90 percent off the expansion products. Otherwise, we're going to lose them entirely."

In speaking with the account executive, I mapped out three parallel conversations, each revealing a different signal. The account team was thinking transactionally, i.e., discounts as a path to retention. The customer was thinking tactically, i.e., deployment blockers they couldn't articulate. Leadership was thinking strategically in terms of expansion revenue at risk. None of them spoke the same business language, and I was going to have to bridge that gap.

I asked the account team to invite me to the next conversation with our customer. Before the meeting, I built a hypothesis: if they hadn't deployed after six months, pricing wasn't the blocker—execution was. I needed to diagnose the real friction point, which meant shifting from a sales conversation to understanding their fear and challenge.

When I sat down with them, I didn't bring pricing sheets or product roadmaps. Instead, I asked a simple question: "Are you seeing value from your deployment, and is it matching your expectations? If not, what is the missing gap?"

The floodgates opened. They explained that the deployment had stalled, their team was overwhelmed, and they couldn't see how our solution fit their actual workflow. They didn't need discounts. They needed help.

I recognized the pattern: they were overwhelmed by scope, not underwhelmed by value. We created a two-week sprint plan. Not six months of implementation. Not quarterly reviews. Two weeks. We jointly defined the minimal valuable outcome they needed, wrote it down, published it, and created a RACI chart so everyone knew their responsibilities. Then we executed on the first two-week sprint, and immediately defined the next.

We didn't plan months in advance. We built trust two weeks at a time. After about six weeks, something shifted. They stopped seeing us as vendors pushing products and started seeing us as partners invested in their success. They eventually deployed fully, bought additional products, and became one of our strongest advocates.

The relationship transformed because we stopped trying to complete transactions and started solving real problems. Cognitive empathy, recognizing that undeployed products signal overwhelming scope and execution barriers, allowed me to focus on solutions rather than negotiations. By systematically diagnosing the real problem across all stakeholders, customers, sales, and leadership, we didn't just solve for one customer. We created a blueprint for turning implementation risk into an expansion opportunity.

THE QUARTER WE STOPPED BUILDING

One of the hardest decisions I've made as a product leader came from listening to a pattern in our quarterly business reviews. In consecutive QBRs, I tracked a recurring signal: More than two-thirds of customer escalations traced back to migration friction. Customers described migrating their operations from on-premise to cloud as consuming enormous time and money. The migration itself provided no immediate value. They had working systems before, and they'd have working systems after. The middle part was just expensive friction and risk. These weren't individual complaints; this was a systemic signal.

Our product roadmap was packed with exciting new features. The sales team had been promising these capabilities to prospects. Engineering was eager to build them. But those customer voices kept echoing: migration is killing us.

I recognized this pattern wasn't just customer feedback—it was a signal that our current approach was creating pain that would ripple across the organization. Before bringing any proposal forward, I needed to map out each internal stakeholder's position as a legitimate signal of organizational risk. Sales would face integrity issues—delays in delivering promised features could damage credibility with prospects. Engineering would question resource allocation—prioritizing utilities over core innovation might seem like abandoning our product vision. Partners might interpret this as a retreat from our competitive positioning.

After weighing these competing organizational risks against customer churn and escalating support burden, the math was clear. Every quarter, we didn't solve the migration problem; we extended the window in which customers second-guessed their investment. We were optimizing for feature velocity while hemorrhaging relationship capital. I created a plan to pause our roadmap for a quarter and build migration tools instead. The case wasn't just about customer pain—it was about how addressing that pain would strengthen our position across every stakeholder group. This approach would create more long-term value than any individual feature could.

Instead of new features, we would build migration tools. Instead of innovation, we would remove friction.

We communicated transparently with customers about the delay, explaining that we were building tools to solve their most pressing problem. Most were not just understanding—they were grateful.

The results validated our analytical approach. Customer satisfaction scores jumped significantly. The migration tools became a key differentiator in sales conversations. "You can start here and get there seamlessly because migration is built into our offering," became a powerful selling point. Most importantly, we reduced the window where customers might reconsider their choice or where competitors might swoop in with alternatives.

Reasoned empathy, treating concerns as data, analyzing stakeholder pain as system signals, created more long-term value than any feature we might have built. I didn't need to feel the frustration to recognize its impact. I needed to calculate it, then let logic steer the solution. By systematically addressing pain points across all stakeholders—customers, sales, engineering, and partners—we didn't just retain customers. We converted them into advocates.

THE SECURITY ARCHITECT WHO BECAME OUR CHAMPION

Back to that hostile security architect. As he began listing his concerns—rapid-fire, jumping from technical requirements to compliance issues to disaster scenarios—I grabbed a whiteboard marker.

"Let's write all of these down," I said. "Every concern, every scenario, every requirement. We're not leaving this room until we've captured everything that's worrying you." I realized that he was signaling risk without a framework to process it. The sales team was interpreting rapid-fire concerns as resistance. They were uncomfortable as we were supposed to be closing, not documenting objections. I understood that I needed to validate every concern as data, categorize systematically, and then address it with logic rather than persuasion.

As that list grew on the whiteboard, something interesting happened. The architect's hostility melted into engagement. He wasn't just listing objections. He was actively offering solutions. For the first time, a vendor was taking his concerns seriously rather than trying to overcome them.

We addressed each item methodically. Some concerns stemmed from misunderstandings I could clarify immediately. Others had mitigation strategies and workarounds that we identified jointly. A few were genuine gaps in our solution.

"For the gaps," I told him, "you're right. We don't have those capabilities today. But if they're really deal-breakers, let's write them into the contract with delivery dates. You become our design partner. You help define the requirements. You participate in our engineering reviews."

His transformation was remarkable. He went from listing a page full of blockers to proactively codesigning improvements, from skeptic to champion. He didn't just approve the deal. He helped us improve our product, strengthen our security posture, and surface issues in design reviews that we would have missed. When he eventually moved to another company, he brought us with him and became an internal advocate there.

Recognizing that rapid-fire objections signal overwhelm, not obstruction, allowed me to turn resistance into partnership. Cognitive empathy—systematically validating his concerns, categorizing them, and collaboratively solving them—transformed the dynamic. By treating his objections as valuable data rather than hostile resistance, we didn't just close a deal. We gained a champion and a friend.

THE OVERWHELMED COLLEAGUE

Not every application of cognitive empathy involves customers or big deals. Sometimes it's as simple as noticing patterns in a colleague's behavior. I had a peer who was constantly busy, always in motion, but never seemed to complete anything. His manager asked if I could help.

I analyzed his work patterns for a day, tracking task switches, meeting cadence, and completion rates. The data revealed the challenge: he averaged thirty-plus context switches per day, said yes to 100 percent of requests, and had no blocks of protected time. He wasn't lazy or incompetent. He was overwhelmed by his overly accommodating approach—and it was creating a ripple effect across the team. His teammates were covering for his incomplete work, breeding resentment. He was working late nights and weekends, but his output remained incomplete.

I didn't give him a motivational speech or try to make him feel better about his situation. Instead, I treated his overcommitment as a system design problem. I showed him my calendar. Blocks of protected time. Scheduled focus work. Clear boundaries.

"The calendar isn't just for meetings," I explained. "It's for managing your attention and protecting your cognitive capacity."

We restructured his workflow together, not through emotional support, but through practical systems. Within three weeks, his metrics transformed: context switches dropped, and completion rate increased dramatically.

Cognitive empathy—recognizing that constant motion signals system failure, not a lack of work ethic—allowed me to focus on structural solutions rather than motivational interventions. I didn't need to feel his overwhelm to diagnose it. I needed to measure it, map its impact, and redesign the workflow. By treating his overcommitment as a solvable system problem rather than a personal failing, we didn't just improve one person's productivity. We created a framework to identify and address cognitive overload across the team.

THE SENSOR, NOT THE STEERING WHEEL

Here's what I've learned about empathetic leadership through a cognitive lens: you don't need to feel someone's pain to address it effectively. In fact, sometimes feeling too deeply clouds judgment and leads to decisions that feel good but don't solve problems.

When I approach partner recruitment, I don't create partnership theater—announcements without substance. I create business plans, co-host webinars, and build actual integration strategies. Partners don't need me to feel excited about their success; they need me to contribute to it.

When someone seems abrupt in a daily interaction, I don't need to feel their frustration to recognize systemic stress. Recognition of their humanity doesn't require absorbing their emotions. It requires acknowledging that their experience exists beyond my interaction with them.

My cognitive empathy might register as near-zero on traditional emotional assessments. Still, it has helped me transform stalled deployments into success stories, turn product roadmap delays into competitive advantages, and convert hostile skeptics into longtime champions.

Leadership doesn't require feeling what others feel. It requires understanding what others need and having the courage to address those needs directly, even when it means uncomfortable conversations, paused roadmaps, or admitting that your solution has gaps.

Empathy is the sensor that tells me something matters. Logic and reason are the steering wheel that determines where we go. And in my experience, that combination doesn't just solve problems. It builds relationships that last.

About Baber

For over twenty years years, Baber Amin has demonstrated exceptional leadership in cybersecurity and identity security management. He has worked with Fortune 500 companies and innovative startups developing cutting-edge identity security solutions, specializing in biometrics, Non-Human Identity, and AI security and safety.

Baber's leadership philosophy centers on the belief that technical excellence and human connection are inseparable—that the best security solutions emerge when customers feel valued, heard, and empowered to solve complex challenges through true partnership. He approaches leadership with the understanding that people do their best work when treated with dignity and respect, and that sustainable business results flow from environments where collaboration thrives and diverse perspectives are welcomed.

Throughout his career, Baber has led identity and access management initiatives that transformed complex technical challenges into tangible business outcomes. He is particularly passionate about bridging the gap between technical and business stakeholders, translating complex security challenges into language that resonates with people's real concerns. His approach builds trust and psychological safety, creating conditions where diverse perspectives drive breakthrough results. He believes empathetic leadership means truly understanding what motivates team members and customers, then channeling that insight into meaningful impact.

When not focused on cybersecurity innovation, Baber enjoys cooking and experimenting with new ingredients, running triathlons, and serving his local community.

CHAPTER 17

THE QUIET POWER OF LISTENING: LEADING THROUGH LIFE'S HARDEST MOMENTS

BY NINA KELLY

In the summer of my eighth year, I thought I would volunteer at my great aunt's school, Shady Oak Park Recreation Center. Rosalie Kelly and Dr. Poret, both from Houma, Louisiana, thought it would be a great thing. This new school in the United States of America allows mentally and physically handicapped children from institutional settings to remain in their family homes. The newly formed organization is now called ARC, a national program that has transformed the lives of children with disabilities. ARC enables these special individuals to live and create independent lives with the assistance and guidance of this foundation.

I had recently moved to Houma, Louisiana, because my mother underwent abdominal surgery, hemorrhaged, and failed to survive. Too young to lose the strongest anchor in life, I searched for a meaning. This sudden loss uprooted me from a known world and family home in Texas and brought me to live with my great aunt, Rosalie Kelly, my father, and the Kelly family home.

It seemed natural to volunteer, as my heart yearned for comfort and purpose. On my first day there, a little girl exactly my age and size, sitting in a wheelchair, caught my attention. She suffered from both mental and physical challenges. I felt an instant connection with her. We both had our challenges. She had physical and mental challenges, and I was very hurt and lost from my mother's death. I resonated with her; we were both small children, with different issues, seeking comfort. We gravitated together.

I spent my time helping her and assisting with her quality-of-life needs. I thought it would make her life easier. I pushed her chair, helped to feed her, washed her hands and face after her meal, and strolled her around the building.

My great aunt pulled me aside. "Why would you take away her independence?" she asked. "If you do everything for her, you are not helping. Be a good listener and encourage her, guide her, help her, but allow her to develop her strength and skills."

I learned something that has remained with me through the decades. When working with people facing tragedy and impossible choices, sometimes the most powerful thing you can do is step back, listen, and allow others to maintain their dignity. I learned valuable lessons of compassion, encouragement, and listening.

WHEN EMPATHY MEETS IMPOSSIBLE CHOICES

Twenty years later, I walked into a small country hospital as an organ procurement coordinator for LSU Medical School. It was the early 1980s, when organ donation wasn't as prevalent as it is today. My role required requesting a grieving family to consider organ donation at the moment of their traumatic loss.

This foggy morning, an 18-wheeler had crossed the highway and collided with a car. The driver, a mother and her daughter, were headed to school. Both suffered severe head trauma and were declared brain dead from the accident.

I had to inform the husband that he had lost both his wife and daughter. When I entered the room, I always said a prayer first to search for the appropriate words. I explained organ donation and what would happen in the next few hours. I left the room to allow him time to make such a decision.

When a person is declared brain dead, they are managed medically to keep the vascular organs functioning, for potential transplantation.

Once I returned, he looked at me and said, "I can donate everything but their hearts. I just can't donate that. Please forgive me."

My heart felt such sorrow. I had experienced the pain that follows the death of a family member from a very young age. "There is absolutely nothing to forgive," I told him. "Even if you did not want to donate at all, that would be perfect."

He wanted others to live through the loss of his beloved family.

I learned something profound that day: empathy isn't about having the perfect words. It's about being present in the pain. Listening without rushing to speak and allowing people to be present with their pain of loss in their darkest hour. The resilience of the human spirit in times of tragedy never ceased to amaze me.

THE HURRICANE THAT TAUGHT ME TO TRUST

I stayed in New Orleans during Hurricane Katrina as president and CEO of the Children's Bureau—the 114-year-old agency that took Louis Armstrong off the streets and gave him his horn. I knew the inner-city children would need assistance.

The city thought it had withstood the hurricane, only to be notified that the 18th Street Canal breached on August 30, 2005. The streets began to flood. All communications were down.

I attempted to drive my car from the ravaged city. I meandered through the streets that began to fill with water. I made it to an overpass across from the Superdome. I parked the car; there were about twenty people on the ramp. The screams from people begging for water and the deafening helicopters dropping supplies created chaos. It was twelve noon in hot and humid Louisiana weather.

A very thin woman, one of the twenty individuals, offered me a wet towel. I thought she was being kind. The sun burning down on the concrete proved unbearable. She had soaked it in something that would instantly burn my face. I learned her intent to harm me. Desperate people do desperate things. The scar remains on my face.

Frightened, I knew that when night came, I would fear for my life.

A large African American man who witnessed the incident approached me. "If you give me a ride, I will get you out of here."

I looked into his eyes and asked, "Are you a good man?"

"I am a very good man. Now we must go."

With no time for hesitation, I gazed into his eyes and witnessed his goodness alongside his fear. He also sensed that at nightfall the situation would change.

We traveled for six hours down old country roads. "You keep saying I am your angel, but I believe in dragons," stated my car companion.

Due to my background as a mythologist, I responded, "Do you know the Chinese believe dragons are very strong and help people?"

He smiled. That broke the ice between us. We found common ground. Mr. Gibson told me he had saved twenty people that day by placing them on rooftops. After six hours together, I dropped him off in Lafayette. He would inform his family that they had lost their homes. This troubled him deeply, bringing the news to his mother, wife, and children.

Our parting words: "Just think, Mr. Gibson, you saved twenty lives today."

He responded, "No, I saved twenty-one."

Stunned from the events of the day, I had forgotten to count myself as one of those people. Yes, he saved me from a potentially dangerous night.

Two strangers met during the tragedy, both traumatized and both facing potential harm. We listened to each other's stories, found common ground in the hurricane aftermath, and survived together. Mr. Gibson saved my life.

THE DOCTOR WHO NEEDED A DIFFERENT APPROACH

For a period of time, I worked nights in the pediatric ward in Lafayette, Louisiana. I made rounds with the doctor, learning everything I could. He demonstrated his incredible diagnoses and neurosurgical skills, saving many children.

One day, parents brought their child to the emergency room, thinking he had a severe sinus infection. Dr. Rivera examined the child and delivered his diagnosis bluntly, "Your child has a blood clot in his brain. We must operate immediately. If we don't, he's going to die right now."

The parents were shocked by how impersonal he was with his delivery of a diagnosis.

I requested a moment with him. "You've just shocked them. They think their child has a sinus infection. You're focused on saving the child, but your presentation is rather harsh."

"Don't you understand it's critical?" he angrily remarked.

"I know. But these are parents and not medical personnel who understand the seriousness of the situation."

I went back to the family and explained that the doctor's urgency came from wanting to save their son's life.

After that, Dr. Rivera considered the parents' emotions. We both grew from those experiences. I learned the value of team cooperation.

THE PRACTICE OF PRESENCE

When I was twenty-five years old, a man came into the hospital after attempting to end his life. He had cut both wrists and both ankles after having driven down a country road and hoping to bleed to death. A stranger driving down this lonely road found him slumped over the steering wheel and rushed him to the hospital. When he awoke, he dropped into a deep depression.

I remember every day on rounds, he cried and wanted to die. Spending so much time with this man, I mostly listened as he explained why he did not want to live. My heart expanded with empathy and compassion. Now he had to face his future.

I could only offer a listening ear. He felt he had embarrassed his family. He struggled with the fact that he had lived. How would he face the aftermath of his actions?

Those long listening hours and the insight he gained as he faced the gravity of his actions made me wonder why he could not find another solution. I often reflect on how many times people reach a point of desperation, not knowing which way to turn. Time is the precious element needed to reflect before any action. Each of us has had moments of desperation deep within, but we are afraid to go on that journey to discover what we might find. He struggled to face his fears and what brought him to such desperation.

With time and the support of a strong medical team, he slowly began his healing to find the strength to walk through his dark night of the soul. Slowly, he discovered the light on the other side. I witnessed this man struggle daily on his journey alone. No family came to visit him. In the end, he was stronger than ever and found a purpose to live. He would eventually help others through his tragedy. I learned the indelible lessons of the fragility of the human heart.

THE GRAIN EXPLOSION THAT CHANGED MY PERSPECTIVE

A massive grain explosion occurred, severely burning multiple men. They were brought to the hospital, and the burn medical team began the initial trauma care.

These patients were in shock. Soon, the reality of their condition dawned on them. Will I ever recover? Where do I go from here? The immediate call to action is to save the patient; all these men were in traumatic shock. But in very short order, they realized they were totally disfigured from the explosion, and that created another crisis.

My heart resonated with the condition these men found themselves in at this time. They were hanging on to life, in shock, severe pain, and barely in touch with the reality of what had happened. Their lives were altered for an extensive period.

Very young, I stood, staring at the scene, wondering how long it would take for these men to recover. They had to endure the unbearable pain caused by the severe burns. Next came the long, slow recovery of burnt flesh and that healing process.

The medical team knew immediately that this would be a long recovery if everyone lived, but one thing at a time. First, save the patient. The physical care of the patient, the emotional support for the family, addressing the financial concerns, the long and slow recovery, and the post-traumatic stress. This would not be an easy journey.

WHAT LEADERSHIP REALLY MEANS

Throughout my life in service to humanity, I have learned the greatest gifts we share are compassion, empathy, and the resilience of the human spirit in times of tragedy. These forces of nature can carry anyone through whatever one encounters.

Empathy serves as one of the greatest tools for success if handled properly.

The little girl in the wheelchair taught me to step aside, allowing her to develop her own strengths through resistance and persistence.

The grieving husband demonstrated that resilience appears during the most challenging moments in life.

Mr. Gibson taught me that strangers appear as the saving grace. Then comes the moment to ask the right question.

Dr. Rivera taught me that even the most skilled and brilliant people can learn from others. Take those precious moments, share insights and experiences, and use them to help others.

The burn victims' experience gave me the overall insight that crisis medical management without seeing the whole person leaves a gap in the overall healing process.

The young man who attempted suicide deepened my compassion for strangers. We never know what suffering lies deep within the individual's heart.

Today, as I reflect on my time on earth, I realize that life lessons present themselves every moment of each day if we are willing to be present, to listen, be nonjudgmental, and discerning. Learn from those who have grown in wisdom, and adapt to the ever-changing circumstances.

Empathetic leadership means having the courage to be fully with others in their pain, fear, and confusion. The ability to listen before action. The strength to allow others their dignity, even when you want to help. The humility to learn from everyone you meet, regardless of their circumstances.

When you lead with empathy, you don't just change outcomes. You change lives, including your own.

I have found that the answers I searched for are often right in front of me when I take a moment to pause. This is easier said than done. In the space we give to others to find their strength, we often discover our own. In the trust we build by honoring their humanity, both parties evolve.

That eight-year-old girl learned a life lesson from her great-aunt, Rosalie Kelly, that she carried for a lifetime: listen, care, assist, but always allow the individual the opportunity to find their own path and strength, which alone can be one of the greatest gifts you give another.

Listen to yourself. Listen to others. Be present. The rest will follow.

About Nina

Nina M. Kelly, Ph.D., is a mythologist with an emphasis in depth psychology. She is a bestselling author and has received Mother's Choice Awards for her three children's books. She's an Emmy Award-winning film executive and producer, humanitarian, storyteller, and cultural and arts activist. She holds a doctorate from Pacifica Graduate Institute. Dr. Kelly's post-doctoral certifications include a master's in dream pattern analysis and archetypal pattern analysis from Assisi International Institute. She also holds certifications in Hypnotherapy from St John's University, Jack Canfield's Train the Trainer, and Eckhart Tolle's The Power of the Presence, along with additional continuing education in psychology, mythology, and religious studies.

She has held numerous leadership positions in her community. Dr. Kelly served as President/CEO of the Children's Bureau of New Orleans, President/CEO of the New Orleans Opera, and President/CEO of Southern Repertory Theatre. She was also Vice President of the Shreveport Opera and the Fundraising Chair for Loyola University School of Music in New Orleans, Louisiana. She has sat on many nonprofit boards of directors.

Throughout her life, she has dedicated her time to the power of story and healing, and continues to grow through ongoing education.

Dr. Kelly has received many awards, including the Atticus Award for her services to her community. She is most appreciative to her children, Barry James Cooper, Jr., Wendy Ann Hawkins, and her grandchildren, Morgan, Madeleine, Hudson, Tudor, Lark, and Christopher, as they serve as her inspiration. She acknowledges the individuals and mentors who have shared their wisdom and graciously offered guidance as she walks through this life.

Connect with Nina:
Nina@honeybeetreehouse.com
www.HoneyBeeTreeHouse.com

CHAPTER 18

THE ALCHEMY OF UNDERSTANDING: HOW EMPATHY TRANSFORMS RESISTANCE INTO RESULTS

BY SASKIA DE WINTER

In the sweltering heat of a Mexico City training room, with broken air conditioning and mandatory attendance breeding resentment, I discovered one of business's most powerful truths. Empathy isn't just a soft skill. It's the hardest currency in human development and organizational transformation.

The room crackled with hostility. Corporate executives sat with crossed arms, their body language screaming defiance. They hadn't chosen to be there. The schedule was imposed. The facility was uncomfortable. And here we were, my team and I, tasked with teaching them about human development and empathy—the very thing their organization systematically denied them.

WHEN UNDERSTANDING BECOMES THE STRATEGY

That first day could have been a disaster. Traditional training wisdom would have had us push through, stick to our agenda, and assert our expertise. Instead, we stopped. We listened. We asked mirror questions, those powerful reflective inquiries that help people see their own thoughts more clearly. "What I'm hearing is that you feel unheard in your own organization. Is that right?" "It sounds like you're being asked to give what you're not receiving. How does that feel?"

The magic didn't happen immediately. Trust rarely does. But something shifted in that stifling room when they realized we weren't there to impose another corporate mandate. We were there to understand.

By the second day, the same executives who had arrived in rebellion were leaning in, asking questions, sharing vulnerabilities. The training that began as an obligation transformed into a revelation. They weren't just learning about empathy as a concept; they were experiencing its power firsthand.

What made the difference? We taught them not just how to be empathetic, but how to teach empathy to others within their organization. We gave them tools to create the very thing they craved. The success wasn't measured in completion certificates or satisfaction scores. It was measured in the tears of recognition when one director said, "This is what we've been missing. This is why we're burning out."

THE COURAGE TO LET GO

Sometimes empathy demands we release control, especially when the stakes are highest. I faced this truth when parting ways with a team member who held critical confidential information: twenty different passwords, internal financial data, and strategic insights that could devastate our business if mishandled.

Every instinct screamed to lawyer up, to protect, to control. Instead, I chose to listen. Really listen. Not to gather ammunition for a legal battle, but to understand their perspective, their fears, their needs.

"I felt a complete lack of control," I remember thinking as we navigated those treacherous conversations. My hands would shake as I reviewed proposals that could either save or sink us. But empathy became our North Star. We crafted solutions that honored both parties' concerns, creating win-win scenarios where conventional wisdom saw only zero-sum games.

When the signatures finally came, when we avoided lawyers and litigation, when confidentiality remained intact, and both parties walked away whole, the relief was profound. But more than relief, I felt validation.

THE EXPERTISE PARADOX

Perhaps nowhere is empathy more challenging than when facing those who believe they have nothing left to learn. I encountered this with a group of top-level directors who were also professional coaches. They arrived at our corporate training armed with their own methodologies, their own certifications, their own unshakeable confidence.

The first sessions were brutal. They questioned our professionalism, challenged our credentials, and dismissed our approaches. The easy path would have been to assert dominance, to prove our superiority. Instead, we did something radical: we became students.

"Tell us about your tools," we said. "Show us your methodologies. What works best in your experience?" We took notes. We asked genuine questions. We modeled the very openness we hoped to inspire.

The transformation was remarkable. By showing authentic interest in their expertise, we created space for them to show interest in ours. What began as a battle of methodologies became a beautiful exchange of wisdom. We trained that group for over six months, not because we insisted we were right, but because we demonstrated that flexibility was more powerful than righteousness.

WHEN FOLLOWING LEADS TO LEADING

A mid-level management team presented another paradox. Their director had very specific ideas about how they should be trained—ideas that conflicted with our proven methodologies. He pushed back hard, insisting on his approach.

Initially, we tried to *fix* his theory, to show him why our way was better. Then empathy whispered a different strategy: What if he actually knew something we didn't? What if his insider knowledge of his team's dynamics was precisely what we needed?

We shifted our approach entirely. "We'll follow your exact instructions," we told him, "and we'll weave in our tools where they complement your vision." It was a risk. Our reputation was built on our methods, not on following someone else's blueprint.

The result exceeded everyone's expectations. By honoring his expertise while contributing ours, we created a hybrid approach that delivered measurable results beyond what either method could have achieved alone. The director was pleased. The team was equipped. And we learned that sometimes the best way to lead is to follow with wisdom and strategy.

THE UNIVERSITY OF UNCONDITIONAL LOVE

But perhaps the greatest MBA in empathy came not from boardrooms or training facilities, but from hospital corridors and museum bathrooms. For thirty-seven years, I watched my mother navigate life after four brain hemorrhages and six surgeries left her partially deaf, incontinent, suffering from nervous tics, and often disconnected from reality.

She taught me that empathy isn't about grand gestures. It's about infinite patience with small, essential things. Food. Sleep. Hygiene. Joy. Family. Music. Nature. Nothing else.

I remember the day at the Centre Pompidou in Paris. We were enjoying the art when she had an accident, the kind that would mortify most people, that could destroy dignity in an instant. The museum was closing. I couldn't remember the French word for *diaper* despite my fluency. Panic could have consumed me.

Instead, I ran. Through Parisian streets, searching for a pharmacy. Back to the museum, now closed, where my mother and her nurse waited in a third-floor bathroom, I negotiated with security guards, calm despite the crisis, focused only on preserving my mother's dignity.

When I finally reached her, when we resolved the situation and left the museum, she looked at me with such gratitude, not the kind you express in words, but the kind that lives in the eyes of someone who has been truly seen and cared for in their most vulnerable moment.

That look taught me more about business than any Harvard case study. It taught me that empathy isn't a luxury we indulge in when times are good. It's the foundation upon which all meaningful human connection is built.

THE ROI OF UNDERSTANDING

In business, we're often told that empathy is soft, that understanding is inefficient, that compassion doesn't scale. My experience proves the opposite. Every time I've chosen empathy over efficiency and understanding over being right, the returns have been exponential:

- The hostile training group became our longest-running client
- The departure that could have destroyed us became a model for ethical transitions
- The coaches who questioned our expertise became our greatest advocates
- The director who challenged our methods became a collaborative partner

But the returns aren't just measured in retained clients or avoided lawsuits. They're measured in the leader who calls three years later to say, "That training changed how I lead." They're measured in the organization that transforms its culture because one team learned how to listen.

THE PRACTICE OF POWERFUL PATIENCE

My mother's thirty-seven-year journey with illness was my doctorate in patience. Watching her relearn to walk, again and again. Celebrating small victories—a clear word spoken, a steady step taken, a moment of lucid connection. She taught me that empathy isn't a sprint; it's an ultramarathon of presence.

Each day brought its own lessons. Morning routines that once took minutes stretched into hours. But in that slowness, I discovered something profound: when we stop rushing, we start seeing. I noticed the determination in her eyes as she recuperated strength during physical therapy. I heard the pride in her voice when she managed three words in a row without stuttering. I felt the joy radiating from her when she recognized a piece of music from her youth.

These observations transformed how I approach business. In negotiations, I notice the slight hesitation before someone agrees to uncomfortable terms. In training sessions, I spot when confusion shifts to understanding. In conflict resolution, I discovered that silence contains unspoken concerns waiting for permission to emerge.

This patience transforms business interactions. When a client pushes back, I remember my mother trying to walk. When negotiations stalled, I remember waiting for her to form words. When understanding seems impossible, I remember that connection often comes not in the first attempt, or the fifth, but in the faithful showing up, again and again.

I once spent six hours in a single negotiation session with a client who kept circling back to the same concern. My team grew restless. Traditional wisdom said to force a decision or walk away. Instead, I remembered my mother taking twenty-five minutes to button her shirt, and I stayed present. On the seventh discussion of the same point, something shifted. The client finally felt heard enough to reveal their real fear: a previous vendor had bankrupted them with hidden costs. Once we addressed that trauma, the deal closed in minutes.

The business world loves to talk about leverage, about power dynamics, about winning. But in high-stakes negotiations, I've found that empathy provides the ultimate edge. Not because it makes you soft, but because it makes you smart.

When you truly understand what drives the other party, their fears, their needs, their unspoken concerns, you can craft solutions that seem impossible to those thinking in traditional win-lose paradigms. The team member with our confidential information wasn't trying to hurt us; they were scared. By addressing the fear rather than the threat, we found solutions that protected everyone.

Empathy in negotiation isn't about giving in. It's about getting to the core of what really matters to all parties and building from there.

BUILDING EMPATHETIC ORGANIZATIONS

The corporate training that began in that sweltering room taught me something crucial: individuals can learn empathy, but organizations must structure for it. Those executives weren't lacking in compassion; they were trapped in systems that penalized understanding and rewarded ruthlessness.

We taught them to be empathy ambassadors, to create pockets of understanding that could grow into cultural transformation. We showed them how to teach others, model vulnerability, and reward connection over mere production.

The implementation wasn't theoretical; it was practical and immediate. We helped them design meeting structures that began with check-ins about human challenges, not just business metrics. We created communication protocols that prioritized understanding context before demanding results.

One executive transformed her weekly team meetings. Instead of diving straight into KPIs, she began with a simple question: "What's really going on for you this week?" The first time, silence. The second time, awkward small talk. By the third week, a senior manager shared that his teenager was struggling with depression. The team's response, genuine support rather than uncomfortable silence, marked a turning point. Productivity didn't decrease; it soared. When people feel seen as humans, they bring their whole selves to work.

Another director restructured his performance reviews to incorporate *empathy indicators*—moments when team members supported colleagues, times they chose understanding over efficiency, instances where they created psychological safety for others. The message was clear: how you achieve matters as much as what you achieve.

The ripple effects were profound. Teams that had operated in silos began collaborating naturally. Innovation increased because people felt safe enough to share half-formed ideas without fear of ridicule.

The organizations that thrive in our interconnected world aren't those with the best strategies or the most resources. They're the ones that understand that business is, at its core, humans serving humans. And humans serving humans requires empathy as its operating system, not as an add-on feature.

THE INVITATION TO TRANSFORM

As I reflect on these experiences, from corporate training rooms to personal crisis moments, I see a common thread. Every breakthrough came not from asserting expertise or maintaining control, but from the brave act of seeking to understand before being understood.

This isn't easy. In a world that rewards quick decisions and decisive action, empathy asks us to pause. In a culture that celebrates expertise, empathy asks us to remain students. In negotiations designed for winners and losers, empathy insists on finding third ways.

But the results speak louder than any argument. Six-month contracts for single trainings. Peaceful resolutions to potentially devastating departures. Collaborative innovations from defensive standoffs. And through it all, the profound satisfaction of leading through connection rather than coercion.

My mother gave me the greatest business gift imaginable. She taught me that when we strip away all pretense, all positioning, all power plays, we're left with the basics: care, patience, dignity, joy. These aren't separate from business success—they're the foundation upon which sustainable success is built.

The invitation is simple but not easy: In your next challenging conversation, negotiation, or conflict, pause. Ask yourself not "How can I win?" but "What don't I understand yet?" Listen not for weakness to exploit, but for humanity to connect with.

Because in the end, the companies that change the world aren't those with the best products or the biggest budgets. They're the ones brave enough to see business as it really is—humans serving humans, with all the messiness, beauty, and possibility that entails.

The sweltering training room in Mexico City taught me this truth, my mother's journey etched it into my soul, and every negotiation since has confirmed it: Empathy isn't a soft skill. It's the hardest currency in the business of being human.

And in a world crying out for connection, for understanding, for leaders who see beyond the bottom line to the human line, that currency has never been more valuable.

The question isn't whether we can afford to lead with empathy. The question is whether we can afford not to.

About Saskia

Saskia de Winter doesn't train leaders. She rewires how they think, decide, and act under pressure.

For more than two decades, Saskia de Winter has worked where leadership is tested for real: in boardrooms, sales floors, negotiations, and moments where results matter and excuses don't. She is the Founding Partner and General Manager of Saskia de Winter Training, a Mexico-based firm that has transformed leaders, teams, and cultures across Latin America, the United States, and Europe for the last 25 years.

Trained as a Physics Engineer (Ithaca College and Cornell U.) and later as a Gestalt and Humanistic Psychotherapist, Saskia brings an unusual combination to the business world: analytical precision paired with a deep understanding of human behavior. Her education spans five countries, including the United States, England, Scotland, Israel, and Mexico, and includes entrepreneurial leadership, sales psychology, high-stakes negotiation, ontological and team coaching, creativity and innovation (SUNY Buffalo), and neuro-linguistic programming.

She has advised and trained leaders from global organizations such as Abbott, Motorola, Universal Studios, Coca-Cola, Essity, and Saint-Gobain, helping them navigate growth, complexity, and change. Her work has driven measurable outcomes: double-digit sales increases, national performance rankings, strategic expansion across Latin America, and the development of new products and leadership pipelines.

Saskia is known for working beyond the obvious. She doesn't offer formulas or motivational shortcuts. She designs highly customized interventions that address what most companies avoid: beliefs, conversations, emotional intelligence, and decision-making under uncertainty. Her approach has helped organizations earn social responsibility certifications, align executive teams, and sustain growth in volatile environments.

Her thought leadership has earned her international recognition, including being named a Forbes leadership mentor and a featured speaker at the Consciousness Festival in Barcelona. She also serves as President of her generation at IPADE, the most influential business school in the Spanish-speaking world.

Fluent in five languages—Spanish, English, French, German, and Italian—Saskia brings a global perspective shaped by culture, discipline, and curiosity. Outside the corporate world, she is an open-water swimmer and a 3D animation enthusiast. She also produced an award-winning short film called "*Caterpillars*" (Orugas).

She is the author of *Square Minded*, a visual book of chess-inspired cartoons, and *Uncertainty Generates Abundance*, a provocative exploration of leadership in unpredictable times, and on thinking differently. This book is not about playing it safe. It's about learning to lead when certainty disappears, and results still matter.

Connect with Saskia:
http://www.saskiadewinter.com
info@sasdw.com
mx.linkedin.com/in/saskiadewinter/
Facebook: /SaskiaDWinter
Youtube: SaskiadeW/

CHAPTER 19

THE HARD TRUTH ABOUT EMPATHY IN BUSINESS

BY JEFFERY MIGLICCO

I used to believe empathy was a weakness. Sitting in my office at 2 a.m., watching my business crumble around me, I couldn't afford to worry about feelings, mine or anyone else's. I had three kids to feed, debt climbing toward six figures, and a family member who'd already bailed me out once. The last thing I needed was to go soft.

That mindset cost me a previous business already, ended countless business relationships, and put a strain on my family life. Only after I risked everything, including my pride, did I realize empathy is not a weakness. In fact, I completely misunderstood the power of empathy until someone showed it to me personally during a critical phase in my career. It's about being strategic enough to see past the immediate transaction to the long-term value of an empathetic human connection.

HARD LESSONS

My first business was the first mobile billboard advertising company in Houston. At twenty-three years old, I'd landed a contract with one of the nation's top banks. They wanted to expand our campaigns to Dallas, San Antonio, and Austin. The opportunity was massive. Unfortunately, to grow my business, I needed more trucks, but I was unable to obtain financing. Despite profitable operations and signed contracts, no bank would loan $560,000 to a very young, entrepreneurial *kid* who looked like he should be in college, not running a company.

I went to my biggest client, the bank that loved our service, and pitched them directly: "Finance the trucks you want me to use for your campaigns, and creatively we can use your direct marketing funds to cover the debt, basically guaranteeing the notes." They refused. The perception was my biggest hurdle. The business model was sound. I couldn't reach the scale numbers without the necessary assets to make a real splash. Then luck dealt me a bad card. Hurricane Ike hit, destroying 80 percent of Houston's billboards. Our contracts evaporated during the rebuild, and eventually, I ran out of cash and sold the business for parts. Young energy and confidence had just learned a hard lesson.

Here's what I missed at twenty-three: I never tried to understand why the banks couldn't take that risk. I never inquired about their internal pressures, the restrictions of their loan committee, or what would have made the decision easier for them. I focused so rigidly on the business model that I failed to understand their positions and the risks associated with the deal.

THE MOMENT EVERYTHING CHANGED

Luckily, a newspaper article about my previous business caught the eye of a medical device manufacturer executive who called me in. After four interviews and many prayers, I took a director of sales position. With a large sales team reporting to me, a steady paycheck, and no more entrepreneurial adventures, the path ahead seemed smooth. Then one of my customers approached me about starting a similar medical device company. My response was immediate: "Absolutely not!" I tried to talk them out of the idea and told them I need time to recover and, to be honest, get back on my feet financially after years of prioritizing the business over my personal life.

But they did something I'd never experienced. They showed amazing empathy, understood my concerns, and asked one simple question. Money aside, comfort aside, would you bet on yourself if these obstacles were not there and you had to build this business? I recognized the tactic, but the confidence they were showing in me moved me. That fire, which allowed me to endure all the pain and suffering through the last business, lit up again. "One hundred percent, I can build this business," I said.

That question changed everything. They listened to my fears about financial instability and once again taking the reins on an amazing business model as a young entrepreneur, and my family's exhaustion from previous blunders. "We're betting on you," they said. "All of it. This doesn't work without you. If you're willing to bet on yourself, let's go!"

I would take a 50 percent pay cut but gain an equal equity stake in the business. Naturally, you can't be an entrepreneur without taking risks. Any smart, still-married man makes this decision with his wife. I recognized the stress it would put on my family. My wife and I discussed all the issues, challenges, and potential long-term opportunities, and it all came down to the same question. Do I believe I can do this, and is this the path I feel God is leading me down? Yes!

I knew this was the right move, and more importantly, their empathetic approach reassured me that together this partnership would endure the challenges to come. They showed me something I'd never seen in business: empathy as a precision instrument for getting things done.

WHEN UNDERSTANDING BECOMES LEVERAGE

Not all empathy feels good. Sometimes it means acknowledging uncomfortable truths on both sides of the table.

We had a customer whose contract value was roughly seven figures annually, who decided to put our contracts out for bid after seven years of partnership. We'd made pricing concessions during COVID, absorbed cost increases without passing them on, and essentially subsidized their growth. This was a slap in the face.

Business is business; it's clear there were other motivating factors we did not see. Their management team demanded cost reductions. Their CEO, someone I'd known for years, was under pressure to show immediate savings. They weren't disloyal. Forces beyond their control were squeezing them.

I called their CEO directly: "I understand you're under pressure to reduce costs. Your board probably demanded that you explore options. However, I need you to understand something as well: if you force this bid process, we will also have no choice but to raise prices. We've subsidized your growth for four years. This partnership has been a pillar of our company, but we cannot continue to erode our margins and increase support for this program. The warning was clear. I understand your goal, but you also have to understand our challenges. This could be a bad move for you as well."

Then I did something risky. I laid out exactly why no other vendor could match our service at any price—not as a threat, but as a business reality they needed to understand. I explained the infrastructure we'd built specifically for them, the institutional knowledge no one could replicate, the switching costs they hadn't calculated. Even the location of our distribution centers was wildly beneficial. No other vendor in the market could match it at that present time.

"Look, if you want a cheaper container, you can always find a lower price if you look hard enough, but it sounds like you haven't considered what you would be losing," I told him. "If you move forward with the bid, that transition may actually cost you more, even if we win."

They went through with the bid process anyway. We raised our prices as promised. They stayed with us at the higher rate. I knew the pressures they were under to complete the process, and I had positioned the deal for an increase, regardless of the circumstances. Empathy isn't always about being nice. It's about understanding reality from multiple angles and finding the path that acknowledges everyone's actual needs.

THE FAMILY GAMBIT

The hardest test of strategic empathy came from family. My family member, a young guy who was a great analyst but definitely an introvert, needed a job. I had a sales position open. Everything about this position would be a challenge for him, but my gut was telling me he was unique. I know how driven this kid is, and his learning capacity was off the charts. However, his challenges were steep: constant rejection, required charisma, and demanded confidence he didn't possess in business, yet.

I hired him, but not out of obligation. I saw something others missed: this introverted analyst would eventually return to analytical work, but if he understood sales from the inside and the power of identifying real customer needs, he'd be unstoppable. I told him directly, "I'm giving you two years. You're going to hate most of it. But when you come out the other side, you'll have something no other analyst possesses. You'll understand what drives revenue from the inside out. After two years, you'll need to move on to something else. This is a stepping stone for you, buddy. Class is in session!"

Those two years were brutal. Cold calling by phone without the ability to visibly assess your customer for positive or negative inflections is hard. Despite being in an uncomfortable position, this guy had grit. More importantly, he learned he could do things that were outside his comfort zone in the business world.

Today, he works as a financial analyst, but with a twist: he's the only analyst in his firm who truly understands what sales teams need. He builds reports answering questions reps didn't know how to ask. He translates data into stories that close deals. That two-year investment in his discomfort created a unique professional who bridges two worlds.

THE MULTIPLICATION EFFECT

Here's what I've learned about empathy after losing two businesses, rarely seeing my family, and finally building a successful business: Empathy isn't about feelings. It's about seeing the entire chessboard, not just your pieces, but understanding why your opponent moves theirs.

When you understand what drives people, not what they say drives them, but the real underlying pressures, you can solve problems others can't even see. That customer who threatens to leave isn't disloyal.

But here's the critical distinction: strategic empathy requires you to understand these hidden drivers without allowing them to paralyze you. You still make hard decisions. You still cut underperformers, lose unprofitable customers, and say no to raises you can't afford. The difference is you do it with full understanding of the human cost, and you structure those decisions to preserve dignity and long-term relationships wherever possible.

THE COMPOUND INTEREST OF HUMAN CONNECTION

Every business book talks about compound interest in finance. Nobody discusses it in relationships. But that's exactly how strategic empathy works. Small investments in understanding people's real needs pay exponential dividends over time.

Was that the customer we confronted with uncomfortable truths? They continue to be a phenomenal seven-figure customer to this day. That family member I trained in sales? He's on his way to becoming an actuary at his current company.

You can't calculate the ROI on these decisions in quarterly reports. They show up years later in opportunities you couldn't have predicted, problems that solve themselves because someone remembers how you treated them, and talent that chooses you over higher bidders because they trust how you'll handle the tough moments.

THE PRICE OF ADMISSION

Let me be clear: this approach forces you to spend more time than you may be willing to on your team. You should use strategic empathy with all employees, but especially with those who you believe are vital pillars that can contribute to the long-term future growth of your company.

If you can't afford those costs, don't pretend to practice strategic empathy. False empathy, acting like you care when decisions prove you don't, is worse than honest ruthlessness. People can handle hard truths when you deliver them directly. They can't forgive manipulation disguised as concern.

When a certain person or employee is worth that extra investment, show them strategic empathy, and something remarkable may happen. This is the edge: building and maintaining real talent. After you have recruited, paid top dollar, invested in all the benefits and all the bullshit it takes to keep people these days, you'd better understand what makes them tick, what makes them get up in the morning, and what drives them through the hard times.

THE IMPLEMENTATION REALITY

You want the practical steps? Here they are, stripped of feel-good nonsense:

First, when someone approaches you for something they want, such as a raise, promotion, or a contract change, pause before responding. Ask why they are not happy with their job, paycheck, or whatever they are trying to improve. Most of the time, the driver is an online survey telling them they're underpaid or a coworker who shared a paycheck, whatever it is. Most likely, they didn't think it through before coming to your office and understanding what the real problem is. This is where you use strategic empathy. The request is rarely the real issue.

Second, when you have to make a hard decision about someone, consider the message it sends to everyone watching. Sometimes, keeping an underperformer costs less than the cultural damage of removing them. In other cases, maintaining an underperformer may also promote a culture of *acceptable* effort versus exceptional effort, and you must let them go as soon as possible.

Third, when dealing with difficult customers or partners, state their position back to them better than they've stated it themselves. Explain your position with equal clarity. Most business conflicts come from each side assuming the other understands their reality. Chris Voss has an outstanding Master Class showing how to utilize labels that work well here when applied strategically. Labeling an emotion often prompts the other party to reconsider and adjust their tone to avoid sounding rude or emotional.

Fourth, invest in people's growth even when, especially when, they'll likely take those skills elsewhere. The reputation as someone who develops talent will attract more talent than any recruiting budget. You can try to only work with top talent and pass over those who you think are not worth the time investment, but at the end of the day, what kind of leader do you want to be?

Finally, when empathy and economics conflict, calculate the total cost, including reputation, culture, and future opportunities, not just the immediate financial impact. The spreadsheet is often deceiving you about the true cost of human decisions.

Strategic empathy isn't about being nice. It's about being smart enough to realize that in a world of commoditized products and automated services, the only sustainable competitive advantage is how you handle the moments when being human is expensive.

Learning from my hard learned experiences, what kind of leader are you today? What kind of leader do you want to be in your business, life, or relationship?

At the end of the day, we can't measure leadership by titles or quarterly results, but by the impact we leave on the people around us. Strategic empathy is the compass that allows us to grow personally, develop future leaders, and build impactful businesses that thrive. I hope each of us will choose to lead with empathy–not as a tactic, but as a way of being, because when we do, we create stronger teams, purpose-driven people, and futures that are brighter than we could ever imagine.

About Jeffery

Jeffery Miglicco is the CEO and Co-Founder of PureWay Compliance, Inc., a national healthcare and medical device company dedicated to improving patient and healthcare facilities' injection safety and experience. Under his leadership, PureWay has grown to serve more than 200,000 locations nationwide and ships over 600,000 medical devices annually.

Beyond PureWay, Jeffery has founded and scaled multiple companies across industries, including a logistics company and a mobile billboard advertising company. He is passionate about building companies that make a meaningful impact on businesses and consumers — from medical device programs that directly serve patients to pioneering innovations that anticipate new demands in emerging markets.

Outside of business, Jeffery is a devoted husband to his high school sweetheart and a proud father of four children. A man of faith, he is a practicing Catholic and brings discipline and endurance into all aspects of life, having once completed an Ironman triathlon. He earned both his BBA and MBA from the University of Houston.

Readers can connect with Jeffery on LinkedIn at linkedin.com/in/jeffmiglicco or at JeffMiglicco.com.

CHAPTER 20

AN ARCHITECT'S VIEW ON DIGNITY, DESIGN, AND THE BOTTOM LINE

BY ROBERT MURPHY

I was about ten the first time I walked into what we then called an "old folks' home." My Nana's broken hip in her eighties had relegated her to a bedridden future, and my parents frequently drove us to visit her in the Preston Springs Hotel in Cambridge, Ontario.

To a child, the place felt like a kindly old ship run aground. The lobby was grand but faded. The corridors smelled vaguely of boiled vegetables and disinfectants. Ashtrays sat on side tables like small metal ponds. The residents, mostly women, moved slowly, or not at all.

But here's what stayed with me. Everyone knew Nana's name, Effie. They knew she liked her tea hot and strong. They tucked her in with a softness that told me she belonged to them as much as to us. The building was tired, and the care was imperfect, but the message was clear: "You're safe. You matter."

I didn't have words for it then. I do now. That feeling was empathy in action, expressed through people, routines, and the bones of an old hotel repurposed for elder care. It would take decades to understand how much that first visit was shaping my life.

Architects aren't usually trained to begin with feelings. We're taught to start with site, program, budget, and code. But that early experience with Nana was the start of a different blueprint for me—one where dignity, small comforts, and unspoken emotional needs mattered more than square footage.

Years later, I wouldn't just design seniors' communities; I would develop and invest in them. I've been a shareholder and an architect in multiple retirement homes and in a 230-acre seniors' continuum-of-care community. I've sat on both sides of the table—studying monthly statements and labour reports while remembering that first smell of boiled cabbage and floor polish at Nana's bedside.

That combination, lived experience plus ownership responsibility, has given me one simple rule that now guides every decision in our firm: lead with empathy.

Not as a slogan, but as a discipline that shows up on the floor plate and, eventually, on the bottom line. Empathy as an architectural method.

Empathy can sound soft. In practice, it's how my team gathers information that drawings alone never reveal.

We walk sites at 7 a.m. to see who's already working and how they actually move. We follow a personal support worker's cart through a full medication pass. We sit with a daughter in the parking lot after she's just helped her father move into memory care.

The test is simple. Does this building still work on a bad Tuesday at 3:15 p.m. when the weather is awful and two team members have called in sick?

When you've also been responsible for operating results, you notice how those human realities show up in staffing costs, overtime, incident reports, and turnover. Empathy stops being a soft virtue and becomes a hard-edged diagnostic tool. It tells you where the building is helping and where it's silently making everyone's day harder.

Two early lessons outside of architecture taught me what that really means.

DON'T JUDGE THE BOOK—READ THE BOOKMARK

My father and grandfather were both in the automobile business. As a teenager on the lot, I was comfortable around the cars, less so around the customers. Dad was fluent in both.

One afternoon, two customers arrived almost at the same time. One wore a sharp suit. The other stepped out of a city bus in oil-stained work boots. I assumed I knew who would buy the nicer car.

Dad greeted them identically and asked the same three questions: Where are you driving most days? Who's usually with you? What do you need this car to do for you on a bad morning?

Then he sent them on the same test-drive loop, each in a car that fit the answers, not the wardrobe.

The well-dressed customer loved the new convertible but wanted to "think about it." The man in work boots came back from driving a sensible, used sedan, walked around it once, and said, "This will do—I'll pay cash." It could obviously haul tools, kids, and groceries. It would start on cold mornings. It fit his real life.

Later, Dad rested his hand on that sedan's roofline and said, "Don't judge the book—read the bookmark. Sell people what their life points to." He didn't mean income. He meant point of view. My job, he taught me, was to stand where the other person stands until their best choice becomes obvious.

In our office, that means we don't design what looks clever in a rendering. We design what fits the lived realities of residents, families, staff, regulators, and operators. We read their bookmark first.

WHAT'S YOUR 6 O'CLOCK BOAT?

My second lesson arrived years later, with a rather prickly client who seemed impossible to please. Every meeting ended with, "I'll get back to you," followed by weeks of silence.

At one design session, I tried something different. Instead of jumping straight into floor plans and pro formas, I asked, “What does a good day look like for you?” He barely responded. So, I narrowed it. “It’s Tuesday. It’s 6 p.m. Where are you?”

He sighed and said wistfully, “If it’s a very good Tuesday, I’m on our sailboat with my son, trying to teach him how to make it safely back to the harbor before it gets dark.”

There it was, his 6 o’clock boat—a quiet, very human picture of success.

We wrapped that meeting up in twenty minutes flat. We made a short list of decisions he really needed to make. I left him space to go find his boat, literally and figuratively.

That conversation didn’t give me another design constraint. It gave me something much more useful: a way to respect what really matters to a decision-maker. Ever since, I quietly ask myself, *What’s their 6 o’clock boat?*

When you design with that in mind, you write emails differently. You sequence decisions in a way that protects people’s time, energy, and dignity. You build trust faster. And in seniors housing, where hard choices and complex approvals are the rule, that trust keeps projects moving.

BLUEPRINTS, BODIES, AND THE BOTTOM LINE

Empathy without execution is just sentiment. The real work is translating what we learn into physical moves that change daily life and, ultimately, operating results.

I’ve spent enough time watching a PSW rush between residents to see how the wrong layout steals time, energy, and patience. A dining room that looks beautiful in a brochure but forces long detours with a hot cart will cost you staff goodwill and, over time, staff retention. A “cozy” lounge used as a pass-through becomes just a noisy corridor where no one can truly rest.

These can all be fixed by what I call micro moves—small design decisions that add or remove friction: a wall shifted by two feet that turns an awkward corner into a clear sightline, or a hand-wash sink placed where staff naturally pause, rather than around the corner.

Individually, these may seem minor. Together, they determine whether staff feel constantly behind or slightly ahead, whether residents withdraw or engage, whether families walk in thinking "This feels right" or "Something feels off."

As an architect-owner, I've seen those micro moves show up in the numbers: fewer falls, less overtime, more stable teams, better occupancy, stronger net operating income. The building is never the whole story, but it is always in the story.

DESIGN THAT PROTECTS DIGNITY

Whenever a family arrives for a tour, there's always a hidden conversation happening under the polite one. On the surface, they're asking about square footage, amenities, and price. Beneath that, they're wondering: Are we failing Mum by not keeping her at home? Will Dad be parked in a corner and forgotten? If I move in here, who am I now?

If we ignore that layer, we design clever facilities that people emotionally resist.

So, we start by saying the hard things out loud—with our clients and in our own design meetings. We acknowledge loss, fear, and guilt as part of the brief. Then, build in micro moves that protect dignity, making it easier to say yes when the time comes.

Arrival sequences that breathe. Instead of stepping straight from parking lot into chaos, we design a small, calm threshold where families can pause, regroup, and not feel like they're blocking traffic while Dad finds his balance.

Trial-friendly suites. Flexible layouts and simple storage allow a resident to "try on" the community with familiar furniture and objects, without a huge upfront commitment or disruptive renovation.

Clear, humane wayfinding. Rather than signs that feel institutional, we use light, colour, and recognizable landmarks to help residents orient without feeling "managed."

These details don't just make move-in day kinder. They protect dignity every day, quietly.

DESIGNING FOR FAMILIES AND STAFF

Seniors don't arrive alone. Love shows up in minivans, on lunch breaks, and through video calls between shifts. If we design only for residents and ignore their circle of support, we've missed the system we're actually serving.

For families, we create places where they can:

- Wait privately for difficult conversations, not perched on a hard chair in a public hallway.
- Share a coffee or a quiet meal with their loved one that doesn't feel like a hospital cafeteria.
- Step outside briefly without feeling they've abandoned the person they came to see.

For staff, dignity is equally non-negotiable. A tired PSW who has nowhere to sit for five minutes, no daylight in the break room, and a constant obstacle course between rooms will eventually leave, no matter how strong your mission statement is.

We design buildings that:

- Make the good choice the easy choice. Hand-wash sinks where they're instinctive, storage where it's needed, circulation paths that shave steps instead of adding them.
- Offer real respite. Staff rooms with daylight, acoustical separation, and enough space to exhale—not a repurposed closet with a microwave.
- Treat staff as professionals, not an afterthought—dedicated work areas for charting, team huddles, and confidential conversations.

When staff feel seen in the layout, they're able to extend that same respect to residents and families. Resident dignity and staff dignity rise together.

PROGRAM-READY SPACES (IDENTITY AS THERAPY)

One of the most powerful tools we have is designing spaces that are ready for identity the moment the doors open.

Outside of architecture, I spent ten years rebuilding a 1940s Tiger Moth biplane from what was literally a wreck. Piece by piece, it came slowly back to life. When it finally flew again, I used it to donate charity flights to veterans and seniors' organizations as a fun(d) raiser.

What surprised me wasn't the nostalgia. It was the way people remembered themselves once in that cockpit. A withdrawn veteran would suddenly start talking about missions, instructors, and comrades-in-arms. The plane wasn't just transportation, but a trigger for identity.

In seniors' communities, we can create similar "analog time machines on the ground" spaces that invite residents to step back into roles they recognize. That can look like: A small workshop that smells of wood and oil, where someone who once worked with their hands can tinker safely. Or, a modest performance corner with a real piano and decent acoustics, where a former music teacher can lead a sing-along.

These don't have to be big capital spends. They do have to be intentional, designed from day one to hold programs, not just furniture.

When we combine empathy for who someone has been with careful programming and design, we see higher engagement, fewer behavioural incidents, and more reasons for families to visit. Identity is a therapeutic asset. The building can either support it or erase it.

LOOSE FIT, LONG LIFE

Regulations, care models, and market expectations are always changing. If you build a seniors' community as a one-trick pony, you inherit a very expensive problem ten years later. Our approach is "loose fit, long life." We design for:

- Suites that can flex between independent, assisted, and memory care with minimal disruption

- Amenity spaces that can shift from a quiet lounge to a small group activity without a construction project
- Service areas sized and located to absorb new equipment or workflows as care evolves

From an owner's perspective, that flexibility shows up as avoided renovation costs and less operational downtime. From a resident's perspective, it means they can often stay in the community they know as their needs change.

Empathy, in this sense, is also about the future: respecting the people who will live and work in the building long after the ribbon-cutting and designing so they aren't trapped by decisions we made today.

OPERATIONS: WHERE EMPATHY GETS MUSCLE

Architects produce visible artifacts. Operators live with what those artifacts make possible, or impossible, every day. A beautifully detailed lounge that is impossible to staff safely at night becomes an empty set. A courtyard that looks wonderful but is hard to supervise quietly becomes a risk. A kitchen designed without input from the food service team becomes a daily compromise.

That's why, in our practice, empathy doesn't stop at move-in. We stay in conversation with operators, walk the building after it's been lived in, and pay attention to what's actually happening. We model flows, we listen to maintenance teams, we track how reality diverges from assumptions, and feed that learning back into our next project.

It's not glamorous, but it's where empathy grows muscle and memory. Over time, that loop is what creates buildings that are kinder and more profitable.

WHY LEAD WITH EMPATHY

At its core, seniors housing sits at the intersection of four groups with different fears and hopes:

- Residents who want safety, purpose, and dignity
- Families who want reassurance that they've done the right thing

- Staff who want to do good work without burning out
- Owners and operators who need sustainable, compliant, profitable buildings

If you design with only one of those in mind, the system will push back. Empathy is the discipline of seeing all four at once—and then giving that understanding a physical form.

When we lead with empathy, we walk a PSW's twelve-hour shift in our heads before we lock in a layout. We imagine a daughter sitting in her car after a hard conversation and asking what she'll need from the building next. We remember a ten-year-old boy visiting his Nana in a converted hotel and asking, "What will this place feel like to him?"

Done well, this doesn't just feel good. It creates better alignment—happier residents, more confident families, more stable staffing, and stronger operating results. Those outcomes are not opposites. They are, in a well-designed building, consequences of the same decisions.

Every day, my team and I translate lived experience, operational reality, and financial responsibility into floor plans, sections, and details that you can build, staff, and bank on.

Empathy is where we start. Architecture is how we make it real.

About Robert

Robert Murphy is a Canadian architect, developer, investor, and former owner of several seniors' residences who has built his career at the intersection of design, business, and dignity for older adults. As a former shareholder in two retirement homes and the founding developer of the 230-acre Villages of Sally Creek seniors' community in Woodstock, Ontario, Bob understands how design decisions affect staffing, resident experience, and the bottom line.

Over four decades in practice, Bob has led the planning and design of seniors' housing and care projects ranging from modest additions to full campuses of care. As founder of Murphy Partners Seniors Housing Architects, he leads a team that begins every commission with a simple operating principle: Lead with Empathy. They start by standing in the shoes of the people who will live, visit, and work in the building—residents, families, front-line staff, leadership teams, and investors—and then translate those insights into clear, buildable designs that support both human outcomes and financial performance.

Bob's dual vantage point as architect and owner gives him a rare ability to "read the bookmark, not just the book": to see how small moves in layout, circulation, and amenity planning can improve safety, staffing efficiency, culture, and length of stay. He is known for championing hospitality-forward, clinically capable environments; program-ready spaces that rekindle identity and community; and flexible, "loose fit, long life" buildings that can adapt to changing regulations, acuity, and market expectations without constant hard renovation.

A natural storyteller, Bob often draws on early memories of visiting his great-grandmother in a converted hotel, time spent in his family's automotive business, and the decade-long restoration of his 1940 de Havilland Tiger Moth biplane—an open-cockpit aircraft he now flies to raise funds and spirits for veterans' and dementia charities. These lived experiences sharpen his sense of what dignity feels like in practice, especially on a bad Tuesday at 3:15 p.m. when the weather is poor and the team is short-staffed.

You can learn more about Bob, his firm, Murphy Partners Seniors Housing Architects, and his beloved Tiger Moth at:

www.murphypartners.ca

CHAPTER 21

THE CURRENCY OF EMPATHY

BY PRIYANK THAKKAR

I didn't call it rock bottom at the time. I didn't have the language for it yet. I just knew that my body felt hollow and my thoughts had narrowed to the essentials: *Pay rent. Find food. Don't panic.*

I had come to Australia in 2007 to pursue my master's degree in accounting and commerce, believing, as many migrant students do, that discipline and effort would be enough. I had taken a short leave from my job to prepare for exams. They had promised my position would be waiting when I returned. It wasn't. One week without work turned into three. Three turned into five. The job market was tight, especially for migrant students. Cash jobs paid little and offered no security. By the time my exams ended, my savings were gone.

Rent was due in three days.

I hadn't eaten in forty-eight hours. The last five dollars had gone toward bread and juice earlier in the week. On Monday and Tuesday, I drank water. On Wednesday, I drank more water and ignored the way my hands wouldn't stop shaking. On Thursday morning, I stood up too quickly and felt the room tilt. Still, I put on my best shirt, printed my résumé, and walked from shop to shop. Around three in the afternoon, I was offered a job. Relief hit first. Then reality followed close behind. I wouldn't be paid for weeks. Rent was still due. Food was still a problem. Survival doesn't negotiate with optimism.

At six that evening, my phone rang. It was a friend from college who was studying in Sydney. He asked me for a favor. "I've saved about $850," he said. "My roommates know I have it. They keep asking to borrow it, and I don't want to give it to them as they are planning to waste it on booze and gambling. Would you mind if I transfer it to you for a few months? Just hold it for me. I'll ask for it back when I need it." I said yes without hesitation. The transfer came through within minutes, and I immediately bought food. He had no idea that a favor he was asking of me was the lifeline I needed in that exact moment. I gave him the money back several months later and didn't tell him that story for fifteen years.

That night, sitting with a simple meal, I felt something I didn't yet have words for. It wasn't just relief. It wasn't gratitude. It was the unmistakable sense of being held by something larger than logic. Grace, if you want to call it that.

That experience did something permanent to me. When you have known powerlessness, you stop wasting power later. When you have known hunger, you recognize it immediately in others, even when it shows up dressed as stress, frustration, or pride. Empathy, I learned that year, is *born* long before it is chosen. And it shows up not as feeling, but as pattern recognition—the ability to see what someone needs before they can articulate it.

* * *

I grew up watching my father leave for work at 7 a.m. and return from his side business at 10 p.m. I remember him once falling asleep mid-sentence at the dinner table, not from exhaustion alone, but from the weight of carrying a family forward without ever calling it sacrifice. Responsibility wasn't discussed in our home; it was demonstrated. So, when people ask me why I lead the way I do, why people call me at two in the morning, why friends trust me with their crises, why clients tell me they feel calmer after speaking to me, I don't think of personality traits. I think of obligation.

Because when you know what it is to have nothing, having *enough* comes with a responsibility to notice where more is needed. That understanding followed me into my career in finance, property development, and consulting. It shaped the way I dealt with people long before I ever realized it was a philosophy.

One afternoon, a young couple sat across from me in my office. They were buying their first home, an $800,000 property. They were hardworking, hopeful, and exhausted. We had already fought through a rejected loan approval and managed to secure financing by presenting their documents and evidence. Settlement was four days away, and they were still short $7,500. They had already paid a $40,000 deposit. If they couldn't come up with the remaining amount, they would lose the house *and* the deposit. They were devastated. They'd called family and friends, but every option was exhausted. I walked them through alternatives, but each one closed as quickly as it opened. There is a moment in situations like this when people stop hearing solutions and start feeling shame. I recognized it instantly.

Something in me shifted.

I didn't run the numbers again. I didn't draft a contract or consult a risk matrix. I heard myself say, almost before I could think it through, "Don't stress. I'll lend you the money. You'll settle. Pay me back when you can." I transferred the funds, and they got their house. They thanked me repeatedly, but that wasn't the point. I wasn't trying to be generous. I was trying to be *accurate*. Accurate about what was actually at stake. Accurate about the cost of doing nothing.

Empathy isn't reckless. It's calibrated. Chris Voss calls this tactical empathy—the deliberate influence of your counterpart's emotions through understanding. It isn't about being nice. It's about being accurate. Logic tells you what could go wrong. Empathy asks what will be lost if you choose not to act.

Years later, they invited me to their wedding. Nearly a decade after that, the husband called me out of the blue. He was starting a business and needed funding. Trust compounds. This is the difference between kindness and leadership: one feels good in the moment, the other holds weight over time.

EMPATHY OFFERS DIGNITY

People often misunderstand empathy. They confuse it with softness, emotional indulgence, or the urge to make everyone feel better. But empathy without clarity is not kindness, it's avoidance. It's the refusal to tell the truth because the discomfort feels too expensive.

Real empathy is not passive. It is not vague. And it is not weak. It requires presence, restraint, and a willingness to disappoint people in the service of something deeper than approval.

I saw this clearly during a call I received from India at two in the morning.

My cousin had been in a relationship for three years, one that had ended and restarted more times than either of them wanted to admit. She was exhausted. This time, she had decided she was done. Her plan was simple: block him everywhere, disappear from the relationship, and avoid one more difficult conversation. No explanation. No closure. Just silence. I didn't argue with her. I didn't rush in with advice or moral judgments. I listened. That, too, is part of empathy, creating enough safety for the truth to surface. Then I asked a question. "Did he ever threaten you? Harm you in any way?" No. "Do you believe that if you needed help in the future, he would help you?" Yes. "Then," I said, "he is worthy of a conversation." She resisted at first, but eventually agreed.

The next night, my phone rang again. This time, both of them were on the line. He had flown to meet her. They were sitting across from each other in a café, both emotional, both wanting clarity, both afraid of what the truth might require. He wanted me to convince her not to leave. I didn't take sides. Empathy doesn't mean choosing a camp. It means choosing *accuracy.* Instead, I reflected on what I knew. In negotiation terms, I was labelling—naming the emotions beneath her words so he could finally hear them. I told him how she spoke about him when he wasn't there. She had told me that she respected him, admired his discipline, appreciated the way he took responsibility for his life. I made sure he understood something essential: she did not see him as a bad man. Then I asked what Chris Voss would call a calibrated question—one designed not to corner, but to illuminate. "This is the third time this has happened," I said. "Each time, you reconcile. Each time, you end up right back here. Are you willing to live this pattern indefinitely?" He was quiet. "Even if I convinced her today," I continued, "what happens tomorrow? What happens the next time she feels this way? Is this the future you want for yourself?" I didn't attack his character. I didn't minimize his love or his pain. I honored him enough to tell him the truth without cushioning it in false hope. That is what people miss about empathy.

Empathy is not rescuing people from consequences. It's not forcing harmony where alignment no longer exists. And it's not keeping people comfortable at the cost of their clarity. Empathy is telling the truth in a way that preserves dignity. He thanked me afterward. Later, he told me that the conversation helped him see what he had been unable to see while he was inside the emotion—how love had kept him looping in a situation that no longer served either of them. That is empathy with precision. It is a soft skill, yes—but it is not soft.

It is disciplined. It's exacting. And it requires more courage than silence ever will.

THE QUIET MECHANICS OF INFLUENCE

Over time, you begin to notice a pattern in who people call when things fall apart. It isn't always the smartest person in the room or the one with the most authority. It's the person who can hold the emotional weight of the moment without collapsing into it. That's been my role more often than I realized at first, personally and professionally. Family disputes. Business failures. Relationship crossroads. Financial emergencies. Not because I have better answers, but because I prioritize relationships.

Years ago, a business partner called me in distress. He was involved in a property development overseas, and something had gone wrong. He needed $100,000 quickly or the deal—and his reputation—would collapse. The lesson here is not about the money.

I didn't have idle capital sitting around. What I did have was something more valuable: relational trust. I had spent years building credibility with people who knew my judgment and my integrity. I borrowed the funds from those relationships and arranged the solution within forty-eight hours. No contracts. No theatrics. Just character. The project survived. He paid it back. What that moment reinforced for me is this: empathy is infrastructure.

Empathy is social capital. It allows movement when systems freeze. It allows solutions to emerge when fear narrows perspective. And it creates leverage that logic alone never will. But here is the part most people miss: you don't build that capital when you need it. You build it quietly, over time, by showing up consistently, telling the truth, holding boundaries, and responding to people as humans before treating them as problems to solve.

THE IMPORTANCE OF PATTERN RECOGNITION

Sometimes empathy looks like lending money. Sometimes it looks like lending belief.

When I was studying for my master's degree, a close friend, now a successful entrepreneur, was unraveling. He was in Australia. The woman he loved was in India. Her parents had begun introducing her to other potential husbands. They had been childhood sweethearts. He wanted to marry her, but tradition and distance were closing the window fast. He needed to go to India immediately. We went to a travel agent together. The ticket cost $1,300.

He didn't have it.

I checked my bank account and gave him everything I had. I didn't create a plan. I didn't know how I would manage afterward. I only knew that delay would change the outcome of his life. He went. They got married and built a beautiful life together.

This story is easy to misunderstand. It can sound like recklessness or blind generosity. It wasn't either. Empathy is not the suspension of judgment. It is the *refinement* of it.

What I was responding to in that moment was not emotion; it was pattern recognition. I didn't see a man chasing a fantasy. I saw someone who had been consistent, disciplined, and relentless in his commitment. I saw effort without entitlement. Persistence without manipulation. Love paired with responsibility. That matters.

Empathy sometimes looks like faith, but more often it is informed discernment. It is the ability to read people accurately under pressure and distinguish between someone who wants rescuing and someone who is simply blocked by circumstance. There is a difference between enabling and endorsing, and between saving someone from consequences and removing an obstacle so they can act on who they already are.

Empathy, when practiced well, doesn't lower standards. It applies them.

It asks better questions: Is this moment pivotal or merely uncomfortable? Will action here reinforce growth, or postpone it? In this case, the answer was clear. Action mattered. Timing mattered. And for my friend, belief changed his life's trajectory.

THE RESPONSIBILITY TO HOLD THE WHOLE

In my family and my career, empathy often means becoming a bridge. When a relative wanted to marry outside our community, emotions ran high. I didn't take sides. I listened to her hopes, to her father's concerns, to the unspoken fears beneath both. When truth needed to be spoken, I spoke it calmly. Sometimes to her. Sometimes to him. Always with respect.

Later, she told me what mattered most wasn't agreement, it was dignity. She felt heard without being indulged. Challenged without being shamed. That is what empathy looks like when it's practiced with responsibility. Empathy is not neutrality. It's not standing in the middle and avoiding tension. It's taking responsibility for the *entire system*. It asks you to hold complexity without collapsing into sides.

I have failed businesses. I have lost money. I have built things that didn't work. Failure has never frightened me. Indifference has. The moment people stop caring about each other, about consequences, about truth, that is when damage becomes permanent.

Ask yourself: When someone comes to you in crisis, do you rush to fix, or slow down long enough to understand? Do you tell people what they want to hear, or what they need to hear in a way they can receive? Are you protecting peace, or championing truth?

Empathy will never make you less effective. When practiced with discipline, it makes you the person people trust when the stakes are high and logic alone isn't enough. If there is one thing to remember, it is this: Empathy is not a feeling. It's a responsibility. And the question is not whether you have it, it's whether you're willing to carry it when it costs you something. That will define the kind of leader, partner, and human being you become.

About Priyank

In 2007, Priyank Thakkar arrived in Australia as a migrant student with a dream, a work ethic, and very little else. Within months, he found himself unable to pay rent, unsure where his next meal would come from. He worked on construction sites, sold phones and internet connections door-to-door, and took a job as an assistant chef in a fifty-year-old Italian restaurant in Melbourne—doing whatever it took to survive. That season of hardship taught him something no textbook ever could: empathy is born from experience, and trust is the most valuable currency in business and in life.

Today, Priyank is the Chief Vision Officer, Finance Broker, and Director of Prevail Finance, a boutique finance broking firm he founded in Melbourne in 2017. With over twelve years of experience spanning both sides of the lending industry—first as a Bank Lending Manager and Commercial Credit Analyst, and now as a broker and property development consultant—Priyank brings a rare dual perspective to complex financial challenges. He holds a Master of Commerce in Professional Accounting and is a member of the Finance Brokers Association of Australia (FBAA).

Priyank is not just an advisor—he is an active practitioner. He has personally completed more than ten property developments, including townhouse projects, subdivisions, and co-living accommodations. He also acquired a loss-making business and, with the help of friends and a dedicated team, turned it into a profitable operation within eighteen months before selling it for two and a half times the purchase price.

Priyank's approach to relationships and empathy has been deeply shaped by the teachings of Swadhyay Parivar, founded by Pandurang Shastri Athavale (affectionately known as Dadaji). His business acumen comes from a different lineage: his grandfather, his father, and a relentless commitment to learning from books, coaches, and the experiences of others. Together, these influences have made him someone who leads with both heart and strategy. He makes friends effortlessly—whether with children or senior citizens—because he listens first, judges never, and meets people exactly where they are.

As the host of the *SeekersPlus* podcast, Priyank interviews industry experts in property, finance, and business to share insights that help others build wealth and navigate complex decisions with confidence.

Outside of work, Priyank enjoys playing volleyball and kabaddi, exploring new cuisines—a passion that began in that Melbourne kitchen—and spending time with his wife of over fifteen years.

Learn more at:
linkedin.com/in/priyankgthakkar
youtube.com/@SeekersPlus

CHAPTER 22

THE VALUE ARCHITECT: EMPATHY AS A COMPETITIVE ADVANTAGE

BY CHRISTIAN J. SCHÄFER

The CFO's face had gone pale, and his hands trembled slightly as he set down his coffee cup in the gleaming conference room of the UK healthcare organization. We were forty minutes into what should have been a routine enterprise software sales pitch when he said the words that changed everything. "I'm worried that our current ERP system issues might put me at risk of going to jail."

The room went silent. My team and I exchanged glances. This wasn't about lowering costs anymore. This was about a man fearing for his freedom because his organization's current financial systems might not properly account for taxpayer funds.

Suddenly, I understood: every sale is actually a purchase, and people rarely buy what you think you're selling. They buy solutions to fears you haven't even discovered yet.

I'm Christian J. Schäfer, and over my twenty-year career in sales and consulting, I've learned that empathy isn't just a nice-to-have soft skill but a core competence to create business value successfully.

Dave, a former boss from whom I learned a lot, once surprised me by saying that empathy was my greatest strength as a leader. He said, "You care too much" about our clients, our firm's results, and your team's progress. What surprised me wasn't the compliment, but that he saw this as unusual. To me, aiming to understand and fulfil what others truly need had always felt as essential as breathing.

ELEMENTARY EMPATHY EDUCATION

My journey to become a *value architect* started in an unexpected place: the playground of my German elementary school when I was seven years old. I loved Fanta Mango. So did my classmates. But I noticed something interesting. Many of them were too lazy to walk the fifty meters to our school kiosk, where Fanta cost twenty-five cents. Instead, they'd offer me fifty cents for the ones my mother packed for my lunch.

This wasn't about exploiting laziness. It was my first lesson in understanding unspoken needs. My classmates valued convenience more than money. I valued entrepreneurship more than Fanta. By recognizing this difference, I created my first win-win situation. They got their drinks without walking. I got to learn about business. The school got additional kiosk sales. Everyone benefited because I'd taken the time to understand and sell what others really wanted.

This pattern followed me into mandatory military service in the German armed forces. While my fellow cadets dreaded weekend and holiday guard duty, I noticed the pay was double and tax-free. More importantly, I recognized their deep desire for free time outweighed any financial incentive. So, I proposed trades and volunteered for a four-day shift over Easter weekend. They got uninterrupted holiday time with their families. I got excellent pay for reading books during the most uneventful shift imaginable. Again, empathy created value where others saw only obligation.

EMPATHIC PROBLEM-SOLVER

After university, I joined Accenture Strategy Consulting. Consulting taught me to lead myself, my teams, and client engagements. My ambition became to help others make progress in their lives.

Consulting helped me become a structured, open-minded problem-solver who connects the dots and involves people in decision-making and action.

The work required analytical thinking, selling the desire for change, removing obstacles that lead to indecision, and moving others to act.

With increased seniority, my role became more sales-oriented, which meant spending even more time selling ideas, outcomes, and people. I succeeded not by pushing solutions at people but by helping people articulate their problems and choose solutions that fit their needs.

EMPATHY IMPROVES DECISION-MAKING

As a consultant, I learned to recognize when others' needs conflicted with my core values.

Once, a prospective client executive expressed interest in staffing me. The conversation started well until he complained, "Your daily rate is too high. You can just invoice me 50 percent more days than you need for the work at a lower rate, and I'll make sure that it will go through procurement fine."

I responded, "I cannot do that. It's unethical."

The meeting turned icy. We exchanged a few more pleasantries before we concluded that we would not work together.

A week later, I introduced myself to Christophe, a client executive who needed support over the following nine weeks.

I was transparent about an upcoming, already-booked three-week family vacation that I couldn't reschedule. I also shared how I'd ensure his success with the help of a vacation cover.

He responded, "We can make this work."

I asked, "Tell me what motivates you, why do you want to do this?"

He responded, "This isn't about me being successful. This is about doing the right thing for the firm. It's a matter of integrity."

I trusted him immediately, and we worked together successfully.

Christophe became a vocal advocate, recommending Accenture to other decision-makers when we were pitching for other engagements.

Empathy helped me to recognize and refuse an unethical opportunity and choose a better one with a client who also valued integrity.

PROTECTIVE LEADERSHIP

One day, Justyna, a talented consultant on my team, was personally attacked by a client. The client had been sick for three weeks, and Justyna had performed brilliantly in her absence. Too brilliantly. The client felt threatened and replaceable, so she lashed out viciously at Justyna.

Justyna was in tears. We went to the client's roof terrace to talk. I used a framework we taught at Accenture, visualizing a flower with petals representing our various roles, and the center representing who we truly are.

"She's not attacking you," I explained. "She's attacking this petal, your role, because she feels threatened. She's new and still isolated here; she came in from an outside firm, and hasn't really arrived yet."

But empathy meant more than just comforting Justyna. I'd already anticipated this risk and had been communicating it upward to our managing partner. Before the client could complain about Justyna, I'd briefed him: "This happened. Justyna did wonderful work. The client felt threatened and lashed out. I find it highly unprofessional."

When the complaint inevitably came, my boss was prepared. We protected Justyna while understanding that the client's aggression came from fear, not malice. Sometimes, empathetic leadership means seeing the humanity in difficult people while still protecting your team from their worst impulses.

When Justyna allowed me to share her story, she told me, "I still remember that 'flower day' and use the framework regularly in my personal life. Our discussion had a very positive effect on my resilience. I found that even more helpful than the resolution of the client escalation itself."

WINNING WITH EMPATHY

During my last five years at Accenture, I led our firm's regional Client Value Services team for Austria, Switzerland, Germany, and Russia.

We analyzed data to systematically identify our clients' needs and proactively develop, quantify, and pitch value-creation opportunities. Our insights increased our firm's relevance with the C-suite, resulting in bigger deals and more meaningful relationships.

We called our approach shareholder value analysis. We created data-driven empathy. We learned that a business case is also a social instrument. It helps people overcome the massive inertia of the status quo. With it, you're not just quantifying ROI; you're giving people the permission to be brave, to change, and take a risk.

At the time, I also worked on a global program to improve how our people collaborated with and sold to clients. The process started by jointly identifying and prioritizing the right business problem to solve, followed by co-creating and prioritizing solutions that are desirable, technically feasible, and commercially viable.

This systematic and collaborative approach created empathy for our clients' needs, strengthened client relationships, and helped sellers answer the classic sales questions: "Why change? Why now? Why us?"

Humans make business decisions in the context of their own fears, dreams, and pressures. Thus, being effective requires understanding our clients' personal stakes, not just their professional ones. This insight led us to add a fourth question: "Why does this matter to you personally?"

EMPATHIC SALES LEADER

In 2021, Microsoft hired me to lead its EMEA Business Applications Business Value Management team. Six weeks into the role, my boss was fired. I found myself sitting across from my former boss's boss, who looked at me with the expression of someone trying to solve an unexpected puzzle.

The conversation started like this: "Christian, what do we do with you?"

I'd gotten a haircut that morning, wanting to look extra sharp for what I knew would be a career-defining moment. "I'd love to move into software sales. In which industry do you need someone to create clarity, generate energy, and deliver results?"

"Public Sector and Healthcare."

"Sounds interesting. Let's do it."

That split-second decision to embrace uncertainty rather than defend my original role taught me something crucial about empathetic leadership: sometimes understanding others means recognizing when they need you to be flexible more than they need you to be right.

In my new role as a Sales Leader, I oversaw a team of senior Sales Directors and Business Value Managers in Europe, the Middle East, Africa, Asia, and Australia. We used empathy to strategically identify and articulate how clients could achieve better business outcomes by using Microsoft's products and services. Our main objectives were to close multimillion-dollar enterprise SaaS deals and to ensure that our clients' feedback was heard internally to improve our value propositions for them.

A CHRISTMAS MIRACLE

Days before Christmas, we faced a crisis. A client's procurement team informed us they no longer wanted to proceed with our proposed five-year deal to increase their software license volume by 400 percent. Through careful questioning and genuine curiosity about their concerns, we uncovered the real issue. The budget issue was only a problem in year one. The procurement lead worried about overcommitting to licenses without confirmed demand. He feared it would reflect badly on him if he committed to a too high license volume level.

We reached out to the client's manufacturing department head, our key champion, who said: "I alone might need up to 280 percent of the current license volume soon. I'd be willing to run workshops with you in January to solidify demand."

But procurement still wasn't convinced. So, we created something unprecedented: a six-year deal with a "try before you buy" structure. Year one, they'd get 500 percent license access at their current 100 percent fee level, an unheard-of value proposition. During years two to six, pricing would increase to our originally proposed 500 percent fee level, with an opt-out clause if they decided during year one that they didn't need the entire volume.

The client signed on the last working day before Christmas, right before lunch. The January workshops succeeded. They kept the increased license levels for the full term. We'd won by understanding that their resistance wasn't about price, but about fear of making an irreversible mistake.

RETAINING TOP PERFORMERS

One day, Robert, one of my best Sales Directors with over ten years of experience at Microsoft, approached me at the start of our most critical sales quarter. He'd received an offer from a startup that would increase his salary by more than 50 percent. This created a crisis as he was working on some of our biggest must-win deals. Losing him would put our annual sales targets at risk.

Because of the trust we had built, Robert shared his situation with me before handing in his formal resignation. We discussed how much he still loved waking up and working for a company as innovative and global as Microsoft, but that he was under financial pressure because COVID-related supply chain issues had made building his family's dream house far more expensive than originally budgeted.

Within forty-eight hours, I built and received approval for a retention package: a 10 percent immediate salary increase, a one-time payment, and retention stock. The total was still 20 percent below his external offer, but Robert stayed. Why? Because he valued how hard my boss and I fought to keep him. We'd demonstrated that we understood not just his financial needs but also made him feel valued.

Robert closed every critical opportunity that year. The retention investment was tiny compared to the business value he delivered.

PROPHETIC MICRO-EXPRESSIONS

Not all empathic insights are comfortable. However, even uncomfortable insights can be useful.

When a former boss's face showed a microexpression of disgust as we passed each other in the office, I instinctively knew that we had an unspoken issue that we needed to resolve.

A mentor had warned me that with narcissistic, toxic bosses, "You have two options: frame everything you do around how it makes them successful or try to run and save yourself."

I doubled down to deliver excellent work and help my boss and our firm succeed. Whilst my work created impact and received excellent feedback from our firm's board, it wasn't enough to save my job. My boss had a budget problem, and eliminating my role was a straightforward way to fix the budget problem successfully.

Understanding others sometimes means recognizing unspoken signals and preparing accordingly. Empathy isn't only about connection; sometimes it's about reading the room accurately enough to protect yourself.

CONCLUSION: VALUE ARCHITECT MINDSET

During more than twenty years in consulting and sales, I learned that empathetic leadership isn't optional but essential.

My elementary school arbitrage taught me to see value where others see inconvenience. My military service showed me that one person's burden is another's opportunity. My decades in consulting and sales have proven that helping others achieve their goals is the surest path to achieving your own.

This approach has taught me that people rarely resist change itself. They resist loss of control, fear of failure, or threats to identity. When you understand these deeper currents, you stop selling and start solving. You stop pushing and start partnering. You stop talking and start listening to what's not said.

The CFO who worried about jail? We didn't sell him software. We sold him freedom from fear. The procurement manager worried about overcommitting. We didn't sell him licenses. We sold him flexibility and reputation protection. When Robert considered leaving? We didn't just offer him money. We offered him recognition and respect.

Every day, I try to help others make progress in their lives. Not because it's a sales tactic or a leadership strategy, but because it's the right thing to do.

I've learned a fundamental truth: we succeed not despite our empathy for others, but because of it. In a world where artificial intelligence and automation become more common, the ability to truly understand another human being's needs, fears, and dreams becomes more valuable. It's irreplaceable.

As a seven-year-old selling Fanta, I instinctively understood a universal truth that still holds true today: the secret to creating value isn't having the best product or the lowest price. It's caring enough to understand what others truly need and then finding ways to help them get it.

That's not just good business. That's empathetic leadership. And in my experience, it's the only kind worth practicing.

About Christian

Christian J. Schäfer helps enterprise leaders solve their hardest problems. He works with clients across various industries who seek his help to navigate complex change where neither the problem nor the solution is obvious.

Every day, Christian tries to help clients make progress. His motivation is to help clients realize their ambitions. He helps clients prioritize which business problems to solve, then choose and implement improvement measures that deliver business outcomes.

His approach is straightforward: listen deeper than most people listen, identify what others need rather than what they say they need, and help teams move forward together. This sounds simple because it is. But it's also rare enough that it works.

From vision to value, Christian helped clients achieve their enterprise transformation objectives, strategically lower costs, redesign processes and operating models, and achieve more than 20 percent revenue growth. He's led multinational teams across Europe, the United States, and Asia. He's managed programs with multimillion-dollar budgets and overseen enterprise sales worth hundreds of millions in revenue.

During his more than twenty-year career, Christian held various strategy consulting, business development, and sales management leadership roles at Accenture, Microsoft, T-Systems, and Wipro.

Christian holds two Master's degrees, in Business Administration and International Management from the European Business School (EBS) in Germany and from Thunderbird in the USA. He also graduated from Harvard Business School's General Management Program in 2021. He continues to invest in his craft through advanced programs in strategy, sales, and leadership, and mentors young colleagues to achieve their potential.

He lives with his wife Amy and their three young children, Nike, Eames, and Henry, in Berlin, Germany. In his free time, Christian enjoys hiking, traveling, swimming, reading, gardening, and playing badminton.

But what matters most isn't on his CV; he genuinely cares about whether his clients succeed. He's willing to push back when a path won't work. He admits what he doesn't know. He listens to disagreement. And he measures success by whether his client solves their problem, not whether he gets credit for it.

Christian works with enterprise clients seeking a trusted advisor when it really matters, someone who will ask the hard questions, see what others miss, and help their organization move from insight to action to outcomes.

Please don't hesitate to send him a direct message on LinkedIn if you'd like to explore how you could work together to make your organization more successful.

CHAPTER 23

THE BUSINESS MODEL OF EMPATHY

BY KIM MAHAN

I was nine years old, standing in our living room in Oxon Hill, Maryland, watching my mother grab her purse and head for the door. My father had come home late again, reeking of alcohol, and the familiar pattern was unfolding: her voice rising, his defensiveness mounting, and my seven-year-old sister crying. But this time was different. This time, she was threatening to drive herself off the Woodrow Wilson Bridge.

My sister rushed to block the door, tears streaming down her face. "Mommy, no. We love you!"

I sank onto the couch, perfectly still. At nine, I'd already learned to read the room like my survival depended on it—because it did. I understood something my sister didn't yet: Mom wasn't really going to drive off that bridge. Scared and hurt, she desperately needed to know she mattered.

"No, you won't," I said quietly.

The room froze. My mother spun around, her face contorting with rage and hurt. "See? She doesn't love me!"

But she also moved away from the door.

That moment taught me something I wouldn't fully understand for decades: empathy isn't about telling people what they want to hear. It's about understanding what they actually need, and sometimes that means calling their bluff with love.

THE SURVIVAL SKILL THAT BECAME A SUPERPOWER

Many of us who people describe as *extreme empaths* didn't develop this skill by choice. We developed it for survival. When you grow up in a home where you can't trust your primary caregivers to meet your basic needs, you learn to become a human radar system. You track moods, anticipate triggers, and adjust your behavior millisecond by millisecond to avoid the storm.

In my house, falling off your bike and scraping your knee didn't get you comfort. It got you yelled at for tearing your jeans. When I was sixteen and got my front teeth knocked out in a car accident, the first thing my mother said when she walked into the hospital wasn't "Are you okay?" It was "Look at you. All that money your grandparents spent on braces, and now look at you."

This kind of upbringing creates a peculiar skill set. You become exceptional at reading people, at understanding their fears and motivations, at seeing the hurt beneath the anger. But here's the trap: you can get it wrong. You can become so attuned to managing other people's emotions that you forget to manage your own. You can see patterns that aren't there, jump to conclusions without warrant, and react to threats that exist only in your hypervigilant imagination.

It wasn't until I encountered Chris Voss's work on tactical empathy that I understood what I'd been missing: the pause, the validation, and the art of checking your assumptions before acting on them. Empathy without verification is just sophisticated guessing.

WHEN LESS BECOMES MORE

Fast-forward forty years. I'm now the primary caregiver for the same mother who once threatened to drive off that bridge. The progression was predictable yet heartbreaking: first, she moved in with me, but she started snapping at my kids. I transitioned her to independent living, where I'd find her every weekend with blood sugar at 400, candy wrappers hidden everywhere. The next phase was an assisted living center, where I'd stop by daily to ensure she took her insulin, and finally, a dementia unit.

Each move meant less space, fewer possessions, and more expensive care. And here's what stunned me: each reduction made my mother happier.

The woman who had hoarded things her entire life, who assumed everyone was trying to steal from her, who lived in constant fear of not having enough—she transformed. In assisted living, she looked around her small room and said, "This is the best place I've ever lived. My children did something wonderful for me."

But the real education came from watching the nurses in the dementia unit. When Mr. Jones hit Mrs. Smith, they didn't scold him. They redirected: "Mr. Jones, tell me about that time you were in the Army." Then, while his story distracted him, they'd diagnose: "Are you hungry? Are your clothes too tight? Are you cold?"

They knew that beneath every difficult behavior was an unmet physical need.

I started applying this everywhere. When I found myself snapping at a team member, I'd pause: Am I hungry? Am I tired? Are my clothes too tight? It sounds simple, almost silly. But recognizing that we're physical beings with physical needs that drive our emotional states, that's revolutionary in a business world that pretends we're all just brains on sticks.

THE FAILURE THAT LED TO EVERYTHING

By 2012, I'd left my corporate executive role to fix education with an app. Yes, you read that correctly. I was going to fix education with an app. The hubris is almost painful in retrospect.

I'd been in the enterprise IT world, managing global teams, and I'd drunk the startup Kool-Aid hard. Everyone was building apps. Everyone was disrupting something. I looked at my LinkedIn profile with all its impressive credentials, then looked at my actual life—high school dropout, single mom of three, survivor of more trauma than I care to list. I realized my real leadership qualities didn't come from my degrees. They came from my struggles.

So, I spent a year teaching myself Java, burning through my retirement savings, maxing out credit cards to buy groceries, and building what turned out to be a poor man's version of Evernote. Thirty thousand dollars and twelve months later, I had to face the truth: good ideas are easy, but bringing them to life is hard. And more importantly, I wasn't the right person to bring this particular idea to life.

That failure was the gift that gave rise to MAXX Potential.

BUILDING EMPATHY INTO THE BUSINESS MODEL

When I pivoted from my failed app to founding MAXX Potential, I asked myself a different question: What does the world actually need, and what am I uniquely positioned to provide?

The answer came from integrating every part of my experience—from high school dropout to corporate executive, from welfare recipient to world traveler, from single mom struggling to survive to IT leader managing global teams.

I posted an ad on Craigslist: "$10-an-hour IT Apprenticeship." Within forty-eight hours, I had over one hundred applications—everyone from GEDs to PhDs. My first hire was someone like me: a high school dropout working as a short-order cook who'd scored in the top 10 percent on his GED and emailed at 8 a.m. on a Saturday morning. Clearly driven. Clearly smart. Clearly, someone for whom traditional education wasn't the right fit.

Today, he's a six-figure software engineer at one of Richmond's top consulting firms.

But here's where empathy becomes operational: everyone told me I had to charge these apprentices. "That's how boot camps work," they said. "That's the model."

No. Boot camps make money off students whether or not those students succeed. Their incentive is to fill seats, to tell everyone they should be in tech because that's how they get paid. Our model is different because I built it on understanding what people actually need:

People need income while learning. People learn differently. People have untapped potential. Employers need results, not charity.

We pay our apprentices from day one because they're doing real work for real clients. They're not students; they're consultants-in-training adding actual value.

THE NONPROFIT TEMPTATION

The real test of this empathy-based model came when I couldn't see payroll. We were five years in, had multiple six-figure contracts, but were still learning cash flow management. While drowning in financial stress, I got a call from one of Richmond's most influential power brokers: "Come by for a whiteboard session."

I drove across the river, desperate for help, hoping for investment. Someone had already filled out the whiteboard by the time I arrived. MAXX Potential sat in the center with arrows pointing to it from everywhere, including local capital, universities, and foundations.

"Here's the thing," they said. "We love the idea of MAXXPotential.edu. Become a nonprofit. Look at all these grants."

Every practical bone in my body wanted to say yes. We needed the money desperately. But I understood something they didn't: making our apprentices *charity cases* would destroy everything we were building.

"No," I said, probably too forcefully. "We're earning money. This model works."

You could feel the tension in the room. I may have burned bridges that day. But when I went back to my leadership team—all credentialed, all struggling alongside me—and told them about the nonprofit offer, their response was unanimous: "No. We're not a nonprofit."

"Well then," I said, "we better get profitable."

And we did.

WHY EMPATHY ISN'T SYMPATHY

Here's what most people get wrong about empathy in business: they confuse it with sympathy. Feeling sorry for someone doesn't help them. The people who helped me most in life didn't coddle me. They pushed me. They saw I could do better and weren't afraid to tell me.

When someone applies to MAXX Potential claiming they love technology, we don't just take their word for it. We give them a real project with no instructions and watch what they do. Do they light up? Do they go home and research solutions? Or do they struggle and deflect?

It's actually kinder to say no quickly if someone won't be successful. We're not doing anyone any favors by giving them a $15-an-hour job in tech if they'd be happier and more successful as a nurse, in manufacturing, or in another field entirely. The sooner we say no, the sooner they can find where they actually belong.

This is operational empathy: understanding that everyone who comes to us is stuck in the "can't get a job without experience, can't get experience without a job" trap, then building a model that solves that specific problem while respecting their dignity and potential.

THE MULTIPLICATION EFFECT

Today, MAXX Potential has hundreds of alumni. Some were with us for six months, while others stayed for several years. All earned while they learned. All contributed real value. We didn't lock them into contracts or require them to repay us.

When I was an IT executive looking for talent, consulting firms would pitch me their people, and I'd ask: "Why are your people better than his people?" I wanted to know: How do you find them differently? Train them differently? Treat them differently?

I built MAXX to be the consulting firm I wished existed when I was in that executive chair—one that could answer those questions with integrity and honesty.

Our people are different because they chose the harder path. They didn't take out loans in the hope of finding a job. They earned their way in. They didn't sit in classrooms. They solved real problems. They didn't get credentials; they built portfolios.

More importantly, they're not charity cases that companies hire to feel good. They're valuable team members that companies compete to recruit.

THE FEAR BENEATH EVERYTHING

A Darden professor once banged on my desk, demanding to know what I was afraid of. Under that pressure, the truth escaped: "Being wrong."

That fear drives more bad decisions than anything else in business. People hoard knowledge because they're afraid of being replaced. They resist change because they're afraid of failing. They accept less than they deserve because they're afraid of not having enough.

My mother taught me this, first through her negative example, then through her transformation. The woman who hoarded everything, who trusted no one, who lived in constant fear—once her basic needs were met, she became generous. She offered food to visitors. She told stories of triumph instead of persecution. She found peace.

The lesson for leaders is profound: address the fear first. In every difficult conversation, every resistance to change, and every performance issue, there's usually fear underneath. Fear of not being loved. Fear of not having enough. Fear of being wrong.

Get the fear out of the room, and everything else becomes possible.

EMPATHY AT SCALE

The real test of empathetic leadership isn't whether you can understand one person's needs. It's whether you can build systems and structures that address human needs at scale.

I designed every element of MAXX Potential with empathy: paying apprentices immediately addresses financial stress. Self-paced progression respects different learning styles. No contracts or debt removes the fear of commitment. Real work from day one provides dignity and experience. Clear pathways to employment offer hope and direction.

This isn't charity. It's understanding that when you address people's basic needs and alleviate their fears, they can focus on growth and contribution.

The resistance to becoming a nonprofit wasn't about tax status. It was about protecting this ethos. As a nonprofit, our apprentices become "that good thing we supported." As a for-profit, they're valuable assets we created. That distinction matters more than any grant money.

THE INTEGRATION

Empathy without action is just emotional tourism. True empathetic leadership requires integrating understanding into every business decision, every system design, every strategic choice.

It means pausing to validate assumptions instead of reacting to perceived threats. It means addressing the physical and emotional needs beneath difficult behaviors. It means building business models that solve real problems for real people, not theoretical markets.

Most importantly, it means having the courage to say no—no to quick money that compromises values, no to opportunities that don't serve people's real needs, no to the easier path that would make you feel good but wouldn't actually help.

The nine-year-old girl who calmly told her mother "No, you won't" understood something fundamental: sometimes the most empathetic response isn't what people want to hear. It's what they need to hear, delivered with love and understanding.

That's not sympathy. That's not soft. That's the hard edge of real empathy, the kind that builds businesses, transforms lives, and creates lasting change.

Because empathy isn't about feeling sorry for people, it's about understanding them well enough to help them become who they're capable of being. And then building the systems, structures, and opportunities that make that transformation possible.

That's the business model of empathy. It's not easy. It's not quick. But it works.

About Kim

Kim Mahan learned to read people before she learned to read books. Growing up in an environment where survival often depended on anticipating the next emotional storm, she honed what she now calls "operational empathy"—the quiet art of grasping what people truly need, even when their words say something else entirely.

That skill propelled her from high school dropout to leading global IT teams at GE and Genworth Financial. But it was a gut-wrenching failure, pouring her savings into a "build an app" startup that fizzled, that forced her to ask a sharper question: What does the world actually need, and what am I uniquely positioned to provide?

The answer became MAXX Potential, an apprenticeship consulting firm that has quietly upended the "pay your dues in debt" trap of traditional training programs and credentialed pathways. From day one, apprentices earn as paid consultants-in-training, sidestepping the fears that keep so many sidelined. Hundreds have launched from MAXX Potential into roles at Google, Amazon Web Services, Capital One, and beyond because someone finally saw their potential and built a path around the barriers, so they could earn while they were learning and deliver market value.

Kim has poured the same fierce energy into co-founding grassroots efforts such as the RVA Tech Women's Conference and the Techsters program for middle school youth, and into serving on the YWCA board of directors and chairing Richmond's technology council. These weren't boardroom checkboxes for Kim; they were her way of paying forward the beliefs that got her past her own rough edges.

Empathy, for Kim, isn't a buzzword or a feel-good checkbox—it's the muscle that lets you label unspoken fears, then design systems to dissolve them. It's helped her turn personal resilience into collective momentum, proving that real leadership starts with getting out of people's way so they can become who they're meant to be.

Today, she's steering MAXX Potential into the wilds of AI and automation, not to replace humans, but to unleash them. She lives in Richmond, Virginia, where Irish dance keeps her feet light, lifelong learning keeps her curious, and time with her children and grandchildren reminds her why any of this matters.

Learn more at: MAXXPotential.com
kimmahan.com

CHAPTER 24

THE BACKING VOCALIST'S REVOLUTION

BY SUE TOMAT

Vince leaned forward, his head tilted slightly, eyes and mouth forming a gentle smile. His hands lay open on the desk between us, his posture upright yet welcoming. I had been with this Queensland government organisation for only a few days, riding high on my recent Australia Day Council Achievement Award. Two years earlier, the Deputy Premier had thanked me in Parliament for my work on the demutualisation of the state's insurance office, the first step towards corporatizing it.

I had just given Vince a draft document. It was the kind of document I'd perfected over ten years of legal practice, the style that I believed had earned me recognition and this very position. I expected praise, or at least approval.

Instead, Vince picked up my document, his expression thoughtful rather than impressed, as he flipped through the pages I had labored over, each one crafted to showcase my expertise through complexity.

"Why do you write like this?"

The question hung in the air like a challenge wrapped in kindness. For ten years, I had written like every lawyer I knew with complex sentences, what I thought was impressive vocabulary, and density that I felt announced importance. I thought it was fabulous, but I was deluded. Here was Vince Hebbard, one of the three most senior leaders, suggesting everything I knew about professional communication was wrong.

My bewilderment must have shown. "Your writing smacks of insecurity," he continued in that caring tone.

The words landed like a thunderbolt. Insecurity? I was at a career peak, fresh off government recognition. How could my carefully crafted writing suggest insecurity?

"Please help me understand how my writing makes me appear insecure," I said, curiosity overcoming bruised ego.

Vince delivered the truth that would reshape my entire approach and career: "You look like you're trying to impress somebody, and only the insecure feel the need."

I saw the spectacular irony instantly. My ego-fueled need to impress through complex writing achieved the opposite effect. Every dense paragraph, every elaborate construction broadcast insecurity. The tools I thought established credibility were undermining it.

Twenty-three years later, running my business, GumLeafGreen, I trace everything to that conversation. Vince's intervention didn't just change how I write; it transformed how I see the relationship between communicator and audience. True expertise doesn't announce itself through complexity; it reveals itself through clarity and simplicity.

What struck me wasn't just what Vince said but how. His body language communicated care, creating psychological safety for difficult feedback. He asked direct questions without vague statements that create anxiety. He read my bewilderment without pressing for answers I didn't have. Most importantly, he highlighted how I was harming myself rather than what he didn't like. This was empathetic leadership—the easier thing would have been saying nothing to me.

That day, I discovered what I came to call "audience logic"—organizing communication around what matters most to readers and listeners, not what seems logical to writers or speakers. I'd noticed how corporate readers consistently skip to the end of documents, hunting for recommendations, conclusions, or other important information first. Why put last what they read first?

This became the foundation of everything I would build. But first, I had to learn to stop being the lead singer and become the backing vocalist, making others' success the driver of my own.

WHEN DAVID BEAT GOLIATH

Scott Pascoe sat across from me in PPB Advisory's office, facing a seemingly impossible challenge. As a partner at this small Australian restructuring firm, he needed his voice heard above the Big Four accounting firms: PwC, Deloitte, EY, and KPMG. The Federal Government had invited stakeholders to submit opinions on overhauling insolvency laws. Every major firm would compete for attention.

"I want to ensure our submission gets noticed," Scott said. "Our submission will be one of hundreds. I'd like to see if audience logic can get us noticed."

The traditional approach would follow the template everyone used, including an executive summary, background, analysis, and recommendations. Every submission would look identical, distinguished only by letterhead.

We agreed to organize it the way government bureaucrats actually think.

This required real courage from Scott. This was a public submission scrutinized by competitors, officials, and the entire profession. His partners had recently seen positive results with my audience logic approach, but this meant putting their credibility on the line publicly.

We rebuilt the submission from scratch, considering multiple audiences. We thought about bureaucrats who would synthesize hundreds of submissions. We considered affected citizens and professional critics. We structured it around the questions officials would need to answer, in their preferred order.

The stakes couldn't have been higher. The Big Four had resources, relationships, and precedent. We had only a different way of organizing information.

Then the call came from Canberra in Australia.

Scott was invited first to meet with government representatives, before any Big Four firm. They told him directly: the quality of his submission was why he was first. Not firm size or connections. The document itself had cut through because it was organized around their needs, not conventions.

This victory demonstrated that empathetic communication could level impossible playing fields. A small firm beat the Big Four not by playing their game better, but by recognizing the game needed changing.

THE MEDIATION THAT SAVED A CAREER

Aaron's hands trembled as he placed documents on the table. One of Australia's largest retailers had requested his removal from their mediation team. His prestigious law firm was fighting to keep him on. The mediator was a former High Court judge. His career trajectory hung in the balance.

Rather than diving into documents, I asked about his background. His father was a successful barrister who commanded courtrooms with elaborate arguments. Aaron seemed to have unconsciously adopted his father's style, which served him through law school but was failing him now.

"Mediators need to quickly understand differing positions, the reasoning for those positions, and find common ground."

The solution required Aaron to abandon everything he thought he knew. Instead of building elaborate and lengthy arguments, we would answer the mediator's questions in the same order the mediator would ask them in the mediation. Instead of impressing with complexity, we would impress with empathy and clarity.

This was a massive risk. Aaron was betting his career on an approach contradicting his training and his father's example. We worked through his anxiety together, acknowledging how unnatural this felt. Every instinct told him not to get to the point but lead to it, to add complexity, to sound more "lawyerly."

I introduced him to audience logic. The document we created looked nothing like a traditional legal document of this kind. It simply answered the mediator's questions in the order the mediator would ask them.

The mediator's response, delivered before both legal teams, was: "This is the best mediation position paper I have ever seen."

A former High Court judge declared Aaron's work the best among thousands he'd read. The firm promoted him shortly after. Aaron became a passionate advocate for audience logic, teaching others what could have cost him his career to learn.

TRANSFORMING RESISTANCE INTO ALLIANCE

Abraham's face flushed red in the video conference, voice rising: "This is not how we do things! This contradicts our templates!"

I was presenting reworked legal templates and advice following the template to a State Legal Office leadership team, showing how audience logic could help them compete with private law firms under a new government mandate. Each division leader had given me their best work, which I had transformed using an approach that made traditional legal writing look ineffective.

Others sat in uncomfortable silence. Two later apologized for Abraham's behavior. But I understood his reaction because I had been there with Vince. The existing templates represented years of investment and professional identity.

Annie, the office head, faced an impossible situation. The mandate was clear—compete commercially. But a key member of her team was in revolt. The safe path would have been abandoning the project.

Instead, Annie chose empathetic leadership.

"We'll acknowledge in every workshop that the template will be reconsidered," she said. "We'll honor it for now while showing additional possibilities and testing them with clients."

Annie attended two workshops herself. The first was a regular session; the second was a leaders-only session. By positioning herself as a learner, she created psychological safety for everyone. She showed that changing the approach wasn't admitting failure but demonstrating growth.

Abraham attended a regular session, too. As others left, he approached me. My pulse quickened—his earlier hostility fresh in memory. But his expression had changed.

"I've been to many writing workshops," he said quietly. "This was one of the best."

Those words, from someone with every reason to maintain opposition, demonstrated the power of empathetic leadership to transform resistance into alliance. Annie went on to lead two other government organizations, engaging me to work with both.

THE PATIENCE OF STRATEGIC EMPATHY

Alistair held an executive position in the UK operation of one of the world's largest insurance companies. Five years after the headquarters adopted GumLeafGreen's board reporting template, regional operations followed suit. Success at the group level should have made regional adoption straightforward.

Alistair refused to sign off on his reworked report, sending team members to give me illogical feedback instead of meeting personally. The improved quality was obvious—already approved by Group Board leadership. Yet his resistance strengthened.

I recognized the signs: refusal to meet, emotional objections despite clear improvements—fear of losing face. Alistair had built his career on traditional reporting. Accepting change might feel like admitting decades of doing it wrong.

The easy solution was escalation. His manager could mandate adoption. But forcing change would guarantee failure. Even if Alistair complied, his resistance would undermine implementation.

"We won't use Alistair's reports in workshops," I told sponsors, accepting risk to my reputation. "We'll use examples from five years ago plus the new examples from the other regions."

When workshop time came, no UK participants attended. Either Alistair was blocking the participation despite accommodations, or they were too afraid to attend due to his wrath.

"Let them exclude themselves," I counseled. "Let other European operations succeed first."

For a year, the UK remained outside while colleagues transformed their reporting. The contrast became impossible to ignore. When the UK operation finally got on board, a full year later, the dynamic had shifted. Instead of being forced, they had acquiesced.

This required believing empathy and time could accomplish what force never could. It meant accepting short-term failure for long-term success, understanding that maintaining dignity while changing creates allies rather than enemies. It proved that what is true and effective in reality eventually prevails.

THE REVOLUTION WITHIN

Looking across these experiences, from Vince's gentle correction to Alistair's eventual acceptance, I see the pattern defining empathetic leadership. It's not about being soft or avoiding conflict. It's about understanding human needs deeply enough to achieve what force never could.

When Vince told me I wrote like I was insecure, he could have said nothing. When Scott faced the Big Four, he could have played it safe. When Aaron faced career stagnation, when Abraham raged against change, when Alistair refused to budge—the easier path would have been avoiding human complexity.

But empathetic leadership means doing the harder thing. It means understanding that most often behind resistance lies fear, behind aggression lies insecurity, behind silence lies struggle. It means organizing everything—words, structures, approaches—around what others need rather than what we want to provide.

I call myself a backing vocalist now, not from lack of capability but from discovering where satisfaction lies. Every success in these stories is collaborative. Scott's triumph was mine. Aaron's promotion was my celebration. Annie's courage became my inspiration. This is what Vince taught me, though it took years to fully understand. When he created psychological safety for difficult truth, when he showed how insecurity sabotaged effectiveness, he wasn't just correcting writing. He demonstrated that leadership's most powerful force isn't authority or expertise. It's willingness to understand another human being deeply enough to help them become who they're capable of being.

Twenty-three years after launching GumLeafGreen, I still return to that room, to Vince's gentle smile and open hands, to the question that changed everything. "Why do you write like this?" wasn't about writing. It was about seeing ourselves as others see us, understanding unrecognized needs, and having the courage to change at the peak of success.

The revolution isn't in techniques—audience logic, collaborative assertiveness, strategic patience. The revolution is recognizing that our success is inseparable from others' success, that empathy isn't weakness but strength, that the backing vocalist who helps others shine creates more beautiful music than any soloist ever could.

This is empathetic leadership: doing the harder thing, understanding the unspoken need, discovering that when we organize ourselves around others' success, we achieve our own in ways we never imagined possible.

About Sue

Sue Tomat has spent over 25 years guiding professionals to sharpen their thinking so they can make better-informed choices about how best to communicate and collaborate to enable success. This includes thinking empathically, independently, and realistically. Inspired by Galileo Galilei since childhood, she encourages people to do what truly works, which often involves challenging conventional approaches.

As the founder of GumLeafGreen, Sue has built a global reputation for delivering training, coaching, and consulting services that transform how people think, communicate, and collaborate. Her expertise is sought after by clients in all sectors and across a wide range of industries worldwide. She works with a diverse set of individuals, from directors and CEOs of listed public companies to students seeking internships.

Sue's honours degree in law and over 10 years as a commercial lawyer in Australia laid the foundations for her expertise and also offered valuable insights into her blind spots and how to improve. She finds joy in helping others excel and believes the greatest teachers are those who have lived the lesson, not just read or theorised about it.

Sue is also passionate about rewilding landscapes, including the land under her custodianship, to better support both wildlife and human communities. She enjoys spending time in wild landscapes with loved ones, including her whippet, to boost creativity, clarity, and resilience.

Learn more at:
www.gumleafgreen.com

CHAPTER 25

WHEN EMPATHY MEETS THE BOTTOM LINE

BY JEFF HUNG

The Venezuelan tenant stood in front of me, his entire body vibrating with rage. His hands clenched and unclenched as he struggled to contain an explosion that had been building for weeks. Living in my South Columbus mobile home park had become unbearable for him. The predominantly Mexican community had made it abundantly clear they didn't want him there. Every interaction, every glance, every whispered conversation reminded him that he was unwelcome, unwanted, an outsider in what should have been his home.

"They hate me," he said, his voice breaking between fury and despair. "Every single one of them hates me. I can't walk to my car without someone saying something. I can't let my kids play outside. This isn't living."

I could feel the situation spiraling toward violence. His whole body was coiled like a spring, ready to snap. This wasn't just about late rent or property damage. This was about a human being whose fundamental need for belonging had been systematically crushed. His agitation escalated with every word, his voice rising, his gestures becoming more erratic. I knew that whatever I said next would either defuse this bomb or light the fuse. Every muscle in his body screamed that he'd been living in survival mode far too long.

At fifty-three years old, I've spent decades as a businessman and real estate investor specializing in what most people consider the absolute bottom of the barrel: mobile home parks. Industry professionals call it the least sexy and least appealing type of real estate investment. People regularly label me a slumlord without knowing anything about how I actually operate. But standing there with this desperate man, I wasn't thinking about property values or liability issues. I was thinking about Maslow's hierarchy of needs and how this man had been pushed so far to the edge that his basic needs for safety and belonging were completely unmet.

I made a decision that would have made any property management textbook author cringe.

"Get in my truck," I said, my voice cutting through his emotional storm.

He stared at me, confusion temporarily replacing anger. "What?"

"You heard me. Get in the truck. Now."

I drove him to the nearest store without explanation. During our earlier conversation, before things had escalated, he'd mentioned that he needed clothes and basic toiletries but couldn't afford them. His family was struggling on every level. I walked through the aisles with him, filling the cart with everything he needed. Shirts, pants, soap, shampoo, toothpaste. Two full bags of necessities that most of us take for granted. When we returned to the park, I handed him the bags.

"Why?" he asked, his voice barely a whisper now. "Why would you do this?"

"Because I can," I said. "And because you need them. Now listen carefully. Take the rent money you owe me and use it to leave tomorrow morning. Find a place where you feel welcome. Find a community that accepts you and your family. This isn't the right place for you, and that's okay."

This wasn't about rent. This wasn't about a neighbor dispute. This was a man whose basic human needs—belonging, safety, dignity—had been stripped away. When those evaporate, all that's left is raw instinct.

And I'll tell you something most people never learn: When a person feels they've lost their tribe, they become capable of anything.

I never saw him again. But I know that in that moment, when violence seemed inevitable, when the standard playbook would have called for eviction notices or police involvement, choosing radical empathy over standard operating procedure changed the trajectory of at least two lives.

This approach to business doesn't come from any MBA program I know of. It comes from studying with the Black Swan Group, learning from Chris Voss and Brandon Voss about tactical empathy and high-stakes negotiation. Their teachings have fundamentally reshaped how I view every business interaction. But more importantly, this approach comes from understanding that every business transaction involves human beings with complex needs, fears, and motivations. When you truly grasp this, everything changes.

THE DEAL THAT ALMOST DIED

Three years before the Venezuelan tenant crisis, I faced a completely different high-pressure situation. I was closing a seven-hundred-forty-five-thousand-dollar real estate deal with a buyer named John, whose billionaire brother was financing the purchase. Everything was set. The paperwork was ready. The money was in escrow. Then, at the last possible moment, John refused to sign.

Sitting across from him at the closing table, I could see the internal battle playing out on his face. His jaw clenched. His pen hovered over the signature line, but wouldn't drop. This wasn't about the property or the price. This was about family dynamics that had probably been building for decades. This was about a younger brother taking money from an older brother who'd made it big, and all the shame and resentment that came with it.

Most people would have started with logic, explaining contractual obligations, threatening legal action, or trying to strong-arm him into signing. Instead, I took a breath and opened with something completely different.

"John, I hear we're having a difficult day."

His shoulders dropped visibly. The defensiveness that had been radiating from him melted slightly. For the first time in that meeting, someone had acknowledged his emotional reality instead of just pushing for the signature.

"It's not easy dealing with family and money," I continued, keeping my voice soft. "Especially when one person holds all the cards. That dynamic changes everything, doesn't it?"

He nodded, and we talked, not about the contract, but about brothers and childhood competition, about expectations and the weight of family obligations. I listened without trying to solve or redirect. Only after he felt truly heard did I gently introduce the time pressure. His brother's financing had an expiration date. The sellers had other interested parties ready to move.

By validating his emotional experience first, I'd earned the right to present practical constraints. John took a deep breath, picked up the pen, and signed. The deal closed. Seven hundred forty-five thousand dollars changed hands. But more importantly, I'd learned that empathy isn't separate from business success. It's the foundation upon which all sustainable business is built.

LEARNING FROM THE BOTTOM UP

When developer Leon Siegel first showed me the mobile home property, I saw what everyone else saw: run-down trailers and massive headaches.

"Forget what it looks like," Leon said. "Can you see six thousand dollars in monthly cash flow?"

That number changed my perspective, but not just financially. I saw an opportunity to provide stable housing for people with few options. The stigma of being labeled a slumlord would follow me, but the chance to make a difference while building wealth was too important to pass up.

My real education came from a tenant named Gaspar Rivera, a jolly-looking, heavy-set Mexican man who lived in the single-family house on the property. For weeks after buying the park, I'd collect rent and leave quickly. One day, Gaspar stopped me.

"Why do you drive off whenever I try to talk to you?" he asked.

I admitted I was uncomfortable, unsure of my safety.

Gaspar laughed warmly. "This community respects the landlord. No tenant would harm you here. But respect goes both ways. These aren't just rent checks. These are people with feelings and families."

That conversation revolutionized my approach. The property transformed from a cash cow into a community. Gaspar became my unofficial property manager, helping tenants find jobs and mediating disputes. Under his leadership, the tenants organized a system in which each contributed $100 monthly to a rotating fund. Every month, one family received $2,600 for emergencies.

Another tenant paid rent by selling empanadas and tacos to returning laborers. The park thrived through mutual support. I learned to collect rent by walking through the community and talking with residents. This wasn't property management. This was community building.

WHEN SYSTEMS FAIL, HUMANITY PREVAILS

The true test came when five housing inspectors, led by Christopher McWhite, descended on my park. They cited violations on seventy-seven units without warning.

Standing in environmental court in Columbus, Georgia, I heard the judge declare me "clearly in violation." They took me into custody. I had to call someone to bring money for the fine. The humiliation burned, but it opened my eyes. McWhite was a crusader working to clean up blighted areas. His methods were harsh, but his mission had merit.

Instead of fighting, I reached out to Rebecca Wiggins, head of the inspector department. I invited her to see the improvements we were making.

During our walk-through, a dog charged at us. Without thinking, I stepped between Rebecca and the dog, kicking it away. She was visibly shaken, convinced I'd saved her life.

But what mattered more was that I'd discovered Rebecca sang in the choir of a Baptist church I followed. When we met, I spoke about our shared faith. I told her I'd turned this whole situation over to God.

The combination of shared values and that protective moment transformed our relationship. I never had another problem with inspectors. They gave me forty-five-day periods to address issues instead of immediate citations.

THE WISDOM OF UNEXPECTED TEACHERS

One tenant I call Robo, was consistently delinquent on rent. Every manual would say to evict him immediately. But I saw someone fighting battles beyond financial ones. So I gave him time and worked out payment plans.

Years later, Robo found me. He'd found faith, started a successful painting company, and built a stable life. "You could have evicted me," he said. "But you didn't, and that made all the difference."

This is the paradox of empathetic leadership: decisions that seem to make the least business sense often generate the greatest returns.

Another situation challenged me when I discovered a tenant who was hoarding. This beautiful, sweet lady paid rent on time, but her home was filled floor to ceiling with newspapers and debris. Her children were living in squalor.

The easy decision would be eviction. But those children deserved better. Instead, I called child protective services to get her help. I offered her another mobile home if she wanted to stay. This was about recognizing that providing housing means more than collecting rent.

My business partner once caught me using a negotiation technique from Black Swan Group. I was asking questions using double negatives: "Would you be against me doing this?"

"Why do you phrase things that way?" my partner asked.

I chose transparency. "You're more comfortable saying no than yes. This phrasing makes it easier for you to agree by saying no. It's about making you comfortable."

My partner appreciated the honesty. Trust had been established through transparency.

SETTING EXPECTATIONS THAT TRANSFORM LIVES

The most powerful lesson comes from a study about rats. Researchers found rats placed in water would swim for thirteen and a half to fourteen minutes before giving up. But when repeatedly rescued just before that point, provided with rest before returning them to water, something remarkable happened.

These rats developed an expectation of rescue. When placed back without intervention, they swam for six hours instead of fourteen minutes. The only difference was expectation.

This principle drives everything I do. When I gave Robo extra time, I created an expectation that someone believed in his recovery. When I bought necessities for the Venezuelan tenant, I set an expectation that he deserved kindness. When I worked with Rebecca Wiggins, I established an expectation of cooperation over conflict.

As leaders, we can set expectations that allow people to thrive for six hours instead of drowning in fourteen minutes. But this requires courage to see beyond immediate profit to long-term human impact.

THE CRITICAL BALANCE

After decades in business, after countless negotiations and difficult decisions, I've learned that empathetic leadership isn't about being soft or sacrificing success. It's about recognizing that sustainable success comes from understanding and addressing human needs, even when that understanding requires us to act in ways that seem counterintuitive to traditional business wisdom.

Every interaction is an opportunity to practice what I call tactical empathy, borrowed from my mentors at Black Swan Group. It means having what I describe as a lava-hot burning desire to be completely open to what moves your curiosity about other people. It means seeking the best advice and applying it quickly, even when that advice challenges everything you thought you knew about business.

Most importantly, it means understanding that failure is part of the process of growth. When I stood in that environmental court, taken into custody for property violations, humiliated and frustrated, I could have become bitter and adversarial. I could have hired lawyers to fight every citation. Instead, I chose to learn, adapt, and build bridges. That failure became the foundation for better relationships and a stronger business model.

The Venezuelan tenant crisis could have ended in violence or legal action. The hoarding tenant could have been just another eviction statistic. John could have walked away from that seven-hundred-forty-five-thousand-dollar deal, leaving everyone frustrated and poorer. But in each case, choosing empathy over standard procedure created outcomes that benefited everyone involved.

This is the truth about empathetic leadership that took me decades to fully understand: it's not a luxury for successful businesses. It's the foundation upon which sustainable success is built. When you understand that every tenant, every inspector, every difficult negotiation involves a human being with complex needs and valid concerns, you stop seeing problems and start seeing opportunities for connection and growth.

The mobile home park that others saw as a disgrace became a thriving community where families supported each other. The tenants others would have evicted became success stories of redemption and transformation. The inspectors, others would have fought, became allies in improving housing conditions. This transformation didn't happen through traditional business tactics. It happened through the consistent application of empathy, transparency, and genuine human connection.

As you face your own leadership challenges, remember the rats swimming for six hours. Your expectations for others can fundamentally change their capacity to succeed. Behind every difficult business situation is a human being trying to meet their basic needs for safety, belonging, and respect.

The choice to lead with empathy requires courage, patience, and vulnerability. But in my experience, it's the only form of leadership that creates lasting success for everyone involved. Because at the end of the day, business isn't about transactions. It's about transformations. And transformation always begins with understanding.

About Jeff

From the quiet marshlands of Charleston, South Carolina, in 1972, Jeff Hung's story began—an early experiment in curiosity itself. Tested for ADD as a child, the results were inconclusive, but the evidence was clear: his mind didn't wander, it soared. From dawn fishing trips to dusk hunts, from the rhythm of horses to the discipline of training retrievers, Jeff's world was the outdoors—alive, instinctive, and full of motion.

At age eleven, he enrolled in military school—a place where structure met opportunity. The cadence of drills, the weight of leadership, the shaping of self-discipline—all became part of his DNA. Returning home to graduate from high school, he immediately entered a world of self-direction and freedom.

University was the next stop—a lesson not in academics, but in awareness. Fraternity life and freedom collided, and grades plummeted, but clarity rose. Sitting in an old gun club he had leased to live in and think, he realized success wouldn't come from a classroom—it would come from creation. Business became his new curriculum, and barbecue his first venture. The smell of smoke and sauce became symbols of risk and resilience. Though the business eventually dissolved, the lessons remained—discipline, mentorship, and the art of strategic thinking.

With that momentum, Jeff went abroad. Europe expanded his lens—a bird's-eye view of people, places, and human potential. In Budapest, a dangerous encounter with a local mobster became a turning point, reminding him that leadership means facing down chaos with calm resolve.

Returning home, Jeff turned his focus forward—to real estate. With no experience but relentless curiosity, he learned the language, earned his license, and founded Spelman Hung Capital, LLC. Through intuition, persistence, and shrewd negotiation, he built a seven-figure portfolio of mobile home parks and multifamily properties. His exit through a 1031 exchange catapulted his holdings into a new orbit, propelling him toward commercial assets and single-tenant leases.

Today, Jeff Hung stands at the intersection of strategy and psychology—continuously evolving through stoic philosophy, Neuro-Cognitive intelligence, and Black Swan negotiation principles. As founder of **Excelsior Influence & Advisory Group,** he offers more than advice—he offers perspective. Those who work with him don't just move forward; they rise above.

Learn more at: commandthemind.com
"Command the Mind, Control the Moment, Win the Deal."

CHAPTER 26

THE EXPONENTIAL IMPACT OF ONE SMALL CHANGE

BY JANETTE FILBERT SPIEZIO

Standing in my zero-waste shop, Sustainable Haus Mercantile, in a small town in New Jersey, I watch a customer hesitate over a $24 shampoo bar. She's holding it like it might bite her, turning it over in her hands, skeptical that this palm-sized bar could replace the arsenal of plastic bottles in her shower, or even work for her hair. I've seen this moment a thousand times. What she doesn't realize is that she's not just holding a shampoo bar. She's holding the first domino in a chain reaction that could eliminate 14,000 plastic bottles from landfills and fundamentally transform how she sees the world.

I want to talk about empathy with a Big E. Not the kind where you pat someone on the shoulder and say "there, there." I'm talking about empathy for the planet, for humanity, for our survival, and yes, for beautiful hair. Because here's the uncomfortable truth: if everyone lived like Americans, we'd need five planet Earths to sustain us. Five. We have one. The math doesn't work, and we're running out of time to fix it.

THE REVOLUTION STARTS IN YOUR SHOWER

Here's how I see it: sustainable living is essentially a pyramid scheme, but for good. When one person switches from plastic shampoo bottles filled with unpronounceable chemicals to a quality shampoo and conditioner bar, the impact multiplies exponentially. Let me break down the math.

Let's assume the average person uses twelve bottles of haircare products annually. Even if you didn't switch to bars until age thirty-five, live to eighty, that's 540 bottles you've personally diverted from landfills. But people who love something don't keep it secret. You gift travel-sized bars to your mom, your sister and brother, your two kids, three best friends, two coworkers, and a few book club members. Now we're at 7,000 bottles eliminated. Then something magical happens: everyone wakes up and asks, "If I don't need my shampoo in a bottle, why is my dish soap in one?" Double the impact—14,000 bottles gone. And that's just the beginning.

This isn't wishful thinking. I witness this transformation daily in my shop. My former store Assistant Manager, Hasitha, worked with us for months before trying our bestselling Dip shampoo bars. Her favorite feature was her treasured long, gorgeous hair. Her routine was a tiny amount of regular shampoo weekly and coconut oil on the ends. Despite giving her samples six weeks earlier, she hadn't touched them.

Finally, I pushed. "Just try it," I said. "I've become a superfan. If you don't like it, no pressure. But you need to speak from experience when talking to customers."

A week later, she burst through the door grinning from ear to ear with a confession: "I absolutely love the bars, especially the conditioner. I won't use anything else." Two months later, her hairstylist said she'd never seen Hasitha's hair look healthier. But the real magic happened when Hasitha was explaining Dip to a skeptical customer who accused her of "just trying to make a sale." As the customer walked away dismissively, the shop door opened. A random customer rushed in, announcing, "I need to restock my Dip. I can't live without it!" The skeptic did a double-take, bought a set, and became a regular customer.

THE GREENWASHING MINEFIELD

Running a truly sustainable shop means becoming a detective, constantly investigating what's really behind the *eco-friendly* marketing. Greenwashing, where brands purposely mislead consumers about environmental benefits, happens when packaging uses green colors, nature pictures, certification-like symbols, a name, and a description that suggests the product is good for the planet. This occurs with nearly every major commercial brand. It's exhausting to fight, but it's necessary.

Take laundry strips and pods, those convenient little sheets everyone's raving about. Brands cold-call me weekly, trying to get them on our shelves. They seem perfect: no plastic bottles, minimal packaging, and they dissolve in water. But after reading sixty pages of research (yes, I'm that person), I discovered the truth. Companies make them with polyvinyl alcohol (PVA), a synthetic petroleum-based plastic polymer. By its chemical definition, PVA is plastic.

Every wash sends tiny bits of plastic into our water systems that municipalities can't filter out. In the US alone, we estimate that we use over 17,000 metric tons of PVA annually. Where does it go? Into sludge that becomes *organic* fertilizer on farmland. Through treatment plants into rivers, and the fish we eat. It also goes into incinerators that pollute our air. It ends up in landfills, where it sits forever. We wonder why microplastics show up in our coffee, our blood, and our organs. This is one reason.

Meliora, another sustainable brand whose products we sell, published a newsletter about the concerns of these *biodegradable* PVA strips. They dissolve into tiny pieces. Nanoplastics are now breaking through blood barriers into our organs. The smaller the plastic, the more dangerous it becomes to humans and to the environment, where it becomes impossible to clean up.

WHEN BREAKING RULES BUILDS TRUST

Not all my product decisions follow conventional eco-wisdom. When Kate from Dip called about her shampoo bars, I almost hung up immediately. They use artificial fragrance, which is typically an automatic rejection from me. But something made me listen and talk to her for a full hour.

Her argument challenged my assumptions. Essential oils, she explained, aren't sustainable, to which I agreed. They require massive amounts of plant matter, often laden with pesticides, with little to no regulation or disclosure requirements. If she wanted to build a scalable business that could actually compete with Big Shampoo, she needed another solution. Her fragrances avoid phthalates (one of the truly harmful chemicals in fragrances that keep the scent lasting longer), meet CREDO clean beauty standards, and achieve top ratings on the Yuka app for ingredient safety.

I took the risk. Today, Dip is our bestselling product because customers keep coming back for more of this award-winning brand. We're the number one retailer nationally, and we have just developed a custom Sustainable Haus scent together: Jersey Cherry Blossom + Vanilla. But here's what really sold me on Kate as a partner: every Dip direct-to-consumer order includes a note from Kate encouraging customers to shop at local refill stores instead of buying from DIP online. She actively sends business away from her direct sales to support shops like mine. Why? Because she understands that when someone visits a refill shop for shampoo, they discover a lovely neighborhood shop that sells dish soap bars, laundry detergent powder and liquid, and reusable cloth paper towels. They begin questioning everything about their consumption habits. Both Kate and I think we need more successful, independent local refill shops, changing the communities for the better.

THE ANTI-SALES STRATEGY THAT BUILDS MOVEMENTS

Here's something that shocks customers: I regularly talk them out of purchases. Someone comes in thinking they need new wool dryer balls. "Why?" I ask. If their dog ate them or they've lost them, absolutely buy new ones. But just looking old and ratty? "They last for years and thousands of loads. Save your money."

A customer comes back for laundry detergent after a few weeks, and I will ask them how much detergent they are using per load. I often learn that they are using a large amount. "You're using too much detergent. Laundry detergent is a ratio of water to detergent, so with the High Efficiency machines, we need less detergent. Your clothes will last longer, your wallet will thank you, and you won't end up with detergent residue on your clothes." We may sell less, but we've earned something more valuable—trust.

This philosophy extends to our pricing strategy. We sell rock crystal deodorant for twelve dollars that lasts ten years. Counter cleaner pods for $1.25 that make sixteen ounces of all-purpose spray. Wool dryer balls that eliminate the need for fabric softener sheets forever. These aren't profit centers. They're trust builders. When customers save money on these essentials, they have the budget to try other sustainable swaps. They believe our recommendations. They tell friends about the shop that cared more about their well-being than making a sale.

My corporate background taught me to maximize revenue per customer. My mission-driven present teaches me that building movements requires different metrics. Success isn't the sale. It's the customer who returns monthly for refills, brings their sister next time, posts about their plastic-free bathroom on social media, and starts asking why their workplace still uses disposable everything.

THE RIPPLE EFFECT AT HOME

The most challenging and rewarding transformation happened in my own family. When I shifted toward extreme sustainability, my daughters were in middle and high school. This was possibly the worst time to introduce major lifestyle changes. One daughter insisted on packing lunch in plastic bags inside paper bags with disposable water bottles, throwing everything away after eating. The waste was staggering.

But forcing change doesn't work. Instead, I placed reusable cloth towels next to our paper towels. After a month, I moved the paper towels to an upper cabinet. My daughters asked about the cloth wipes, how to use them, and where the dirty ones go. They could have retrieved the paper towels anytime, but chose not to. Today, neither buys paper towels. Both use bento boxes, beeswax wraps instead of plastic, shop organic produce from farmers' markets, and thrift their clothing and home goods. Oh, and they both use Dip shampoo and conditioner bars.

My oldest daughter, now twenty-eight and living in Los Angeles, just bought a condo. It came with vinyl flooring throughout, which is a toxic petroleum product that off-gases for years. Without my saying anything, she announced, "I can't live with vinyl flooring." Within a week of moving in, she'd torn up every square foot herself, donating it to Habitat for Humanity and restoring the original hardwood underneath.

When my youngest daughter moved to Dublin for a year, her first order of business was finding an organic farmer's market for healthy food and refillable, clean laundry detergent. She brought her own organic cotton thrifted sheets and went to the university swap to source small household items she couldn't bring with her.

There was only one time I insisted on a change. My nail-obsessed daughter was using traditional polish loaded with toxins. "You need to switch to 10-free or 15-free polish," I said, referring to formulas free from the worst chemicals. She called two days later: "I bought new nail polish." That was it. No argument, no resistance. When you build trust through years of not forcing things, the moments you do insist carry weight.

MEETING PEOPLE WHERE THEY ARE

Empathy in business means accepting people exactly where they are, not where you wish they were. Customers arrive with various struggles, such as itchy scalps, allergies, autoimmune conditions, chemical sensitivities, and recent cancer diagnoses. They're scared, frustrated, and desperate for solutions that won't make things worse.

A mother came in whose daughter couldn't stop scratching her scalp. Nothing had worked. I suggested Oneka, our Canadian refillable liquid shampoo, which is unscented, gentle as baby shampoo, and made with herbs from their organic farm. She seemed skeptical but desperate enough to try anything.

A month later, she returned glowing. Two months later, she shared this story: At breakfast, her daughter was scratching again. The mother's heart sank. Had the shampoo stopped working? "Why are you itching?" she asked. "Oh," her daughter replied, "we ran out. I used my brother's shampoo." The entire family converted that day. Sometimes the most profound empathy is simply offering options when someone feels they have none.

We stock multiple solutions for everything because one size never fits all. For deodorant alone, we carry rock crystal, spray, cream, paper tubes, baking soda-based, and sensitive skin formulas. Not everyone will love every option, but everyone can find something that works.

THE MATHEMATICS OF CORPORATE RECOVERY

My journey here wasn't linear. After a thirty-year corporate career in compliance, managing large teams at Prudential Financial, I got downsized. This was the best thing that could have happened, though it didn't feel that way initially.

I could have retired to poolside lounging. Instead, I spent time researching why I couldn't understand the ingredients in my laundry detergent, household cleaners, or personal care products despite being college-educated.

"Plant-derived ingredients" sounds healthy until you realize it tells you nothing. What plants? What process? Why can't they just tell us what's in it? So, I started making my own laundry detergent with saponified coconut oil, washing soda, and baking soda. That's it. No mystery ingredients, no big trade secrets, no chemical names requiring a degree to pronounce.

From one product, I expanded to making over a hundred items myself and source over 3,000 products from other vendors because, let's face it, I may sew beautiful napkins and wipes and make a great laundry powder, but I can't carve olivewood utensils or make stainless steel food storage and baking pans. My Instagram account, @sustainablehaus, has grown to over 100,000 followers, and we ship orders throughout the US daily. People just want honest information and solutions about living sustainably without sacrificing quality or overspending. They also don't want to do lots of research or experiment by trying random brands.

BEYOND INDIVIDUAL CHANGE

After nearly ten years running Sustainable Haus, here's what I know: individual change multiplied becomes systemic change. Every customer who switches to clean-ingredient, package-free products influences an average of ten others. Those ten influence ten more. Suddenly, major corporations notice declining sales of disposable products. Municipalities see less waste. Treatment plants process fewer chemicals.

But this isn't just about environmental metrics. It's about recognizing our interconnectedness—that my plastic bottle becomes microplastics in your seafood, that chemicals in my cleaning products affect your groundwater, that my consumption patterns influence what's available for your children.

True empathy means expanding our circle of concern beyond immediate family to encompass strangers, future generations, other species—the entire web of life of which we are just a small part. It means choosing differently and accepting that convenience today might mean catastrophe tomorrow.

The woman in the shop holding that $24 salon-quality shampoo bar, which will last two to six months, doesn't know she's about to join a revolution. But when she tries it, loves it (it was designed to work on all hair types), shares it, and starts questioning every other purchase, she becomes part of a movement that's growing exponentially. One person, one change, one moment of choosing differently, multiplied by millions.

That's empathy with a Big E. That's how we change course before those five planets are required. That's how we build a future where our children can breathe clean air, drink clean water, and live without wondering what toxic exposure caused their illness.

The question isn't whether you can afford to make sustainable changes. The question is whether we can afford not to. And it all starts with something as simple as a shampoo bar.

About Janette

Janette Filbert Spiezio is an Ecopreneur, Naturist, lover of the planet, and Founder/Owner of Sustainable Haus Mercantile, a zero-waste refill and eco-friendly home goods shop in Summit, NJ.

For over forty years years, Janette has been making her haus and life more sustainable and less toxic. For the past 10 years, she has been helping others do the same, focusing on living a less toxic life by making one change at a time. The tagline for Sustainable Haus is healthy people, healthy home, healthy planet, because the three are inextricably linked. Sustainable Haus offers over 3,000 plastic-free, clean-ingredient solutions for everyday challenges, and Janette is the maker of over one hundred products. The store ships daily throughout the US and to PR, APO, and DPO boxes. Sustainable Haus is one of the largest independent zero-waste, refill shops on the East Coast and likely in the US.

Janette speaks publicly on the dangers of plastics and everyday toxins, the importance of sustainability and zero waste, and, importantly, offers practical solutions. She has been featured on News 12 NJ, Forbes, and Fox News. She is Co-founder and Co-chair of Beyond Plastics New Jersey, a chapter of the national organization, Beyond Plastics, and together they are changing the laws in New Jersey. She is also a Climate Reality Leader. Janette is a first-generation American with two adult daughters, Amanda and Alex. She is passionate about education and uses her Instagram platform, with over 100,000 followers, to teach daily. Her husband, Ethan, is a big supporter.

Janette is mission-driven and works to reduce everyday toxins and plastic for herself and the community. She is an avid camper, organic gardener, creative cook, and master seamstress.

For more information:
www.sustainablehaus.com
www.instagram.com/sustainablehaus

CHAPTER 27

WHAT THEY CAN DEFEND, THEY'LL CHAMPION

BY ALAN HAUSER

The discussion had become a tug-of-war.

To the pharmaceutical team, our companion diagnostic (CDx) tests that identify likely responders were just another budget line item. To us, it was the leverage point, but they couldn't justify it internally. Forty minutes in, wc were still circling the same points.

I paused and brought us back to the numbers.

"Right now, diagnostics show up as an expense on your P&L," I said. "The benefit is invisible. So when you walk into your CFO's office next month, all they'll see is cost. You're asking us to make a bet you can't justify."

The business development lead exhaled. "That's exactly the problem."

"So let's build something you can defend."

That was a "that's right" moment–recognition replacing resistance.

"If we can measure what the CDx changes in your trial outcomes, what would 'fair' look like six months from now when you have to explain it?"

The tone shifted: this wasn't about access to our platform; it was about explaining it to senior leadership–and right now, they couldn't.

Our job wasn't to win the argument. Our job was to give them a scoreboard they could point to with confidence.

This chapter is about building that kind of scoreboard–so they can defend the deal in every room that matters.

THE PATTERN BEHIND THE PROBLEM

After twenty-five years navigating biotech partnerships–from gene editing methods to AI-powered molecular testing enabling precision oncology–I've seen a pattern:

Stalled negotiations.

"Too early" rejections.

Brilliant technologies that couldn't find a partner.

Different words, a common root cause: we were solving for the wrong problem. We focused on proving our value instead of understanding what our partners needed to protect. We told them why the science was important; we didn't show them how to defend yes.

My brother's battle with Burkitt lymphoma is why I entered this field. I watched him endure chemotherapy so brutal that I knew there had to be a better way–but personal mission alone doesn't move markets. When you sit across from a pharma VP, they don't see your childhood, your brother, your resolve. They see a P&L, a portfolio review, and a pitch deck with too many slides. They're thinking:

What will I have to explain?

Who will challenge this?

How will this look if it doesn't work?

Empathy in this context means seeing their scoreboard clearly–before you ask them to put your technology on it.

Defendable deals usually follow a similar sequence. Empathy gives you the information; structure turns it into something they can take to their senior management.

THE DEFENDABLE DEAL FRAMEWORK

1. **Run an accusation audit on their internal constraints.**
Start by naming what feels risky on their side–what they'll have to defend six months from now.

2. **Design for their scoreboard, not yours.**
Build around the metrics and valuation language they report to their CFO.

3. **Build a no-regrets first step.**
Make the first commitment small, time-boxed, and reversible–an option, an experiment, a pilot that ends with no blame.

4. **Give them champion language.**
Provide simple sentences and examples they can repeat to legal, finance, and their boss. If they can't explain it, they can't sell it.

Taken together, these four tools make "yes" easy to defend.

Tool 1: Run an Accusation Audit on Their Internal Constraints

Empathic dealmaking starts by doing their risk calculus out loud. That surfaced with a microfluidics company. Their pitch was, "We sell high-throughput screening platforms to pharmaceutical companies." Investors weren't biting.

In our one-on-one, I asked the question he'd been avoiding.

"Does the technology work?"

"Of course it works," he said.

"Then why aren't you discovering drugs yourself?"

Silence did the rest. I labeled what he was afraid of–looking like he'd moved the goalposts on his investors–and added a dignity clause: *If the data says no, we walk, no blame.* That made it safe to tell the truth.

Accusation audits are about doing their risk calculus out loud before they do. You name the fear in their language: overpaying if you're wrong, a science project instead of a product if you don't define outcomes up front, and moving the goalposts with their board if you haven't agreed what success means. When you do that, you stop being the person pushing risk onto them and become the person helping them manage it.

The guardrail is simple: once they share their fears, your next move is to build something that protects them.

Tool 2: Scoreboards They Can Defend

At Motorola Life Sciences, I had no budget, no headcount, and no managerial authority. The company's original name–Motorola Biochip Systems–captured its identity. Everything centered on our CodeLink DNA microarray chips.

I saw an opportunity for MPGx (Massively Parallel Genomic Profiling), a non-chip approach that could screen multiple genes across many samples at once. Different technology, different workflow, but aligned with how our pharma customers actually worked.

The obvious move would have been to build a killer slide deck and pitch it hard. Instead, I asked:

If someone says yes to this, what will they need to defend?

I started with coffee conversations, not conference rooms. No PowerPoint. Just sketches and questions.

With the R&D lead: "What would worry you most about this?"

With manufacturing: "Where would this break your current process?"

With sales: "What would your team need to explain to customers?"

Each conversation surfaced a piece of their scoreboard. Brand feared market confusion, manufacturing resource strain, sales conflicting messages, and finance needed reversible commitments.

After each round, I revised the proposal–not just the slides. I positioned MPGx as an adjacency, not a replacement: different use case, separate sales play, clean handoffs. I built in stage gates with clear stop/go criteria and simple financial models anyone could audit.

By the time the presentation reached executive management, the deck was already traveling on its own. When leadership did their back-channel checks, they heard the same thing from every stakeholder:

"We helped shape this. Our concerns are addressed."

They weren't just reacting to a pitch; they were defending something they had co-authored. The project was approved. The real win was the scoreboard everyone could stand behind.

Scoreboards work when they:

- Reflect metrics people already care about.
- Show how your value moves those metrics.
- Give your champion a simple line they can use: "We're paying for outcomes, not volume."

Too many metrics will break this. A few well-chosen ones make it work.

Tool 3: The No-Regrets First Step

At Pangene, our homologous DNA recombination program–grounded in science, later honored with a 2007 Nobel Prize–got the same answer across pharma: "Too early." The clinical risk calculus of gene therapy was unforgiving. One adverse event could sink a company. After months of no's, I realized we were asking for a giant leap, not a first step.

At a Licensing Executives Society meeting in Salt Lake City, a cocktail conversation with a transgenic plant executive connected our homologous recombination work, originally aimed at therapeutics, to his company's push to engineer better crops.

We were both PhD techies who'd moved from the bench into business development, so we shifted quickly from science to structure: what his CFO would approve.

Instead of pitching a big collaboration, I asked:

"What would a low-risk way to start look like on your side?"

His answer wasn't a large research program. It was an option.

We built a two-step deal, easy to defend internally: a modest upfront for an option to a license tied to a short corn-and-soy evaluation. If the data disappointed, the option expired. If it worked, they could exercise and convert into a pre-negotiated IP license and co-development partnership.

They signed. That "too early" technology found its first commercial partner by making yes the responsible choice, not the brave one.

With the microfluidics company, the same logic applied. Once we'd named the fear and added the dignity clause, we framed a simple choice for the board: keep selling tools, or run two small, gated experiments. It wasn't a wild pivot–just a no-regrets first step the board could underwrite without losing face. I rebuilt the business plan and deck around a single narrative: "We're following the data." The data came back positive, and the struggling venture raised $12 million in its Series A.

No-regrets steps work when:

- The downside is capped and explicit.
- The learning is valuable even if the answer is no.
- The story is, "We tested this responsibly," not "We bet the farm."

Tool 4: Language That Survives Lawyers

At Motorola, while in-licensing biomarker technology for our eSensor diagnostic chips, we hit a wall that could have killed the deal.

The university licensors had a Most Favored Nation clause with another company: no better terms for anyone else. The original royalty rate was set for single-test reagent kits. Applied to an integrated multigene platform, the fees would have been commercially unworkable.

They couldn't lower the rate without breaking their MFN promise; we couldn't accept it without destroying our business model.

"The MFN locks the nominal rate–we've known that from day one," I said. "So let's keep that rate and change what we measure."

"Go on," the licensing director replied.

"I'm proposing an equivalent-value concept for genomic content," I said. "I've also sent a one-page calculator with a rate schedule and worked examples so both teams can plug in different panel designs and get the same answer."

After a pause, he said, "So when my lawyers ask how this isn't just a rate cut, I can say the rate is unchanged, but the measurement basis is standardized."

"Exactly," I said. "Auditable math, no discount–just a clarified valuation metric."

Another pause. Then: "I can defend this."

"That's the point," I said.

The deal went through. We saved millions, and years later, people were still using the same framework because both sides could explain and defend it.

The issue was never just the number; it was the principle for applying it–something both sides could defend, audit, and teach to their lawyers and tech-transfer offices.

Language that survives lawyers has three traits:

- It's faithful to the original promise.
- It's mathematically and logically clean.
- It gives your counterpart a simple, honest sentence they can use when someone asks, "Why is this okay?"

Without that kind of language, even a fair deal dies in review.

BUILDING THE BRIDGE IN THEIR NUMBERS

To make this concrete, go back to the CDx negotiation at the beginning of this chapter. In that deal, everything shifted once we agreed the goal was a scoreboard his lawyers and CFO could defend. Then the real work began.

With their team, I mapped a decision tree showing where the CDx changed the economics: a higher probability of trial success, more efficient studies, and a cleaner benefit-risk story for regulators and payers. The diagram wasn't the point. Translation was. We converted those effects into risk-adjusted net present value–the same yardstick they used to price the uncertainty of their own drugs.

From that map, we chose a short list of metrics both sides already tracked–response rate in the intended patients, screen-failure rate, and serious adverse events–and tied our economics directly to how those numbers moved. Instead of being paid on test volume, we structured a base fee plus performance tiers when those metrics improved versus the original plan, and a success fee if the diagnostic helped them hit the primary endpoint with an acceptable safety profile.

Everything had guardrails: floors to protect them, ceilings to protect us, and an audit trail. It could all be explained to someone who wasn't in the room. Looking back, all four parts of the Defendable Deal Framework were there, even though we didn't call them that at the time.

The framework gave both sides something they could point to and say, "This is fair–and here's why." With that structure, the discussion stopped being a debate and became a measurement plan. It was one of the clearest demonstrations of a defendable yes I'd seen–and once I saw it that way, I started noticing the same pattern everywhere else.

Coda: The Practice of Seeing

Not all empathy happens in conference rooms.

At a Phoenix tech-transfer conference early in my career, I met Dr. Bert Rowland, a biotech patent pioneer who'd written the seminal gene-splicing patents that launched the industry.

We discovered we were both tennis enthusiasts. He invited me to play the next morning after his keynote. I'd flown in on my own dime to soak up every session, not to skip them.

Later that evening, a colleague pulled me aside. "If Bert wants to play, you play. Don't turn down that invitation."

It clicked: tennis was his unstructured time.

The next morning, while others attended panels I'd planned to see, I was on the court with Bert. That hour of tennis opened a door to a relationship that would prove more valuable than any session at that conference.

Back in the Bay Area, we made it weekly: tennis at the University Club in Palo Alto, then a debrief. I'd bring a couple of questions, listen more than talk, and implement one idea before our next session.

Over the next five years, Bert shaped how I think about IP. He became my mentor, then my collaborator on two startups. His way of working still echoes in how I negotiate and partner.

As I edit this chapter, I'm reminded that this isn't theory. In North Carolina, I shuttled between stroke wards, funeral plans, and helping my mother after my father's death. Back in California, I'm navigating a significant negotiation to create value for the company and its shareholders. In both places, the work is the same: see what people need to protect and help them take a step they can justify.

The practice starts with one simple question: "Six months from now, what will you need to defend about this decision?" In your next meeting, open with that question, then count to seven before you speak again. Write down the first few fears or constraints you hear. Your job is to build one guardrail that addresses the biggest one.

You're not listening for openings to counter, but for the constraints they can't change, the promises they've already made, the people they answer to, and the metrics they're measured by.

Once you understand what they need to protect, you can build bridges instead of battlegrounds: scoreboards both sides can explain, reversible first steps, and language they can use to champion your partnership when you're not in the room.

My brother survived his cancer. The chemotherapy that nearly killed him still did its job. Forty years later, he is living proof that even imperfect solutions can save lives. His journey taught me that brilliance alone can't turn breakthroughs into human benefit.

Understanding does that one conversation, one partnership, one defended decision at a time.

About Alan

Inspired by his teenage brother's battle with Burkitt lymphoma, Alan K. Hauser has devoted his career to turning breakthrough technologies into products and partnerships with real-world impact. A commercialization leader, Certified Licensing Professional, and inventor, Dr. Hauser helps transform innovations–from gene editing and microarrays to microfluidics and AI-powered spatial biology–into practical solutions for research, drug discovery, and diagnostics, with a particular focus on precision oncology.

Alan has negotiated and closed over sixty-five alliances and supported nine genomics product launches, including FDA-cleared DNA testing tools, at companies that ultimately achieved exits valued at more than $2 billion. He also led a multidisciplinary team that generated $150 million in annual pharmaceutical licensing revenue.

As CEO of Health Discovery Corporation (HDC), Dr. Hauser is advancing Support Vector Machine (SVM) methods–foundational machine-learning techniques that separate signal from noise in complex data. Building on HDC's pioneering contributions to SVM, the company's pattern-recognition engine is designed for high-stakes, information-rich applications in precision medicine and diagnostics, industrial analytics, and other domains where accuracy matters.

Alan earned his PhD in Chemical and Biomolecular Engineering from UC Berkeley, completed the executive program at Northwestern's Kellogg School of Management, and undertook additional finance coursework at the University of Chicago and Harvard.

Outside of work, he has completed more than twenty triathlons, including the three segments of the original Hawai'i Ironman, and has mentored over thirty-five STEM students and young professionals, helping cultivate the next generation of innovation-to-commercialization business leaders.

Learn more at: alankhauser.com

CHAPTER 28

THE VOLTAGE OF VULNERABILITY

BY URSULA LEON

The warning came too late.

I stood at the base of a 250-kilovolt electrical bus, staring up at conductors that could kill me in an instant. After ten years as an electrician with the International Brotherhood of Electrical Workers Local in Las Vegas, I'd heard the same safety mantra thousands of times: "Stay away from the bus. Always stay away from the bus." Those silver lines overhead weren't just dangerous; they were death itself, waiting for one moment of carelessness.

But today, my foreman pointed directly at those deadly conductors and said something that made my stomach drop to my steel-toed boots.

"You're going to be working on the bus. Not near it. On it. You'll be standing right on top of those lines."

In the electrical trade in high-voltage work, we have a saying that keeps us humble: you're always ten feet away from death. It's not metaphorical. It's mathematical. High voltage doesn't forgive, doesn't give second chances, and doesn't care about your kids at home or your years of experience. That morning, at the Diablo Canyon Substation, with the sun already baking the metal structures around us, I was about to close the ten-foot safety buffer to zero. Any wrong move at 250,000 volts, and I wouldn't just be injured, I'd be vaporized.

My partner for this high-stakes assignment was a massive guy, easily twice my size, with arms like steel beams and hands that could palm a basketball. In my early years, I might have been intimidated by his sheer physical presence. But when I looked at him that morning, I didn't see the typical macho posturing I'd grown accustomed to after a decade in construction. I saw my own fear reflected in his eyes. We were both rookies at this voltage level, both doing the mental math on our mortality, both wondering if today's paycheck was worth tomorrow's absence.

"I have a wife," he said simply, checking his safety gear for the third time. "I know my wife is always right. She told me this morning to be extra careful. Said she had a feeling."

It was such an unexpected thing to say in that moment of shared terror, but it told me everything I needed to know. This wasn't going to be about who was tougher or who had more experience. This was about two human beings choosing to trust each other with their lives, acknowledging their vulnerabilities rather than hiding them behind false bravado.

That partnership on the bus would teach me something that would transform not just how I work, but how I lead: empathy isn't soft; it's survival. And in an industry where speaking up had nearly cost me everything, I was learning that beneath the hard hats and the tough talk, we're all just trying to make it home alive.

BREAKING TWENTY YEARS OF SILENCE

I started my apprenticeship at eighteen as a girl in a world that didn't want me there. The message was clear from day one: keep your head down, do your work, and above all, keep your mouth shut. As one of the few women on construction sites in Las Vegas, I learned that survival meant becoming invisible. When inappropriate comments flew like sparks from a welder's torch, I didn't take them personally. When I was assumed incompetent before I'd even picked up a tool, I just worked harder, faster, and smarter. I wore my coveralls like armor, covered from head to toe, making sure nobody had a reason to look at me as anything other than another set of hands on the job.

For years, I believed this was just the price of admission and how you earned your place in the brotherhood—even if you'd never truly be a brother.

But silence has a weight, and that weight accumulates over time, like electrical resistance building up in a circuit. After years of witnessing mistreatment—sometimes directed at me for being a woman, sometimes at others for their race or age, sometimes just because someone needed a target—that weight became unbearable. The breaking point came when I was twenty-five, freshly turned out as a journeyman electrician, finally holding the same union yellow ticket as the men around me.

I thought that the yellow ticket, once I completed my union apprenticeship, would change things. I thought competence would be enough. I was wrong.

I finally confronted a foreman about the constant assumption that I couldn't do the job simply because I was a woman. I'd prepared for denial, for gaslighting, for being told I was too sensitive. His actual response shocked me more than any of those would have: "Yeah, you're right. You are treated differently because you're a woman."

That admission should have been a victory. Someone finally acknowledged what I'd been experiencing. Instead, it became the beginning of a year-long nightmare. The acknowledgment didn't bring change; it brought retaliation. The work environment became actively hostile, with a precision that spoke of coordination. Tools would mysteriously disappear when I needed them. Dangerous tasks would suddenly become "perfect for Ursula." Safety equipment would be "accidentally" assigned to someone else. The isolation was surgical, designed to make me quit without anyone having to fire me.

I survived that year, but barely. The cost was enormous both professionally and personally. I spent the next decade beating myself up, convinced it was my fault for not having the communication tools I desperately needed. Years later, listening to Chris Voss's teachings on tactical empathy, I understood I had been trying to fight for respect without first having empathy for myself.

LEARNING FROM THE TOUGHEST TEACHER

Six months into my apprenticeship, when I was still learning which end of a screwdriver was which, I was assigned to work with Kroby. His reputation preceded him like a storm warning—a twenty-year veteran who was brilliant but impossible, one of the best electricians working Las Vegas in Local. He came from Chicago, where quality and craftsmanship are a must. Other apprentices literally requested transfers to different job sites rather than spend a day under his supervision. He was harsh, demanding, and had zero patience for anything less than absolute perfection.

On my first morning with Kroby, he looked me up and down. I could see him calculating all the ways I would slow him down and the mistakes I would make. But something in me refused to be intimidated by his gruff exterior. Where others saw an impossible taskmaster, I saw a man who had earned every callus on his hands, every bit of knowledge in his head, through two decades of excellence in a trade that didn't tolerate mediocrity.

"You're going to learn to think," he told me that first morning, his voice gravelly from years of job site dust, "or you're going to fail. I don't care which. But if you're working with me, you're going to work smart, not hard. Hard work without thinking is just expensive stupidity."

For six months, I absorbed everything Kroby taught me—the mindset of strategic thinking, seeing three steps ahead, and understanding not just what to do but why we did it that way. While other apprentices complained about his impossible standards and harsh criticism, I started to hear the stories beneath his gruffness—stories about his family who depended on him, about the pride he took in buildings that would stand for generations after he was gone, about the crushing responsibility of doing work that could kill someone if done wrong.

Kroby taught me to work like a craftsman, to take pride in even the parts of the job nobody would ever see. But more importantly, he unknowingly taught me my first real lesson in empathy: that the hardest people to work with often have the most to teach, if you can see past their armor to the human underneath who's just trying to maintain standards in a world increasingly willing to accept "good enough."

THE COST OF NOT ASKING FOR HELP

My sister had cancer, but she wore her strength like a shield, just like I wore my coveralls. We came from the same cloth—taught early and often that asking for help was weakness, that handling your problems alone was strength, that needing others was a luxury we couldn't afford. She was always okay, always smiling, always insisting she didn't need anyone's assistance. And I believed her performance because I was performing the same show on my own stage.

The revelation came from the most unexpected source—my massage therapist, of all people. I'd just returned from a job in California, ready to dive back into work, to lose myself in the familiar rhythm of wire and conduit, when he stopped me mid-sentence during what I thought was a casual conversation about my family.

"Your sister is dying," he said, with a directness that felt like touching a live wire without gloves. "Everyone in your family is too close to see it, but I'm watching from the outside. She's dying, and you're about to go back to work like nothing's happening."

I wanted to argue. My sister had just told me she was fine, that I should take the job, that she didn't need anything from me. But something in his certainty, his willingness to say the unsayable, broke through my carefully constructed denial.

That afternoon, I made one of the hardest phone calls of my life. I called my superintendent, Jesse, my voice shaking like I was an apprentice again, afraid of making a mistake. "My sister might be dying. Or she might not be. But I can't have any regrets. I need time off."

Jesse's response surprised me, cutting through years of tough-guy construction site culture in a single sentence. "I lost a brother," he said quietly, the job site noise fading in the background. "Didn't get to say goodbye. Take all the time you need. Your job will be here when you get back."

THE APPRENTICE WHO DARED TO DREAM BIGGER

Years into my established career, I worked with a helper in California who reminded me of myself at that age—eager, skilled, always anticipating the next need before anyone asked. He was everything a foreman could want: fast, reliable, never complained, always showed up early. Everyone told him he should be grateful for the good pay, the steady work, the approval of his supervisors. But during our lunch breaks, sitting in whatever shade we could find on the job site, he'd talk about his real dream: becoming a lineman.

"Everyone says it's too hard to get in," he told me one afternoon, unwrapping his sandwich with hands already calloused despite his youth. "They say I'm already in a good spot, why risk it? Why leave something secure for something uncertain?"

I recognized that voice—it was the same one that had kept me silent for years, the same one that tells us to be grateful for what we have instead of reaching for what we want.

"You know what's really hard?" I asked him. "Waking up in twenty years, still wondering what if. You're not just a good helper, you're someone with a dream. And you have to go after it, because nobody else is going to chase it for you."

He had real reasons to stay safe—his mother had cancer, he was her primary support, and the steady paycheck mattered more than dreams. But I could see in his eyes what I'd felt on that bus platform: the hunger for something more than survival, for work that fed the soul as well as the bank account.

Today, we talk once every two or three years. I see his posts on Instagram—working on high-voltage lines against brilliant blue skies, living his dream as a lineman. He doesn't know that each photo fills me with a pride that has nothing to do with me and everything to do with him. He reminded me that real leadership isn't about keeping good people in place—it's about empowering them to grow beyond what you need from them.

THE EVOLUTION REVOLUTION

After my sister passed, I started writing "love" in my journals every single day. It became my anchor, my reminder that beneath all the armor I'd built over twenty years in construction, love was still possible, still necessary, still the point of it all. When I formed my LLC to manage my rental properties, I named it EVOL LLC—love spelled backward. It felt like a secret rebellion, hiding softness inside something that sounded hard and dangerous.

But the real revolution came when I started developing a consultation concept called EVOL—Empathy, Vision, Ownership, Leadership. The acronym itself tells the story: love backward becomes evolution forward. After two decades of learning empathy through trial by fire, through hostile work environments and life-or-death situations, I want to bring these tools to construction sites across the country.

Who better than a woman who survived twenty years in the trade to train men about empathy without threatening their masculinity? I've seen them at their strongest and their most vulnerable. I've worked beside them when the heat index hit 115 degrees and when the overtime stretched past exhaustion into dangerous territory. I understand that beneath the bravado, they're humans trying to provide for their families, take pride in their work, and make it home safe.

The framework I'm developing is simple but not easy:

- Empathy: See past the armor to the human underneath, including your own
- Vision: Look beyond surviving today to building a career worth having
- Ownership: Take responsibility for your growth, not just your daily tasks
- Leadership: Guide others through understanding, not dominance or fear

HIGH VOLTAGE HUMANITY

Six months ago, if you had told me I'd be co-authoring a book with Chris Voss about empathy in leadership, I would have laughed—not because it was impossible, but because I couldn't imagine my story mattering to anyone beyond my own survival. I wasn't a business owner with impressive metrics. I wasn't an executive with a corner office. I was an electrician who had learned that speaking up came with a cost, and empathy was the currency to pay it.

But that's exactly why this story matters. Because empathy isn't a luxury for those who've already made it—it's a survival tool for those still in the trenches.

Twenty years in the electrical trade taught me that we're all just trying to make it home. Whether we're working on a 250 KV bus or navigating a difficult conversation, whether we're setting boundaries with hostile coworkers or sitting with dying loved ones, we're all just humans carrying more than anyone can see, doing our best with the tools we have.

The voltage is still dangerous. The work is still hard. But now I know that vulnerability isn't the opposite of strength—it's the current that makes a real connection possible. And in an industry built on power, that might be the most revolutionary tool of all.

About Ursula

Ursula M. Leon Hernandez is a union electrician with more than twenty years of experience working on major construction, utility, and industrial projects in the United States. Born in Puebla, Mexico, and raised in the U.S., she built her career through grit, perseverance, and the quiet strength required to show up every day in environments where she was often the only woman—and the only Latina—on the jobsite.

Throughout her career, Ursula has contributed to highly complex and iconic projects, including the Las Vegas Sphere, nuclear and hydroelectric facilities, substations, data centers, and large-scale casino developments. Each jobsite sharpened her understanding of how communication, respect, and human connection directly affect safety, teamwork, and the overall culture of a crew. She learned early that miscommunication, dismissal, and lack of empathy can break down trust just as quickly as any technical failure.

These experiences planted the early seeds of what she now calls EVOL, a movement focused on empathy, emotional intelligence, and human-centered leadership in construction. EVOL reflects her belief that the trades are at their strongest when people feel seen, respected, and heard.

Ursula is not stepping into leadership from afar—she is building this work from the ground up, carrying the hands-on expertise, union values, and field wisdom that shaped her. Her approach blends practical jobsite insight with emerging leadership tools, helping teams communicate more clearly, resolve conflict, and create environments where workers can show up with dignity.

Having navigated adversity, discrimination, and high-pressure environments, Ursula brings a lived understanding of the courage required to speak up and stand strong. She uses her story to mentor other tradeswomen, minorities, and new leaders, reminding them that resilience, emotional intelligence, and self-worth are part of the job.

Ursula's mission is simple: to evolve the way the industry leads. She believes every system, whether electrical or human, functions better when its connections are grounded in intention, respect, and empathy. Through EVOL, she is transforming twenty years of jobsite experience into a new path forward for leadership in the trades.

LinkedIn: https://www.linkedin.com/in/ursula-leon-3aa299124
Website: https://www.evol-lasvegas.com

CHAPTER 29

WHEN UNDERSTANDING CHANGES EVERYTHING: THE COURAGE TO SEE BEYOND THE SURFACE

BY THOMASINA TAFUR

The classroom door clicked shut with a finality that echoed through the hallway. On the other side stood a young Saudi woman, her eyes wide with disbelief. I had just done something unthinkable. I'd locked a student out of my classroom in a country where, as a foreign teacher, my position hung by a thread thinner than the desert sand outside our windows.

My hands weren't shaking from fear, though they should have been. They were steady because I knew something that took me years to learn: true empathy sometimes means making the hardest choice, not the easiest one. And in that moment, standing in a classroom thousands of miles from home, surrounded by young women whose futures depended on more than just English lessons, I understood that empathy without boundaries isn't empathy at all—it's enablement.

THE MISCONCEPTION THAT NEARLY DESTROYED MY EXPAT EXPERIENCE

When I first arrived in Saudi Arabia, I thought I understood empathy. Twenty years at FedEx had taught me to read people, to understand their needs, to navigate complex relationships in a male-dominated industry. I'd even co-founded the FedEx Women's Forum, bringing together female employees from across the country when many senior leaders didn't even want to publicly support our cause. I knew how to build bridges where others saw walls.

But Saudi Arabia taught me that empathy without cultural understanding is like trying to navigate a desert with a map of the ocean. Useless, and potentially dangerous.

Most teachers went to Saudi Arabia for the money—tax-free salary, easy travel throughout the Middle East, and exotic adventure. They'd arrive with lesson plans downloaded from Western websites, ready to transplant their familiar methods into unfamiliar soil. They'd last maybe a year, sometimes less, leaving frustrated and bitter, complaining about students who "didn't want to learn."

I went with a different mission. These weren't just students. They were young women standing at the intersection of tradition and possibility, carrying the weight of their families' expectations while reaching for futures their grandmothers couldn't have imagined. If I were going to teach them English, I needed to understand why English mattered in their world, not mine.

THE POWER OF STRATEGIC OBSERVATION

The first month, I barely taught at all. Instead, I watched. I listened to conversations in the hallways, observed how the Bedouin girls, who traveled over an hour each way to attend university, interacted differently from the city girls. I noticed which students looked exhausted (those were often the married ones, juggling homework with household duties). I paid attention to who spoke up in class and who remained silent, not from lack of knowledge but from cultural conditioning.

One morning, a student named Aisha approached me after class. "Miss Thomasina," she said quietly, "why do you ask us about our lives? Other teachers just teach from the book."

"Because," I told her, "I can't teach you to communicate in English if I don't understand what you need to communicate about."

That conversation changed everything. Aisha began sharing stories about her dreams of working in international business, but also her fear that improving her English might make her seem "too Western" to potential husbands. Other students started opening up about similar conflicts. They wanted opportunities, but they also wanted to honor their culture and families.

This is where most Western teachers failed. They'd either dismiss these concerns as backward thinking or become paralyzed by cultural sensitivity, afraid to push their students toward growth. But true empathy means finding the third way—respecting where someone comes from while helping them get where they want to go.

REWRITING THE CURRICULUM OF POSSIBILITY

I threw out my original lesson plan three times in the first two months. Each iteration moved further from standard ESL curricula and closer to what these young women actually needed. Instead of having them write essays comparing fashion or exercise, I assigned research projects on successful Arab businesswomen. Instead of role-playing scenarios from American textbooks, we practiced job interviews for positions at Saudi companies expanding internationally.

One assignment particularly stands out. I asked them to write essays comparing real Saudi women who'd achieved success internationally with the Western media representations they saw in Chanel advertisements and Disney movies. The room erupted in discussion. For the first time, they weren't just learning English; they were using English to examine and articulate their own identities.

"If you learn my language," I told them, "you'll have options in life. Not Western options or Eastern options—your options."

The shift was immediate and profound. Students who'd been passive became engaged. Those who'd been struggling suddenly found motivation. When you show people you truly see them, not who you think they should be, but who they are and who they're trying to become, they'll move mountains to meet you halfway.

THE MOMENT THAT ALMOST COST EVERYTHING

Which brings me back to that locked door and the student on the other side of it.

Fatima had been one of my brightest students, quick to grasp new concepts and eager to participate. But over several weeks, I'd noticed troubling patterns. She'd copy other students' work, claiming collaboration when it was clearly plagiarism. She'd lie about completing assignments, sometimes producing elaborate excuses that must have taken more effort than the homework itself would have required.

In my twenty years at FedEx, integrity had been nonnegotiable. You could make mistakes, you could fail, you could struggle, but you couldn't lie about it. The supply chain doesn't care about excuses; packages either arrive on time or they don't. Numbers either add up or they don't. Trust, once broken in business, rarely recovers.

But this wasn't FedEx, and Fatima wasn't an American employee who understood these unspoken rules. She came from a culture where saving face often mattered more than objective truth, where family honor could hang on academic performance, and where failure might mean an arranged marriage instead of a career.

I'd shown her empathy. I'd given her extra time on assignments, offered additional tutoring, and created opportunities for her to correct her mistakes privately. But empathy without accountability becomes enablement, and I was enabling her to build a foundation of deception that would crumble the moment she entered the professional world.

The day I locked her out, she'd submitted another student's work as her own—again. When confronted, she'd lied—again. And when given the chance to come clean, she'd doubled down on the deception.

"Fatima," I said, "please leave my classroom."

The silence was deafening. In Saudi culture, public shame is almost unbearable. As a foreign teacher, challenging a Saudi student, especially rejecting one, could be career suicide. If she complained to the administration, if her family had connections, I could be on a plane home within days.

She left, and I locked the door behind her, not from anger, but from determination. The other students needed to see that empathy has boundaries, that understanding someone's challenges doesn't mean accepting destructive behavior.

WHEN EMPATHY MEANS STANDING FIRM

Fatima went straight to the Dean, as I'd expected. What followed was one of the most nerve-wracking days of my professional life. Investigations, meetings, cultural advisors explaining why I'd overstepped, why I didn't understand the Saudi way.

But here's what those advisors didn't know: I'd spent months building relationships with my students. They'd seen me arrive early to help the Bedouin girls who struggled with their long commutes. They'd watched me adapt lessons to honor their culture while challenging them to grow. They'd experienced empathy in action, not as weakness but as strength.

When the administration interviewed my other students, the response was unanimous. Yes, Miss Thomasina was strict about integrity. But she was strict because she cared about their futures. She wanted them to succeed not just in her classroom but in the global marketplace. She held them to high standards because she believed they could meet them.

The Dean ruled in my favor. More importantly, Fatima returned to my classroom the next semester as a different student. The consequence had been the empathy she actually needed. She graduated with honors, and last I heard, she was working for an international consulting firm. She learned from this mistake and apologized.

THE MULTIPLICATION EFFECT OF UNDERSTANDING

That Saudi experience transformed how I view empathetic leadership. True empathy isn't just understanding someone's struggles. It's understanding what they need to overcome them, even when it's not what they want.

This principle reshaped my approach to caring for my mother with dementia. The organized part of me wanted systems and efficiency. But she didn't need a project manager. She needed a daughter who could see past repetitive questions to the fear beneath them.

When she asked for the tenth time what day it was, she wasn't asking about the calendar. She was asking if she still mattered. So I changed, answering each question as if it were the first, entering her reality instead of correcting it. Strategic empathy: understanding her emotional needs mattered more than factual accuracy.

This shift helped me understand my sister's initial resistance to finding Mom a care facility. My sister, struggling with ADHD after caring for our father's final years, wasn't abandoning our mother. She was protecting herself from unbearable pain.

Instead of arguing logistics, I shared my own fear and exhaustion. I explained not just what needed doing but why it mattered, inviting her to engage on her terms.

Today, we're united in our mother's care because empathy taught us to see each other's struggles as clearly as our mother's.

THE REVOLUTION THAT STARTED WITH UNDERSTANDING

During my twenty years at FedEx, as one of the few female sales leaders, I'd experienced the barriers women faced—meetings during school pickup times, networking at uncomfortable venues, and the assumption that ambition and motherhood were incompatible.

One evening, after being the only woman in yet another room of decision-makers, I called a female colleague. She said something that changed everything: "What if there are hundreds of us across the company feeling exactly this way?"

That sparked the FedEx Women's Forum. But creating it required empathy on multiple levels—understanding not just what women needed but why male leadership might resist.

When I approached my boss, I didn't lead with accusations. Instead, I painted a picture: "What if FedEx could tap into the full potential of half its workforce? What if we could become the industry leader in developing female talent?"

"I'll support this," he said, "but you'll need to convince the other senior VPs."

Several leaders saw the Forum as threatening or unnecessary. One told me bluntly that women had the same opportunities as men.

This is where empathy became strategic. Instead of arguing, those of us on a shared project asked questions: What challenges did he face in retaining talent? What would happen if competitors attracted our best female employees? Then we shared specific examples of talented women who'd left for companies with more flexibility and visible female leadership. We helped him see the business case through his priorities, not ours.

After months of conversations, we got approval. The Forum launched with three regional conferences, bringing together hundreds of female employees. We invited male allies from the beginning, making it about development, not division.

FedEx still places a high regard on diversity and inclusion. It's changed the company culture—male managers now actively sponsor female talent, policies have been revised, and the leadership pipeline has strengthened.

All because empathy taught us to engage the system with strategic understanding rather than anger.

THE COURAGE TO SEE CLEARLY

Looking back across these experiences, from Saudi classrooms to FedEx boardrooms to my mother's bedside, I see a common thread. Empathetic leadership isn't about being soft or accommodating. It's about having the courage to see clearly: to see people as they truly are, to see what they truly need, and to see how to bridge the gap between their current reality and their potential.

Sometimes that means adapting completely, like rewriting the curriculum for Saudi students. Sometimes it means standing firm, like maintaining integrity standards despite cultural pressure. Sometimes it means playing the long game, like building coalitions across differences to create systemic change.

But always, always, it means remembering that empathy without action is just sentiment. The Saudi girls didn't need my pity about their restricted opportunities; they needed practical tools to expand those opportunities. Fatima didn't need endless excuses; she needed accountability wrapped in compassion. My mother doesn't need my frustration about her repeated questions; she needs my patient presence. The women at FedEx didn't need sympathy about discrimination; they needed strategic pathways to advancement.

True empathetic leadership requires three kinds of courage:

First, the courage to observe without judgment, to understand before trying to be understood.

Second, the courage to act on that understanding, even when it's risky or uncomfortable.

Third, the courage to maintain boundaries, recognizing that enabling destructive patterns isn't empathy. It's cowardice disguised as compassion.

YOUR MOMENT OF CHOICE

Right now, in your world, someone needs your empathetic leadership. Maybe it's a team member struggling with challenges they haven't voiced. Maybe it's a client whose resistance masks deeper fears. Maybe it's a family member whose difficult behavior stems from pain you haven't fully recognized.

The question isn't whether you can afford to take the time to truly understand them. The question is whether you can afford not to. Because when you have the courage to see people clearly—to understand not just their actions but their motivations, not just their failures but their potential—you unlock possibilities that rigid rule-following never could.

That locked door in Saudi Arabia? It opened more than it closed. It opened Fatima's future by refusing to compromise her integrity. It opened my students' respect by showing them that empathy includes accountability. It opened my own understanding that true leadership sometimes means making the hard choice precisely because you care.

Your locked door is waiting. The question is: Will you have the courage to close it when empathy demands it, and the wisdom to know when that moment has come?

Because in the end, empathetic leadership isn't about always saying yes. It's about understanding deeply enough to know when no is the most caring answer you can give.

About Thomasina

Thomasina Tafur is an Options Trader and Financial Coach, whose experience includes serving as an instructor at Princess Noura University (Saudi Arabia), the world's largest all-women university, and twenty years' executive leadership with FedEx.

A servant leader with the heart of a teacher, Tafur empowers emerging women leaders to advance their careers, fosters global communication, and instills effective negotiation tactics. With her background in options trading and financial coaching, Tafur is an advocate for women's wealth management and Wall Street prowess. Her dissertation, "The Case for Female Leadership on Wall Street," explores how women's unique contributions and leadership styles are a compelling case for increasing female representation in executive roles on Wall Street.

At FedEx, Tafur led initiatives ranging in scope from $10 million to $20 million. She co-founded and co-led FedEx's first nationwide International Women's Forum to empower women to take on greater leadership and decision-making roles within the organization. Because of its success, the program was duplicated in other cities with more than 500 attendees per event. She also won the FedEx 5-Star award for increasing account activation rates by 46 percent and generating $18.5 million in incremental business. Additionally, Tafur was one of two leaders chosen to train FedEx teams in negotiation skills, including the Airline Sales group, the only group at FedEx that both sold and bought.

"When you show people you truly see them, not who you think they should be, but who they are and who they're trying to become, they'll move mountains to meet you halfway," Tafur says about her leadership philosophy. "A true leader takes on the role because they genuinely care about the outcome of the groups they lead," she added.

A world traveler and calculated risk-taker, Tafur immerses herself in new cultures, languages, and practices giving her a global perspective in personal and business dealings.

Tafur holds an MBA in International Business from the University of Miami and a PhD in Global Leadership from Pepperdine University.

Connect with her at www.linkedin.com/in/thomasinatafur or thomasinatafur@gmail.com.

CHAPTER 30

THE PARTNERSHIP RESET

BY OLIVER FERNANDEZ

The tension hit before anyone spoke. A static-filled conference line. A proposal so weak it felt like a dare. A trusted supplier suddenly acting like they wanted out—like they were bracing for rejection.

I'd been in countless negotiations, some friendly, some hostile, some that kept me awake at night. This one felt different: pricklier, cringier. Like walking into a room and everyone stops speaking.

In my world, danger doesn't take the form of shouting or threats. It manifests subtly in communications: long awkward pauses, apprehensive tones, emails that dodge the issues, and executives who suddenly avoid eye contact. These moments can make or break relationships.

I used to think my job was about leverage, pushing until someone caved. But breakthroughs, the real turning points, always came when I stopped trying to win… and started trying to understand the value hiding beneath the surface.

And the first time I felt that shift, that gut-level realization, was during a call that should've been routine… but wasn't.

Before I ever had a name for empathy, I kept running into the same certainty: the real turning points in negotiations weren't the slick presentations or the heated debates. They were the still moments. The pauses. The fragile spaces where someone hesitated just long enough to reveal what they were truly worried about.

I didn't recognize it immediately. I was trained to focus on process, logic, and numbers. But repeatedly, I found myself in conversations where breakthroughs only happened when I stopped talking and started listening for what wasn't being said.

Those moments felt small at the time—a sigh, a softened tone, a silence that lingered—but they changed everything. They were the start of a shift in how I negotiated, how I led, and how I understood people.

And it all began with one quiet moment on a call I assumed would be routine… but became anything but.

THE PARTNERSHIP RESET

The conference call went silent. After nearly a decade of unchallenged partnership, our longest-standing marketing agency had just submitted a proposal so weak it seemed designed to fail. As a Global Procurement executive, I'd seen plenty of supplier relationships deteriorate, but this felt different. They were disengaged, practically begging us to fire them.

I could have taken the easy victory. Here was proof that my new mandatory bidding process had exposed their uncompetitive pricing. Other qualified suppliers had submitted significantly lower bids. This was supposed to be my big win with marketing, my chance to prove the value procurement brought to executives.

But something wasn't right. Something warned me that suggesting another supplier without more justification than a quote could destroy my credibility internally. More importantly, I suspected they'd misunderstood our requirements, thrown off by a bid process they'd never faced before.

I delayed my recommendation, and I picked up the phone. "Is it a good time to talk about your proposal?" I asked. "Just some feedback: I'm not negotiating or anything, and I know we're not very familiar with each other, but you're a long-standing partner, and our supplier relationships are important to us. Judging from your proposal, it feels like you might be feeling blindsided by this new process and how it is unfolding."

The silence stretched longer. Then she sighed. "Yeah, honestly, we thought we were partners. We have been for years. Now it feels like we're being replaced by any random supplier off the street who wins a race to the bottom."

That moment changed everything. By acknowledging her emotion, I'd created psychological safety. Once she felt heard, she revealed how shifting corporate priorities had confused her team. We reframed the entire project as a partnership reset rather than a rebid. They returned a proposal that outperformed every competitor on creativity, cost, and cultural fit. The relationship emerged stronger than ever.

This transformation wasn't luck—it was the deliberate application of tactical empathy—strategically understanding others to advance dialogue and achieve superior outcomes for all.

THE EXECUTIVE OBSTACLE COURSE

Months later, I faced a different challenge. I was leading a high-stakes internal cost-reduction meeting, armed with data showing we'd been leaving money on the table with suppliers for years. My team had prepared aggressive negotiation proposals for all executives. But the executive sponsor across the table was fuming before I'd even started. Her body language screamed confrontation. Tense muscles, crossed arms, clenched jaw, and barely any eye contact. She knew I was about to recommend replacing some of her team's suppliers with more cost-competitive alternatives.

My deck contained irrefutable data. The numbers didn't lie. But I recognized it wouldn't land unless I addressed the emotion flooding the room.

"It seems like you're worried this initiative will make your team look like they haven't been managing budgets responsibly," I said. "If that's not the case, then no offense, but if it is, I want to reassure you that it's not my first rodeo, and it wouldn't be the first time I've heard that."

The air shifted. After a long pause, she said, "That's exactly it."

I'd labeled what everyone else tiptoed around. The risk was enormous. She could have exploded at my presumption. Instead, acknowledging her fear transformed me from threat to ally. Where Finance and my predecessors had encountered only resistance and grief, I found collaboration.

We reframed the entire exercise. Rather than cost-cutting, we agreed to position it internally as our team's co-developing value optimization initiative. This shift in perspective changed everything. She became a coarchitect of the savings plan rather than an opponent. Her engagement increased dramatically, and she emerged as an internal champion, helping drive the initiative forward rather than blocking it at every turn.

The lesson was clear: tactical empathy isn't just understanding. It's about using that understanding strategically to transform opposition into advocacy. It would have been easy to chalk that transformation up to luck. But the pattern kept repeating. Each time I chose understanding over assertion, the dynamic flipped. And nowhere was that more surprising than with a supplier everyone had written off as impossible.

THE MIRACLE OF THE DIFFICULT SUPPLIER

Not every transformation happens in boardrooms. Sometimes significant changes occur in unexpected places.

I'd inherited a supplier infamous for saying "no" to everything. My predecessors had fought them on price, terms, and timelines—every possible negotiation point. The relationship had devolved into trench warfare, with both sides dug in, unwilling to budge.

In our first meeting, I tried something different. I didn't argue a single point. Instead, I mirrored and labeled their concerns.

"You're under pressure to protect your margin, and you're worried we'll keep squeezing," I observed.

He nodded. "Finally, a procurement guy who gets it."

Once he felt understood, I asked a calibrating question to promote more collaboration: "How can we structure this deal so your risk goes down while our cost predictability goes up? I'd have a lot of appreciative folks here, since they're worried about rising costs. I'd prefer to avoid questions about our partnership if your internal costs remain unmanaged and we continue paying more.

One key question changed everything—we built a tiered-pricing model based on outcomes, and his opposition turned into support. Our partnership improved, shifting from conflict to collaboration.

Fixing relationships is hard; fixing a failing project is harder. The next lesson came in a crisis where, despite clear contracts and automatic penalties, something felt off.

WHEN SYSTEMS FAIL, PEOPLE MATTER

The software rollout was already behind schedule when disaster struck. The supplier missed another critical milestone, triggering automatic penalty clauses in our contract. My legal team was prepared to enforce it immediately. IT, however, worried that penalizing the supplier would strain the relationship and lead to more delays through demotivation and higher costs.

Having managed numerous integration projects, I sensed something was wrong beneath the surface. I scheduled an in-person meeting with the supplier, alone, at a neutral location. I was seeking the most honest response possible.

"What's been the hardest part of the last few weeks for your team?" I asked. "Is there anything we can do on our end to ensure success for us both?"

After some hesitation, he revealed that their lead programmer had been hospitalized. The remaining team was covering double shifts, exhausted and overwhelmed. They'd been terrified to tell us, fearing we'd trigger contract termination given how litigious we'd been about the penalties.

"It sounds like you're exhausted and worried about disappointing us, and that a lot of this has been out of your control," I said.

That acknowledgment transformed negotiation into collaboration. We extended the deadline slightly and helped reallocate internal support. The system launched successfully. Months later, they repaid that empathy with loyalty, innovation, and a proposal discount that more than offset the original penalty.

I'd played the long game, identifying the *people* problem behind the *work* problem. Tactical empathy revealed the real problem no spreadsheet could show. But the biggest example of this wasn't with an external partner at all.

It happened inside the organization, with an executive whose initial reaction threatened to kill one of the most impactful projects of my career.

THE INNOVATION THAT ALMOST WASN'T

One of my most important initiatives nearly ended before it began. I'd proposed a fleet car initiative to our CFO, armed with extensive data supporting the ROI. By any objective measure, the project made sense.

The CFO killed it immediately, dismissing it as a "nice to have" that would never yield gains worth the implementation pain.

This confused me. This CFO, like most, lived and breathed ROI. My data was bulletproof. But I remembered how previous procurement projects had generated complaints from executives about wasted hours and disgruntled legacy suppliers. These suppliers had told our drivers that such projects actually increased their costs, and that they preferred spending time helping our teams deliver sales rather than administrative exercises.

Instead of arguing, I asked, "What's the biggest risk you see if we pursue this?"

"It'll bog down valuable resources with barely any return, while making a lot of enemies internally," he replied.

"You feel like this could turn into another symbolic program that fails to deliver," I said.

He leaned back. "Exactly."

I tried reframing: "What if we positioned competitive bids from multiple suppliers as not only a cost-resilience strategy, but also as a supplier solution opportunity—multiple quotes, showcasing all of the best driver features that sales executives can choose from, with measurable ROI?"

He smiled. "Now you're talking."

My tactical empathy had turned opposition into advocacy. He became the program's biggest champion, soliciting support from other executives to ensure the project ran smoothly and on time. The initiative succeeded so completely that it won me a corporate-wide Finance Innovation award, voted on and awarded by our CFO.

That win reminded me that the hardest resistance often hides a simple fear. But fear isn't limited to executives in boardrooms. Sometimes, it shows up silently within our own teams.

THE HUMAN SIDE OF PERFORMANCE

Not all challenges involve external negotiations. One of my strongest procurement team members started missing deadlines. She appeared visibly distracted in team meetings and disengaged during our one-on-ones. Projects were falling behind, jeopardizing our team's objectives.

Traditional feedback wasn't working. Instead of pushing harder, I tried a different approach.

"What is your engagement level right now?" I asked. "Mine fluctuates, but right now I'm at a six personally."

She responded that hers was a two. Work had been demanding lately, and she was exhausted.

"What's been most difficult about your workload lately?" I asked.

She hesitated. Then, with tears welling up, she said quietly, "My daughter has been going through a terrible divorce."

"It sounds like you're trying to stay strong for everyone, but you're burning out," I acknowledged.

That single acknowledgment broke through her walls. We adjusted her workload and provided flexible hours. Her performance soared again. The team rallied behind her, understanding that supporting each other through personal challenges strengthened our professional capabilities. Supporting her reminded me that tactical empathy isn't reserved for negotiations—it's a leadership discipline. And that discipline would soon be tested in one of the most contentious internal relationships I'd ever managed.

THE TWO-QUARTER TRANSFORMATION

My most challenging relationship transformation involved an executive stakeholder who clashed with me on everything—timelines, priorities, tone. He resisted acknowledging or validating any value my procurement team delivered.

After one particularly heated meeting, I approached him in the hallway. "It seems like you're under pressure to deliver visible wins fast."

"Yes! And your team's governance and constant requests slow my team down," he responded.

"Slows you down?" I mirrored back.

"Exactly," he said.

"How can my team help you get those wins your team is after without sacrificing control or leaving money on the table?" I asked. "I'm sure your team isn't immune to the cost-cutting pressures we're all feeling. If so, how can my team facilitate, unburden your team, and create more wins you can get credit for?"

That one calibrated question flipped our entire dynamic. We co-developed a rapid-approval model meeting both our objectives. Within two quarters, he'd become one of my biggest internal allies. His team became internal leaders for the cost-savings achieved and evangelists for our initiatives.

These successes gained him more organizational exposure. Within a year, he was promoted. Thankfully, he became a champion and supported my candidacy for a promotion, which I eventually received. Watching that transformation unfold over two quarters clarified something I'd been seeing for years but had never fully articulated. Every breakthrough—supplier, stakeholder, executive, team member—shared the same pattern.

THE COMPOUND EFFECT OF UNDERSTANDING

Looking back at that first phone call with the legacy agency, I see the pattern that connects all these experiences. That moment when she said, "We thought we were your partner," could have ended with termination paperwork and change management costs. Instead, it became the first demonstration of a principle that would define my career: tactical empathy turns friction into fuel.

Each story shares the same DNA. A moment of conflict or resistance. A choice to understand rather than overpower. A question or observation that acknowledges the other party's reality. And then transformation.

The numbers tell part of the story. The Finance Innovation award, the successful software launch, and the cost savings achieved. But the real metrics are the relationships transformed, the suppliers who became advocates, the executives who became champions, the team members who thrived because someone saw their humanity.

In procurement, we're taught to negotiate hard, to squeeze every penny, to enforce every clause. These tools have their place. But tactical empathy, the deliberate, strategic use of understanding to advance dialogue, consistently delivers superior outcomes. It transforms "no" into "how," opposition into partnership, and friction into fuel for innovation.

The partnership reset with that legacy agency taught me that the most powerful negotiation tool isn't leverage, data, or contractual obligation. It's tactical empathy—the ability to say, "It sounds like you're feeling..." and mean it. Because when people feel genuinely understood, they stop defending and start collaborating. And that's when real value creation begins.

About Oliver

Oliver Fernandez is a trusted advisor to senior executives navigating high-stakes negotiations, complex supplier ecosystems, and large-scale enterprise transformation. With more than two decades of procurement experience across global technology, media, and marketing, and professional services organizations, Oliver has built a reputation for combining analytical rigor with the human-centered discipline of Tactical Empathy—the strategic foundation of his leadership philosophy and the central theme of this book.

Oliver's approach to negotiation and commercial decision-making has been shaped by extensive training at premier institutions, including Harvard, Yale, McKinsey Academy, and his Ivy League MBA. His work has influenced procurement, finance, IT, and marketing leaders globally, helping organizations reduce risk, optimize spending, strengthen supplier partnerships, and build true cost resilience from within.

As the founder of Ollie Coaching, Oliver created the Parsimoney™ Framework, a modern operating system designed for leaders who want smarter spending, better alignment, and more equitable supplier relationships. His system integrates behavioral psychology, influence science, and enterprise strategy—giving leaders tools to make better decisions under pressure and build sustainable value that goes beyond savings.

Oliver is known for his clarity, balance, and ability to translate complex dynamics into actionable insights. Whether resolving stakeholder conflict, navigating vendor escalations, or redesigning sourcing strategy, he brings calm to high-pressure moments and transforms tension into collaboration.

Outside his advisory work, Oliver is dedicated to continuous learning, global travel, and supporting emerging leaders. He splits his time between Canada and the U.S., continually exploring the evolving intersection of negotiation, cost resilience, and human behavior.

Learn more about Oliver online at:
Ollie.coach

CHAPTER 31

DR. NO FROM COMPLIANCE: HOW EMPATHY TRANSFORMED ME FROM CORPORATE ROADBLOCK TO STRATEGIC PARTNER

BY CHRISTOPHER M. WISEMAN

I was sitting across from two New York real estate agents and their attorney, eight hours into a negotiation that had stalled for over a year. Millions of dollars hung in the balance. I'd been director of legal affairs for exactly three weeks, replacing someone who'd held the position for twenty years. My expertise? Data privacy and intellectual property. Commercial real estate? I knew about as much as a fish knows about mountain climbing.

So, I did something that would have horrified any legal professional. I laughed and said, "You're probably wondering what some Silicon Valley schmuck can tell you about Manhattan real estate. The answer is absolutely nothing."

The room went silent. Then, something shifted. The lead agent's shoulders relaxed. The attorney put down his pen. For the first time in eight hours, we weren't adversaries. We were just people trying to solve a problem together.

That moment taught me something that would revolutionize my approach to compliance and legal work: empathy is not a weakness. It's the most powerful tool in your arsenal when everyone else is reaching for their weapons.

THE MYTH OF DOCTOR NO

For decades, compliance professionals have worn the *Doctor No* badge like armor. We're the gatekeepers, the risk preventers, the ones who are the appointed devil's advocates in the name of regulation. We often speak in acronyms such as GDPR, HIPAA, and CCPA, and our favorite word is *noncompliant*. We're necessary evils, tolerated but rarely welcomed.

But what if I told you that this entire approach is backwards? What if the most effective compliance isn't about saying no, but about understanding why someone is asking for the yes?

Let me share what happened when I flipped this script at a semiconductor company during their IPO. I was overseeing privacy compliance across ten countries: the US, Canada, the UK, the EU, India, China, Japan, South Korea, Singapore, and Hong Kong. IPO intermediaries were demanding massive amounts of personal data. The typical approach would be to build walls, create friction, and slow everything down in the name of protection.

Instead, I scheduled an hour with our finance director to understand her world. Not to audit. Not to impose requirements. Just to understand.

"Show me what data flows through your department," I said. "Help me see it through your eyes."

What we discovered together shocked us both. The finance department held massive troves of personal data neither of us had fully mapped—employee records embedded in payment systems, contractor information in vendor databases, executive compensation details scattered across multiple platforms. But here's what made the difference: we discovered it together. I wasn't the compliance officer finding problems. We were partners uncovering shared challenges.

That finance director became the most ardent data privacy evangelist in the company. Not because I convinced her, but because she convinced herself once she understood the landscape. When IPO intermediaries demanded blanket data access, she had the support of the C-Suite and pushed back harder than I ever could have. She negotiated data minimization with the authority of someone who truly understood both the business need and the privacy risk.

MEETING PEOPLE WHERE THEY ARE

The Marines taught me to lead from the front. My father, also a Marine, demonstrated leadership by example. But it wasn't until I read *Never Split the Difference* that I understood the missing piece: you can't lead someone anywhere until you understand where they're standing.

When I joined a major California county government to help oversee program privacy compliance, they asked me to help develop their AI governance framework. I immediately enrolled in an AI certification program and joined the GovAI Coalition. Not because I needed the credentials, but because I needed to understand the tsunami of confusion heading toward every government employee who would have to implement these policies.

AI governance is complex enough to make seasoned technologists sweat. Imagine being a social services case worker or a permit clerk and suddenly being told you need to understand algorithmic bias and data sovereignty. The typical consulting approach would be to deliver a comprehensive framework and wish them luck.

Instead, I asked myself, *What would it feel like to be them?*

They don't need to be passionate about AI the way I am. They need to understand how it affects their specific job, clients, and the challenges they face. So, I created different pathways for different people. Technical staff got detailed frameworks. Department heads got decision tools. Frontline employees got role-specific guidance that connected to their daily work.

What started as feedback on a basic AI policy evolved into a comprehensive playbook with procedures, assessment tools, incident response plans, and customized training curricula. More importantly, it became something people actually used because it met them where they were, not where I thought they should be.

THE SHADOW AI CRISIS

Here's something that keeps me awake at night: Shadow AI. Employees are using unauthorized artificial intelligence tools to handle sensitive government data. The traditional response? Send scary emails. Create punitive policies. Become *Doctor No* on steroids.

But one day, after the fifth request asking, "Is this AI tool HIPAA compliant?" I realized something. These weren't rogue employees trying to circumvent security. They were dedicated people trying to serve constituents better, faster, and more effectively. They were using shadow AI because we hadn't given them compliant alternatives.

So, I changed the conversation. Instead of "No, you can't use that," I started with "Thank you for asking. Help me understand what you're trying to accomplish."

This shift was transformative. I created assessment frameworks that helped employees evaluate their needs. I worked with IT to identify compliant alternatives. I built FAQ resources that anticipated common scenarios. Most importantly, I created what one employee called a *safe space* for them to admit they'd been using unauthorized tools and receive help in becoming compliant without fear of punishment.

Shadow AI usage dropped dramatically. Not because we policed harder, but because we made the right path easier than the wrong one. Employees began coming to us proactively, before we implemented new tools. We transformed from enforcers to helpers.

THE POWER OF STRATEGIC VULNERABILITY

That Manhattan real estate negotiation I mentioned? Let me tell you how it ended. After admitting my complete ignorance about commercial real estate, I reframed the entire discussion.

"Look," I said, "we all want the same thing, a completed deal that works. The challenge isn't that we're opponents. It's that this complex transaction has created complications none of us anticipated. So instead of negotiating against each other, what if we negotiate together against the challenges?"

For eight and a half hours, we worked through issues that had been intractable for a year. Not because I was a brilliant negotiator, but because I was vulnerable enough to admit what I didn't know and empathetic enough to understand what they needed.

We closed the deal within two weeks.

BUILDING TRUST THROUGH UNDERSTANDING

The most powerful transformation I've witnessed came from a family member who'd made a serious mistake involving his former employer's social media accounts. He called me, spiraling, afraid he'd lost everything.

The professional in me couldn't endorse what he'd done. But the human in me understood his desperation to provide for his family. So, I listened. For hours on the phone. For a full day in person. Not judging, just understanding.

Through our conversations, he realized he didn't want to return to corporate life. He wanted to combine his salesmanship with his handyman skills and work for himself. I helped him navigate business licensing, structure his company, and, crucially, gave him his first major project: overhauling my property into a native-plant pollinator garden.

This wasn't charity. It was strategic support. He got a steady income and a showcase project. I got skilled help with a massive undertaking. More importantly, he got to rebuild his identity on his own terms, not society's expectations.

Today, his business thrives. Not because I saved him, but because I understood him well enough to help him save himself.

THE ROI OF EMPATHY

When I consulted with a medical device manufacturer on their Data Privacy Impact Assessment, I could have delivered a standard compliance checklist. Instead, I spent time understanding their world. Data scientists explained how patient trust directly impacted data quality. Marketing teams independently reached the same conclusion. They already understood the link between privacy and business success. They just needed someone to help them operationalize that understanding.

By focusing on the ROI of privacy protection rather than regulatory requirements, we created a program that the organization embraced enthusiastically. Privacy became a competitive advantage, not a compliance burden.

This pattern repeats across industries: when you understand stakeholders' actual needs and pressures, you can design solutions that serve both compliance and business objectives. It's not about choosing between security and efficiency. It's about understanding both well enough to optimize for both.

THE ATTESTATION SOLUTION

During a critical Social Health Information Exchange project involving health records, criminal justice data, and social services information, we discovered teams using unauthorized software to test data sets. All work stopped. Tensions mounted. Relationships strained. The data team manager asked me for a *HIPAA waiver*, something that doesn't exist.

The standard solution would require weeks of third-party software review. Instead, I proposed something different: a two-page attestation where our vendor would certify, under penalty of perjury, that all their software met our legal and regulatory compliance requirements.

This solution took one day to implement. It satisfied legal, compliance, IT, and operations. Most importantly, it transformed the data team manager from my biggest critic to a staunch advocate. He later told colleagues I was the first compliance person who actually understood their operational pressures.

That attestation became our template for similar challenges. But more importantly, that relationship became a model for how compliance and operations could work as partners, not adversaries.

FROM COMPLIANCE TO COMPETITIVE ADVANTAGE

"Seek first to understand, then to be understood." My parents, both educators, raised me on this principle. In my early legal career, when startup clients asked, "What do I do now that I have my business license?" the standard answer was, "We provide legal advice, not business advice."

This never sat right with me. So, I spent months researching startup strategies, creating a PDF guide called "Next Steps in Your Business Planning." I sent it to clients without asking permission.

When the senior partner called me into his office, saying, "Close the door behind you," I thought my career was over. Instead, he said our clients had been incredibly appreciative. "This is above and beyond what most law firms would do. But Chris, next time you get a great idea, just run it by me first."

That experience taught me that understanding clients' real challenges, not just their legal needs, creates value that transcends traditional service boundaries.

THE EMPATHY IMPERATIVE

Here's what I've learned across decades of transforming *Doctor No* into *Doctor How*: Empathy isn't soft. It's strategic intelligence that reveals the most efficient paths to achieving shared objectives.

When you understand why someone needs something, you can often find ways to give them what they need while protecting what you must protect. When you acknowledge the pressures others face, they become more willing to acknowledge yours. When you admit what you don't know, people trust what you do know.

Empathy in compliance isn't about being nice. It's about being effective. It's about recognizing that behind every request for a HIPAA waiver is someone trying to serve patients better. Behind every shadow AI installation is someone trying to work more efficiently. Behind every *unreasonable* demand is a human being facing pressures you haven't seen yet.

The transformation from Doctor No to strategic partner doesn't require abandoning your expertise or compromising your standards. It requires adding one more tool to your toolkit: the ability to see the world through someone else's eyes before deciding whether to build a bridge or a wall.

Most of the time, you'll find that bridges get you where you need to go faster than walls ever could. And when you must say no, you'll say it in a way that preserves relationships and opens doors to creative alternatives.

Because ultimately, compliance isn't about stopping bad things from happening. It's about enabling good things to happen safely. And you can't enable what you don't understand.

About Christopher

Christopher M. Wiseman is a thought leader in tactical empathy and data governance strategy, bringing twenty years of progressive expertise in privacy, security, and compliance leadership to complex organizational challenges. As a co-author of *Lead with Empathy*, he demonstrates how genuine understanding—when deployed strategically in high-stakes environments—unlocks breakthrough solutions and transforms adversarial dynamics into collaborative problem-solving.

Throughout his career, Wiseman has built a reputation for translating sophisticated technical concepts into actionable business intelligence. His work spans the critical intersection of data privacy, security governance, and artificial intelligence—three domains where empathetic leadership increasingly determines organizational resilience and market competitiveness. Whether designing enterprise-wide data governance frameworks, leading privacy transformation for healthcare information exchanges, or building responsible AI governance ecosystems, Wiseman consistently demonstrates how leading with understanding creates sustainable competitive advantage.

His practical expertise reflects a rare combination of deep technical credibility and sophisticated stakeholder engagement. As a certified privacy professional (CIPP/US, CIPP/E, CIPM), Wiseman brings rigorous standards-based knowledge to organizational challenges. His case studies in *Lead with Empathy*—spanning medical device privacy assessments, multi-agency AI governance transformations, and high-stakes commercial negotiations—illustrate a fundamental principle: the most elegant technical solutions fail without authentic human understanding. Leaders who invest in tactical empathy discover paths forward that purely technical approaches miss entirely.

Wiseman's recent work leading governance and compliance for a major California county's Social Health Information Exchange exemplifies his approach. Tasked with consolidating fragmented compliance requirements across twenty-eight regulatory frameworks serving healthcare, social services, and criminal justice agencies, he recognized that regulatory alignment alone would not ensure success. By pausing to understand stakeholder motivations—discovering that data quality and patient trust were inextricably linked—he reframed privacy protections from compliance burdens to strategic business enablers, transforming organizational readiness and accelerating sustainable implementation.

His expertise in artificial intelligence governance and responsible AI implementation positions him at the forefront of emerging leadership challenges. Through organizations such as the GovAI Coalition and as an AI Governance Practitioner, Wiseman helps organizations navigate the intersection of innovation and ethics—where empathetic leadership becomes essential.

When not speaking or advising organizations on governance transformation, Wiseman explores how tactical empathy applies across executive decision-making, crisis leadership, and organizational change. He resides in the San Francisco Bay Area with his fiancée, is a proud father of six adult children, and is an avid hiker, surfer, saxophonist, and jazz enthusiast.

Learn more at **wisemanprivacy.com** or
connect on LinkedIn: **@christophermwiseman**

www.ingramcontent.com/pod-product-compliance
Ingram Content Group UK Ltd.
Pitfield, Milton Keynes, MK11 3LW, UK
UKHW021523300726
14060UKWH00017B/749/J